ADVANCE PRAISE FOR *OTHERHOOD*

"Life doesn't always unfold the way we expect. In this thought-provoking, honest, and often hilarious exploration of 'otherhood,' Melanie Notkin describes the pleasures and pain of coming to grips with the life she actually has—a childfull life, without children of her own. An essential read for anyone interested in what it's like to be a woman today."

—Gretchen Rubin, bestselling author of *Happier at Home* and
The Happiness Project

"Heartbreaking, insightful, and ultimately affirming, *Otherhood* is Notkin's anguished but undefeated post-feminist battle cry on behalf of childless women of a certain age who refuse to settle for a lesser love."

—Jonathan Tropper, bestselling author of *This Is Where I Leave You*

"In *Otherhood*, Melanie Notkin brilliantly reveals feminism's dirty little secret: The most fabulous women today are not finding love, marriage, or the baby carriage. They are creating—in a way *The Feminine Mystique* did not predict—a new, equally extraordinary kind of happiness."

—Karen Lehrman Bloch, author of *The Lipstick Proviso:
Women, Sex & Power in the Real World*

"Melanie Notkin gives a giant comforting hug to the millions of women who don't fit neatly onto the traditional timeline of single girl-dom, marriage and motherhood. She passionately reminds us that there are many paths to fulfillment and happiness in this so-called otherhood where women embrace love, commitment and mothering at different times and in different ways than they had ever imagined. Any woman who has ever felt bad about not being 'on track' will find hope and inspiration in Notkin's readable, compelling book. The experience is like chatting with an old college friend who hands you a mug of tea and kindly reminds you to stop bitching already and get busy creating and celebrating an authentic awesome life."

—Sarah Elizabeth Richards, author of *Motherhood, Rescheduled:
The New Frontier of Egg Freezing and the Women Who Tried It*

"In *Otherhood*, Melanie Notkin takes the reader on an intimate and insightful journey of what it's like to be single, never married, and childless when apparently no one thinks you should be. She courageously invites us into her intimate world, experiences, and feelings, in a way most close friends wouldn't even do. And in doing so, she beautifully highlights the importance of being authentic and true to yourself, even if your dreams and wishes don't come on cue."

—Dr. Robi Ludwig, psychotherapist and TV commentator

"Melanie Notkin's *Otherhood* is empowering and enlightening for a generation of modern women who don't want to settle in order to settle down. This book will resonate not only with single women but also with those who love them."

—Andrea Syrtash, author of *He's Just Not Your Type (And That's a Good Thing)* and *Cheat On Your Husband (With Your Husband)*

"*Otherhood* is a timely book offering up valuable guidance on how to feel appreciated and supported while being self-reliant. Melanie Notkin's genuine love for her reader shines through each page. Notkin is a powerful leader for all women as they enter into 'otherhood.'"

—Gabrielle Bernstein, *New York Times* bestselling author of *May Cause Miracles*

"Melanie Notkin has tapped into the deep need we all have for a new language of love. *Otherhood* is the perfect book for these times—honest, romping, vulnerable, uplifting. Read it now, because everyone will be talking about it soon."

—Bruce Feiler, *New York Times* columnist and bestselling author of *The Secrets of Happy Families*

Modern Women Finding a
New Kind of Happiness

OTHER
HOOD

Melanie Notkin

SEAL PRESS

For my friends, the family I choose

OTHERHOOD
Modern Women Finding a New Kind of Happiness
Copyright © 2014 Melanie Notkin

SEAL PRESS
A Member of the Perseus Books Group
1700 Fourth Street
Berkeley, California 94710

Library of Congress Cataloging-in-Publication Data

Notkin, Melanie.
  Otherhood : modern women finding a new kind of happiness / Melanie
Notkin.
    pages cm

  ISBN 978-1-58005-521-5 (pbk.)
1. Single women--United States--Psychology. 2. Childlessness--United
States. 3. Women's studies--United States. I. Title.
  HQ800.4.U6N68 2014
  305.40973--dc23
                              2013043625

10 9 8 7 6 5 4 3 2 1

Cover design by Van Huynh
Interior design by Tabitha Lahr

Printed in the United States of America
Distributed by Publishers Group West

A note on the people and events in *Otherhood*

The following stories are based on my personal experiences and those of the women and men I know and/or met with for the purpose of research for this book. The chapters are filled with composite characters, women and men whose identifying characteristics have been modified or blended with others to protect their privacy. The exception to this are the experts I have included in various chapters. Experts and true-life personas are identified with their last names (with the exceptions of Stephanie Banks and Harrison Black, composite characters).

Some of the experiences and conversations with the women and men included here have been modified to compress the events. Some events may be out of chronological order.

CONTENTS

INTRODUCTION TO
THE OTHERHOOD

I'm having dinner in TriBeCa with two old high school friends. Both have recently moved to New York City. Charles, the head of finance for a cable network, is happily married with three kids. Bruce is in pharmaceutical sales, father of one, happily divorced and dating around.

We've covered the usual subjects: The weather, work, the wife, the ex-wife, the kids. Appetizers have been cleared. Another bottle of wine has been ordered. And so I'm waiting.

When you're a single woman of a certain age in a place like Manhattan and you go out with friends—friends from out of town, or friends who married long ago; friends who know you and love you, or new friends you've recently met through business—they all want to know one thing.

Bruce leans forward. Charles holds his breath. I know it's coming.

"So . . . is there any special guy in your life?" Bruce asks.

"No guy," I say.

"I don't get it!" he exclaims, throwing himself back in his chair in exasperation. "You're an amazing woman!" Bruce looks at Charles, who nods in agreement on my left.

"I don't get it either," Charles adds, mimicking Bruce's bewilderment.

I know how the rest of this story goes. The main course is now being served and I'm all too familiar with the meal I'm about to get a taste of.

"You're like my friend Jessie, the one I dated last year right after my divorce," Bruce says as he takes a bite of his chicken. "She can't find anyone either and she has everything going for her. She's cute, smart, fun to be around . . . I'm not ready for something serious right now, you know, but if I were, she'd be the girl I date."

Bruce may not be looking for a serious girlfriend, but he's clearly curious about why I don't have a boyfriend. "Since I moved to New York, I've met so many fantastic women. Why are they still single? Why are *you* still single?"

I've got no good answer to Bruce's question. But if you're over thirty-five, single, and a woman in Manhattan, it's going to be asked. My hope is that it's meant to be rhetorical—like when men ask each other why girl-on-girl sex is so damn hot. But that's never the case. Apparently, the fantastic single woman needs a fantastic explanation for why she's still single.

"I just haven't met the right guy yet," I say nonchalantly.

"Really?" Bruce says. "But you're cute, smart, successful . . . you can't find a guy who wants to date you?"

I ignore the unintended insult that it's the men who are rejecting me rather than the other way around. I know Bruce means well.

"I meet men," I go on, now by rote. "Just not anyone I want to be with long-term."

"I just don't get it," Bruce says. "I can name ten women I know, one more amazing than the next, who are all single. No kids. And they'd make great moms. I feel like the guys should be lining up."

Bruce looks around the room, clearly in thought, trying to figure it all out. There's nothing left for him to blame but my career. Which

> Often, a woman's involuntary childlessness, such as mine, is misinterpreted as having come about by choice. In fact, I've always envisioned motherhood as part of the romantic wholeness of marriage and family—and in my mind, it still is inseparable from love. Without one, I haven't had a chance at the other.

is a good sign. It means we're almost done. "Do you think it's because you've been too busy with your business?"

Anyone who knows me knows that the idea that I chose a career over marriage and family is about as preposterous as the idea of choosing an elephant as a household pet. Yet people love to point at that very elephant in the room, declaring, "*J'accuse!* You're a career woman! You've left behind familial pursuits for your job!"

"It's true, I'm busy with my company," I say to Bruce, perhaps a little defensively, "but I'm also always out meeting people, more than I ever met while working in corporate America. And when I do meet someone I like, I make the time. The problem is not my career."

At that point, if I'm lucky, Bruce and Charles will give up. But often—and, true to form, on this night—the dating questions are followed by the baby questions.

"Don't you want kids?" Bruce asks. There is judgment in his tone.

Often, a woman's involuntary childlessness, such as mine, is misinterpreted as having come about by choice. In fact, I've always envisioned motherhood as part of the romantic wholeness of marriage and family—and in my mind, it still is inseparable from love. Without one, I haven't had a chance at the other.

"I very much always wanted children, but I wanted to have children with a man I love. Now that I'm in my early forties, I'm not sure if it's in the cards for me." I've gotten used to saying this without disappointment. Or at the very least, hiding it.

There's an awkward silence. Bruce sighs and Charles peers over his shoulder, pretending to look at something across the room. It seems these two men are finally ready for a change of subject.

Men, in fact, tend to go pretty easy on women like me when talking about fertility; somehow they can intuit the boundaries. Other women, not so much. Here's how the questions keep coming just a week later while I'm out for cocktails with a married mother of two:

"Did you freeze your eggs?"

People ask about egg freezing—which can cost $12,000 to $15,000 in a place like New York City—as if it's something you pick up in the dairy section at the supermarket: "Did you remember to freeze your eggs?" No. I did not freeze my eggs. Not because I was naïve or because I didn't want to take responsibility for my fertility, but because by the time egg freezing became a really viable option for women, I was already forty.

And from a colleague at a breakfast meeting the next day:

"Would you have a baby on your own? You could totally do it. Celeste is expecting, you know. She couldn't meet a guy and went out and got herself pregnant."

I wonder when single motherhood became the sole barometer of one's true desire for children.

"You don't even have to go to a sperm bank," my colleague continues. "Do you know some gay guy who'd have a kid with you?"

No. My life is not an episode of *Will & Grace*.

From a new female acquaintance:

"Ever think of just sleeping with someone and—oops!—getting pregnant?"

The "oops baby" is not an uncommon term today, the implication being that it might not have been an "oops" at all. (Women tend to have figured out how to use birth control by their midthirties.) No, I have never considered that. Deception is not the way I'd want to begin a lifelong partnership with the father of my child.

And lastly, from a female business acquaintance comes the scientific "proof" that I will indeed, one day, meet expectations:

"My friend's sister's cousin had her first—twins!—at forty-five. You have lots of time. The way reproductive technology is these days, you'll meet someone and then have kids. Don't worry."

I'm not worried. I'm just out for a cocktail. I'm just having coffee. I'm just attending my breakfast meeting.

Back at dinner with Charles and Bruce, Charles pushes this idea that women—meaning me—still have attractive options. "My colleague Bridget is really fantastic and the head of her entire division at the network," he says as he waves to the server for another round. "She hasn't met anyone and is considering a baby on her own. I admire her so much. I mean, what an incredible thing to do. She's determined to be a mother."

I smile wide, as if I agree that Bridget is indeed a courageous woman. And I do. But inside, I feel small.

Bruce chimes in again about Jessie. "She's got the most amazing attitude about life. She's so sweet. And if I do say, damn hot. She just moved out west for some TV show she got a part in. Where were women like that when I was looking to get married the first time? I'll say it again: How did *you* not get snatched up back then?"

"Who knows?" I say with a shrug. "We're all just doing the best we can, right?" I smile and finish my wine. I don't let it show that I no longer presume life will be as I once imagined.

I motion to the server for the check. It's time to move on.

But walking home, I can't help thinking back on how I've gotten to this point. I have always wanted to get married and have children. As a little girl, I was constantly refining my plans for my backyard wedding. When I was twelve, I purchased baby-name books in anticipation of the son and twin daughters I imagined I'd one day have. In my teens, I was a camp counselor and frequent babysitter, often stopping by to visit my charges even when I wasn't on duty. I'd already thought a lot about the type of mother I would be—loving, generous, and supportive of my children's autonomy.

When I was twenty-three and interviewing for my first job in New York City, I inquired about maternity benefits to make sure the employer was right for me and my expected lifestyle. I focused my career in the nonprofit sector, hoping it would allow me more flexible hours. And I dated only men with traditional values.

By age thirty, I'd moved into the for-profit sector (so that I could afford life in New York as a single-income dweller), ultimately landing at a global beauty company in my midthirties where my hours were only getting longer. As my job responsibilities as a senior executive grew, so did my requirements to travel overseas. I loved my career but grew increasingly anxious about what it meant for dating and, eventually, for my future family.

At the same time, I suddenly found myself beginning to suffer the prejudices of being an "older" single woman. At thirty-four, a male friend said he wanted to set me up with a man our age but held that I was just "too old." At age thirty-six, another man told me he'd (reluctantly) date me since I could probably still "pop one out." Just weeks before that, a man I had been seeing told me flat-out that he could not continue to date a woman my age. While he and I had never discussed marriage or children, he felt that a woman between the ages of thirty-five and forty was too desperate about her biological clock. "It's just too much pressure," he admitted. It seems he had heard my clock ticking as loudly as I did.

In the midst of all this, I became an aunt. Aunthood has undoubtedly provided an outlet for my loving, maternal urges. My desire for children of my own, however, did not wane with the birth of each niece or nephew. My heart still aches for my very own baby to hold in my very own arms, my loving husband by my side.

I am now in my early forties, still single, and understand the likelihood is that I won't give birth to children of my own. But my story is only one of millions of stories of childlessness due to being single or finally finding the right partner at late age. My generation of women expected to reap all the social, economic, and political equality our mothers did not have. The husband and children they did have, we just assumed we'd inherit those as well. And yet for so many of us, those things have proven elusive.

The rise of childless women may be one of the most overlooked and underappreciated social issues of our time. Never before have so many women lived longer before having their first child, or remained childless toward the end of their fertility.

People today often presume that when a woman like me is childless, it's probably by choice. Not true. Me and my fellow childless-not-by-choice women are perceived as an exception, not a norm. Not true. Society so often dismisses us—sisters, daughters, friends, and coworkers—as outliers. In reality, none of this is true.

In fact, an American woman today is virtually as likely to be a

> 66 The rise of childless women may be one of the most overlooked and underappreciated social issues of our time. Never before have so many women lived longer before having their first child, or remained childless toward the end of their fertility. 99

mother as not. Nearly half—47.1 percent—of all American women of childbearing age do not have children of their own, whether or not we're married, according to the U.S. Census publication *Fertility of American Women: 2010*. That's a steep rise from 35 percent in 1976. Meanwhile, a study by the Centers for Disease Control and Prevention shows that 80 percent of all unmarried women are childless. Perhaps the most compelling part of that study, though, is the fact that 81 percent of those unmarried, childless women say they plan or hope to have children one day.

So why is it that when these hopes and dreams don't come to fruition, for whatever reason, we're chastised as if we've actively chosen this fate? A 2011 report from the U.S. Census Bureau, for example, labels the trend of women having their first child at a later age "the delayer boom"—as if marriage and family are life stages that we're intentionally, even selfishly, putting off. Meanwhile, pop culture portrays us time and again as being naïve about the length of our fertility, or we're belittled in the mainstream media for being "too picky" in our quest for a mate. All this further supports the assumption that our childlessness is something we've either chosen or, even worse, deserve.

Right now, we've got a collective case of "mom-opia"—the myopia of seeing the world through mother-colored glasses, seeing motherhood as the only normal, natural way to be a woman—and it's blinded us, all of us, to the reality of what's really going on. The assumption that the significant majority of women are or will be mothers is false. When we continue to assume it's true, we rob ourselves of the chance to understand why this shift, the social and emotional impact of our childlessness, intentional or unintentional, has come about, and how this "new normal" is going to impact our relationships and our lives for decades to come.

My own experience of not becoming the woman I expected to be—neither married, nor a mother—and the similar experiences of my cohorts, friends, peers, colleagues, and the multitudes of women who connect with me through my work, inspired me to explore the story further, deeper.

I wanted to more intimately understand the truth about who we are, not the stereotypes we're assumed to be. I wanted to understand why we are where we are today, in this time, and how our expectations— our assumedly natural paths toward love, marriage, and motherhood— have eluded us.

We have gone without definition or visibility for too long. I am offering "Otherhood" as a name for our misunderstood group of women doing our best to live full and meaningful lives despite the frustrations of some of our most cherished longings. We, the Otherhood, who have yet to find our rightful, equitable, requisite place in society, deserve one. Our otherhood denotes our state, our condition, our character, our nature, and our tribe.

Otherhood uncovers, explores, and examines the experiences of this overlooked and misunderstood segment of contemporary women. Part anecdotal storytelling, part inspiration, part reportage and part manifesto, *Otherhood* sets out to get to the heart of the issues, enliven the societal consciousness, and trigger conversation in and around our tribe.

The experience of the Otherhood is not mine uniquely, of course. It is the story of a generation of women who followed the path their mothers and aunts prepared for them: Getting a good education, finding the means to support themselves, and setting out to find love, get married, and have children. The motivation to get a degree and a job, of course, were not politically motivated or a way to wave a feminist flag. They're simply the things many women do in life. (And if we don't all have the college degree, certainly we all need to have jobs.)

But as we got closer to thirty, then thirty-five, then forty, still looking for love, marriage, and, for many of us, motherhood, other people imposed a political or even radical tag on our very normal decision to earn a living. At some point, we were called "career women," an anachronistic term that a generation ago described those women who worked when most women did not.

Today, the typical woman of the Otherhood is still single (or single again, following a divorce) long past the time when she thought she'd be settled down—whether that means that she's in her late twenties or midforties. She probably feels that her personal growth has been stunted, that she's become alienated from her peer group, that she's fallen short of the expectations of family and friends (on top of her own), and that a great number of people around her presume, falsely, that she's chosen her lifestyle and treat her accordingly. She might seem enviable for the perceived glamour of that lifestyle—her career, her income, her freedom, her sex life— even if "glamour" may be an entirely erroneous perception. And at the same time, she is also often misperceived, sometimes even vilified, as careless and selfish, superficial and undisciplined, cold and solely career-focused.

Most of us childless women in our thirties and forties—and if not most, then certainly a great many—simply want to find the right, loving relationship before making the lifetime commitment to have kids. Once upon a time, love and marriage had to happen first, as far as societal values were concerned; now, for the modern woman, that same desire for a romantic union as a necessary precursor to having children gets deemed an unacceptable life choice.

How did we get here? How did so many of us—all of whom wanted and still want love, marriage, and children—not reach our goals? How did *I* get here? Was it, in fact, specific choices I made, knowingly or unknowingly, that led me to this fate? Or could it simply be fate itself; was I somehow destined to be single and childless? Whether by pop culture, our families, or our peers, why are we midthirties-and-older, single, childless women scrutinized so unsympathetically, harassed for sticking by our convictions and invalidated as just plain less than everyone else? How has our status shaped our lives and the choices now available to us, and moving forward, just how attractive are our options for love, dating, marriage, and children? How are we coping, and do we have proper personal and societal mechanisms for support? And, it bears repeating: How did we get here?

We weren't prepared for this situation. Most girls growing up in the 1970s and '80s were often encouraged by both parents to aspire to a higher education and more professional opportunities than our mothers were offered. We believed that we'd have the husband and children mom had and the earning potential she didn't.

A woman in our mothers' generation was stationed in society by her husband, her children, her wealth, and her traditional family lifestyle: The '50s generation had married younger and had children earlier than even their parents had. As men came home from war, women left their wartime jobs to focus on family. It was not uncommon for a woman to leave college for marriage. Careers were

out of fashion while housewifery was in vogue. But by the early
1960s, things had changed dramatically. Women pressed for more
than a family life. They aspired to higher education and better jobs
with equal pay. The new heroine/archetype looked more like Gloria
Steinem than June Cleaver.

But still, modern feminism was never about forsaking love, marriage, and children for a career outside the home. It was driven by a
need of those who suffered the ennui of being homebound, not just
because of family ties but because of social, political, and economic
inequality with men. The prefeminist woman was unable to live life
to her potential. But as Betty Friedan stated in the epilogue to her
seminal 1963 book *The Feminine Mystique:*

> *"The more I've become myself—and the more strength,
> support, and love I've somehow managed to take from,
> and give to, other women in the movement—the more
> joyous and real I feel loving a man. I've seen great re-
> lief in women this year as I've spelled out my personal
> truth: that the assumption of your own identity, equal-
> ity, and even political power does not mean you stop
> needing to love, and be loved by, a man, or that you
> stop caring for your kids."*

And yet today, the one thing a woman cannot do without scrutiny,
without being made to feel *less than*, is to aspire to have a family while
waiting for love. Instead, she is branded a "career woman," perhaps
a more politically correct version of "spinster" or "old maid." She's
"picky." She's "too independent." She's "cold-hearted." She's "not
mother material." The latest studies show that even as progressive
lifestyle choices gain acceptance, nearly 40 percent of Americans still

think childlessness is fundamentally bad. The independent, childless woman does not feel like a qualified member of the social order, but rather is made to feel hopeless, hapless, and just plain old *less than* everyone else.

For many women, *Sex and the City* remains the dominant pop cultural portrait of our supposed lifestyle. One, if not *the*, important difference between Candace Bushnell's world and the women of Generation X is that women are no longer primarily concerned with expressing our freedom, sexual and otherwise. Today's struggle is about our desire to know there's something more to life, something deeper. Unlike the women of the generation that precedes us, we are not engaged in a battle of the sexes. Our battle is within. It's existential.

Until now, the never-ending national conversation on "having it all" has applied only to married mothers who also have or aspire to have careers. Just as there's no definitive answer as to whether or not those married mothers can have it all, there is also no easy solution for us women of the Otherhood, single and approaching the end of our fertility, when we find ourselves at a different crossroads. Indeed, it's our opportunity costs—giving up on one thing to pursue another—that weigh on the women of the Otherhood the most: Do we continue to wait for love, even if it comes too late for a biological family? Do we try to have a baby on our own? Should we stay with men we love who do not want children? Should we partner up with men we *don't* love but who *do* want children? Do we walk away from the very career opportunities and higher incomes feminism afforded us in an attempt to prove we are not prioritizing career over family? Or should we focus our energies on other parts of our lives—starting businesses, pursuing artistic or creative passions, or starting over in new places? As the eleventh hour approaches, how do we decide?

I know well the burden of this crossroads. As I began nearing forty and the end of my fertility, I questioned my life's meaning.

For empathy and support, I turned to a group of female friends who shared my circumstances. Our collective situation was an inevitable and invariable topic of discussion. Like our peers, coworkers, family members (and, yes, some complete strangers), we also wondered why we—dynamic, accomplished ladies—were without promising romantic prospects, prospects with whom we could start a family, and what we could do about it. The same universal questions emerged at just about every gathering: "Where are the men?" "Would you date a guy who doesn't want children?" "Would you have a baby on your own?" "Did you freeze your eggs?" And so on. We bemoaned the pressure we felt from loved ones "concerned" with our inability to get married and have kids. We considered some newly ripening alternatives, like single motherhood. And we spoke of our nieces and nephews with proprietary love and affection, pouring our maternal instincts into those children we were fortunate enough to have in our lives.

Our conversations were so consistent that I became certain my friends and I couldn't be the only ones having them. Mustn't there be other brunch tables, other cocktail lounges around the country where women were sharing similar concerns?

When I began to investigate, the answer was a clear and resounding yes. Being a part of this tribe, I had to ask myself: How did I not know this? How did we not know of each other?

From this epiphany, in 2007 I founded Savvy Auntie, a lifestyle brand that celebrates modern aunthood and embraces the nearly 50 percent of American women who are not mothers, specifically the one in five American women I've dubbed PANKs, or Professional Aunts No Kids, who have a special bond with the children—nieces, nephews, godchildren—in their lives. This overlooked segment of women deserved a meeting place, a tribe all their own.

Through my website, as well as my columns on *The Huffington Post* and PsychologyToday.com, I came to know the women of this tribe and engage in pointed, lively, and penetrating conversations with them, and I began to better understand our common experience in all its layers and vulnerabilities. And I was overcome by the universal lack of sympathy for my childless cohorts, whether they are aunts or not. We are so often perceived as cold, selfish, unfulfilled, feckless, sad, blasé about our fertility, and too choosy for our own good. On an even more profound level, we are made to feel unnatural, unwomanly, discredited, and devalued. Even the term "childless" is (literally) so belittling that, research has shown, it undermines the very health and well-being of the women it was coined to describe.

While on SavvyAuntie.com I focus on being child*full* (because we aunts and godmothers choose to fill our lives with the children we love), it has become clear that in order to be completely authentic about our modern experience, I must discuss the other side of the coin as well. We are indeed also child*less*. The diminutive is, at the very least, honest. And it is time to acknowledge its truth and its effects.

In the summer of 2011, I wrote a piece for *The Huffington Post* entitled "The Truth About Childless Women." In it, I described dealing with my own "circumstantial infertility," the term I use to describe women who cannot have children because of circumstance rather than biology. Often the circumstance is that they're single with no partner with whom to have children. I wanted to give a name to my situation and offer a voice for women who feel "less than" because of their inability to become mothers despite their desire:

The grief over not only not being a mother, but now also suffering from feeling 'less than' simply because I hadn't found love (or mutual love), was at times overwhelming. And as I saw couples younger than I getting sympathy for their biological infertility, I wondered why all I got were accusations of not doing enough, not trying hard enough . . .

. . . The assumption that's out there is that all women who don't have children simply don't want children, but there is a place between motherhood and choosing not to be a mother. And tens of millions of American women are there... My circumstances have left me infertile but they have not left me non-maternal. I love the children in my life with boundless adoration. If I was not meant to be a mother to 2.1 kids, then perhaps I was meant to be motherly to many more . . .

Although it's been over two years since that column first appeared online, I still receive countless, self-described "tear-stained" emails from women who feel their perspective has finally been represented, that their voice has finally been heard, in this and other posts I've published.

Among the daily letters, comments, Tweets, and emails I receive from women, some are heartwarming and convince me of the value of the community we're building. "There is such power and peace in knowing you're not alone," they tell me. Others share happy discoveries of the joy and satisfaction they've found in other kinds of relationships and "mothering." Many simply gleefully type, "That's me!" in response to an online discussion or under a digital poster that celebrates Auntie's Day, the day I founded in 2009 to celebrate and honor aunts and godmothers, much like Mother's Day honors mothers.

But many of the private notes I receive—most, if I'm being truthful—are heartbreaking. "I don't know what I did wrong" and "I can't believe this is my life" are frequent sentiments. Others recount agonizing dilemmas. "The man I love has two kids and doesn't want more," one commenter told me recently. "I had no idea how much my biological clock would take over . . . now I cry myself to sleep." She concluded with, "At this point of desperation, I am thinking it would be better to be on my own raising a family than to stay begrudgingly, blaming my partner for not 'allowing' me to have children." Another reader confessed just the opposite: "I feel like denying my child a father I loved would make me miserable . . . I choose to keep hoping for love."

If not a mother and/or a wife, who are we? What will be our legacy? And what do we do now?

No matter how we got here and no matter where we want to go from here, we all converge in this place and time, this Zeitgeist, with one story. Our story. The story of the Otherhood.

MODERN WOMEN

Wynn, Rachel, Jacqueline, and I are at the Modern, talking about old-fashioned dating. Time and again, I hear how women are turned off by men who can't plan a date, or a "proper date." It's become a phenomenon; the boys are not rising up and the women are taking the fall. And few men realize how they are turning women off. And how easy it is to turn us on.

"He made me plan every single date," reports Wynn, a single, forty-year-old fashion PR executive. She's exasperated after her fourth and final date with a forty-two-year-old CPA she met at a friend's birthday party. "He said, 'Let's go for sushi. Pick a place in Midtown West and I'll meet you there after work.' And for some strange reason, I did, never mind that I was going to be working in SoHo that day and felt like Italian. At the end of the date, he said we should go out again this week and asked me to email him with what I wanted to do and he'd meet me there. I told him I was tired of planning our dates! He said he just doesn't know cool places like I do. I emailed him the next day with a link to Yelp and said, 'Use this for the next girl you date.' I know that was harsh, but I'm sorry, he was being lazy."

Rachel, a single, thirty-nine-year-old beauty-industry executive, has a similar story about a guy she was recently set up with by a friend. "I thought he sounded really interesting because he's a successful entrepreneur who sold his first business a couple years ago, but I should've known better when he asked me out for a 'casual' cup of coffee. What the heck is a 'casual cup of coffee?' Do I have to stand up and drink the coffee out of a paper cup? Did we have to buy it from a coffee cart? How much more casual can coffee get?" The two wound up meeting at a Starbucks near Rachel's apartment. "He actually reminded me throughout the date how generous it was of him to do that because he lives all the way in Brooklyn." Rachel sighs as she rolls her eyes.

I know these types of men. I've dated several of them, and far too often, I've acquiesced to their inability to court me. They make me feel as if a date is a favor they're doing me, so I should in turn make it as uncomplicated for them as possible.

Picture this: My date is forty-seven, divorced, two kids. He's a partner at a major Midtown law firm. He's clearly had to solve a problem or two in his life. He had connected with me on Facebook, as we have lots of mutual friends, and to his credit, politely asked me out during a brief phone call. He was charming enough, so I agreed. Things were looking up.

But then things went downhill. "I'm happy to come to your area of town," he said on the call, thinking he was being generous. "But I don't know any places near you. Maybe you can suggest something?" That was the give-and-take: He'd meet me in my neighborhood, but I had to actually plan the date—as if we had to make it even.

Here's the thing about New York City: It is only thirteen miles long and about two miles wide. Claiming unfamiliarity is indefensible, and besides, all he had to do to find several potential locations for a date was to search online. Or poll his Facebook buddies. Or ask a friend. Or ask his assistant. Or pick up *New York* Magazine. Or ask any New Yorker for his or her opinion.

Divorced men in their late forties with small children and a big job can find a solution to the problem: Where should we eat?

I call it the "Client Test." If I were a client of his, or a potential client, he would have secured a reservation at a restaurant convenient to me, or at an impressive venue we'd both enjoy. Instead, I'm asked to plan the date. Courtship goes out the window.

"There are lots of great places near me," I said innocently, then added, "I'm sure you'll think of something," trying to put the selection back on him, giving him the opportunity to try again.

When he picked me up on a Sunday evening at 7:00 PM, I didn't know if the date was to be for drinks or dinner. In fact, I had no clue what to expect. And it seems, neither did he. We rounded the corner, and he said, "Well, this is your area of town. You're in the driver's seat now. Where should we go?"

And with that, my lady-parts went soft.

Under my breath, more disappointed than anything, I muttered, "Let me put my penis on so I can think." I had gone to the trouble of putting on an adorable dress, curling my hair, putting on makeup . . . I didn't want to be in the driver's seat in my five-inch wedges. Wynn is laughing as I tell this story at dinner. "That's perfect! What did he say?"

"He didn't hear me. I said it under my breath," I admit. "But I was already disenchanted. He's a grown man. He's a partner at a law firm! Why do I have to plan his date? He asked *me* out. And wait, it got worse."

"Worse than having to choose the restaurant?" Jacqueline, a single, thirty-five-year-old real estate agent, asks.

"I didn't know if we were eating or just having drinks," I explain. "Either would have been fine, but I had to ask. And frankly, I wished I'd known *before* the date, so I'd know whether to eat beforehand. So I had to ask him if he preferred drinks or dinner. He said, 'I could eat.' It's like I wasn't even standing there."

"Oh, my God," gasps Rachel in disbelief. "Why don't some men understand that one of the most attractive things they can do is simply pick the restaurant? We generally don't even care which restaurant they choose. Just choose one!"

Rachel is right. Of all the women I interviewed, no matter their ethnicity or background, no matter how independent or where they were in their careers, each one had the very same issue with dating: They just want the man to plan a date. It doesn't have to be a fancy date or an original date. It just had to be a plan. If our date says, *Meet me after work at The Dutch at eight,* we're thrilled. If he says, *Whatever you want to do is fine with me,* we're depleted.

"Oh, Rachel, there is nothing sexier than a decisive man," Wynn says. We all nod in agreement.

The server asks what we'd like to drink. We scan the wine list together and, without hesitation, decide on a bottle of 2009 Napa Valley Sauvignon Blanc for the table.

"So then what happened?" Wynn asks.

"Would you believe I had to ask him what type of cuisine he prefers?" I ask in reply. "Not that he cared what *I* might have been in the mood for. And then, here's what happened next: We walked up and down Columbus Avenue as he looked at menu after menu to decide which place he liked the most. He couldn't even decide on which restaurant he wanted to eat at! And every time we walked into a restaurant to see if there was a table available, he let me go ahead and speak with the hostess. It was like he was being taken out on the date, not vice versa." I'm still not done. "And the even crazier thing?" I continue. "The *very same thing* happened two weeks later with another guy. It was a setup with another divorced dad of two. When he texted for the date, we texted about pizza for some reason, and so he suggested pizza for our date. It was kind of cute and a perfectly good choice. But then when he picked me up, he said, 'Let's have sushi.' I'm a little annoyed because I had sushi for lunch and was looking forward to great pizza. But hey, I'm going with it, right? The thing is, he hadn't made a reservation anywhere and the sushi place that was to his culinary satisfaction was booked up and again, like the last date, he literally said to me, 'Well, this is your neighborhood. You're in the driver's seat now. Where should we go?'"

"No way!" Wynn says. "Did your penis go soft again?" she asks with a giggle.

"This time, I said it loud and clear. 'A woman doesn't want to always be in the driver's seat on a date. She wants the man to drive once in a while.' It was the first time I can recall deciding that, since I was never going to be with this man, he might as well learn a lesson for the next woman he takes out. But he didn't know the area, he claimed, being from Long Island, and he acted like I was being impossible. And so, once again, we traipsed up and down Columbus Avenue until he settled on a restaurant he thought he'd like best."

The server presents a beautiful bottle to our table and offers Wynn a taste. She looks at the wine as it is poured into her glass, closes her eyes to sniff it, tastes it tentatively, then, a few seconds later, swallows. She opens her eyes wide and bright. "This is excellent!" she exclaims. "It's oakier then I normally find in a Sauvignon Blanc, which caught me off guard, but I absolutely love it. Girls, enjoy!" The server agrees with Wynn's assessment of the oakiness and pours a glass for each of us.

I smile thinking how much I appreciate how my friends put effort into making sure we all enjoy our time together. We may not always meet men who court us, but we are excellent at courting our friendships.

I'm embarrassed to say, we toast to chivalry, and Wynn is laughing. "Why are you laughing?" I ask, starting to laugh myself. Wynn has this infectious laughter about her that I just adore.

"This wine reminds me of a story. I went on a blind date a few weeks ago, before I dated the CPA," she starts, and I know it's a good start because it's Wynn's story. Wynn has great stories. "And not only did he somehow arrange it so that we met in the middle between his workplace and mine—I believe his exact words were 'equidistant location'—but when he suggested drinks, he was unable to come up with a venue. Not wanting to spend the day on the phone until he finally came up with something, I bluntly suggested Stone Rose at the Time Warner Center."

"Oh, I like that place," Rachel offers. "Great views of the city. And it's a really nice after work drinks place." Of all my friends, Rachel is the one who most often tries to see the best in every situation.

"Exactly," Wynn says, "but I didn't like that I had to pick the place and have him decide if it was a good choice. His exact words were, 'Well, that sounds OK, if we don't think of something better.' I wanted to say, 'I'm sorry if my perfectly equidistant suggestion doesn't meet your needs.'"

"What's with men and meeting in the middle?" Jacqueline asks rhetorically. "What happened to accommodating a woman?"

"The venue issue was not even the main problem," Wynn says. "I ordered a Manhattan and my date—and I say this literally—my date ordered a 'white wine,' like it's a wedding and he has a choice between red or white. Now, I don't mind that he ordered white wine, per se. It was that he—"

"—didn't know which *kind* of white wine he wanted!" Jacqueline says, knowing where Wynn was going with this.

"Exactly. The poor server had to ask which white wine he wanted. It was embarrassing. *Just fake it!* I thought to myself. *Just say 'Chardonnay' with confidence. Even if you don't know the difference between a Chardonnay and a Pinot Grigio! Just say one!* But he had no idea what he wanted. He just stared at the five or six white wines listed by the glass like a kid looks at a multiple-choice question on an exam, having no clue what the answer is. Look, I'm not saying a man has to love wine or liquor, but if you ask a woman out for drinks, have a drink in mind," Wynn says. "And preferably, make it brown. Every man should have a brown drink they like. Or at least tolerate."

"What happened to men who knew how to order a drink?" Rachel asks. "It's really attractive when a man is decisive about his drink."

"I was out with a man recently," Jacqueline says. "We met at a wine bar. He had no idea how to order wine. And when I asked the server if I could taste my selection before committing to it, my date was annoyed. 'It's Merlot,' he said. 'Like you're really going to know the difference.' But I *do* know the difference. And we're at a wine bar. This is what they specialize in! Anyway, I happen to have really liked what I tasted, and you know what he said when the server asked what he wanted to drink? 'I'll have a beer.' He took me to a wine bar and ordered a beer. Norm is the new normal," she says, referring to *Cheers*.

"That's the problem," Wynn says. "Men see lazy men on TV and the movies, you know, the slacker-types, and think that it is OK to behave that way because the guy in the show or movie always gets the girl. But yuck, that so does not work for me."

"I wish men understood that courting us is like foreplay," I say. "We all know that dating is foreplay for sex in general. If we like you, we'll probably end up sleeping with you at some point. So what I want to say to men is, 'Imagine that dating is sex.'

"Let's say the man comes over for sex, like it was dating. And he stands at the doorway not knowing what to do next. With a lack of confidence or assuredness, he says, 'I've never been to your apartment before. Where do you prefer to have sex? Do you want to do it in the living room? The dining room? I hear people think the kitchen is pretty cool.' And you finally say that the bedroom is best. And once you get there, he starts again with more indecisiveness. 'So, do you want me to undress you? Do you want to undress me first? Do you want to kiss first?' And you finally get naked and he says, 'So do you like it on top? On the bottom?'"

I slap my palms against the table. "All we want is for the man to know what he wants for himself, because I know what *I* want, dammit. Know what you want! Know that you want *me!*"

"I agree," Rachel says. "But it just sounds so, you know, unfeminist."

"Oh, fuck feminism," Wynn says uncharacteristically. "At least what became of feminism."

I must admit, I think Wynn's got a point. I recently reread Betty Friedan's seminal book, *The Feminine Mystique,* and I do believe that feminism somehow became something different from what Betty intended. She never intended for women to eschew love, marriage, and motherhood for career. She actually wrote that being all the woman she could be—with equal social, political, and economic rights—didn't mean she stopped needing to be loved by her man, or to love her man, or to love her children. Feminism was never about "having it all." It was about—it *is* about—having the opportunities and choices women were not privy to before, like the types of careers men had with pay that equaled theirs. The choices Betty wanted for us were

> 66 I recently reread Betty Friedan's seminal book, *The Feminine Mystique*, and I do believe that feminism somehow became something different from what Betty intended. She never intended for women to eschew love, marriage, and motherhood for career. 99

never supposed to be work *or* family, love *or* loneliness, motherhood *or* Otherhood. They were simply to be choices. No one expected not to suffer the opportunity costs of whatever choices we made.

As if reading my mind, Wynn asks aloud, "Is this fallout from feminism? Did men think that because we wanted the things men already had a right to, that somehow they now have a right to become like women?"

"Biology does not trump social equality," I argue. "I am a man's equal at work, but when it comes to dating, I want to be courted. That doesn't mean we're both not human. But I am a woman. And I want a man. A manly man. And when a man is decisive about the date, the venue, his drink, it makes me know he'll be decisive in bed. It reminds me he knows who he is. He's an equal. I know who I am."

"Exactly," Rachel says. "We don't need poems or flowers. We just want the man to choose the venue, make a reservation if needed, and know how to treat us to a sophisticated date. We're grown-ups. Date like a grown-up! Somehow, that's so rare it's become an aphrodisiac!"

The server is ready to take our order. We agree to order a number of dishes to share. We're in this together.

"But I also notice they might take what you are saying literally," Rachel says. "They think because they've taken you out on a nice date that you'll have sex with them or make out like crazy with them.

But like sex, I like it slow. I want to say to them, 'Relax. Slow down. Take your time. Enjoy the moment. Let it evolve naturally.' I'm not saying I haven't slept with a man on the first or second date. And I'm not saying I regret it either. I just wish the ones where I'm not sure where it's going . . . where I'm just getting to know him . . . that they would stop pushing it. It's not that I'm too weak to say no, it's just that it's a turn-off when they start kissing your ear the minute the check comes. Yuck. There's no mystery in that."

Jacqueline has a theory. "It's their ego talking. They want credit for doing the right things and then they expect their gold star in the form of sex."

"Totally! I found myself having to tell him what a great restaurant he chose at least four or five times the other night on a date," Rachel says about another recent date she went on that was a little more upscale than her "casual cup of coffee" date. "I told him I don't eat meat and he chose a Greek restaurant with a number of fish and vegetarian dishes. And that was really thoughtful of him. But he wanted me to tell him that all night long, saying, like, 'Take a look at the menu, is there something you can eat here?' like he didn't know there was. And then he said, 'I wanted to make sure this restaurant had plenty of choices for you. Did I pick a good place?' And then he said to the server, 'My date doesn't eat meat. There are choices here for her, right?' I mean, he was treating me like a child and wanting me to tell him time and time again how smart and considerate he was."

"As women, so many of us are born nurturers," Jacqueline says. "I don't want to be the one to make sure you are making sure I'm having a nice date. I nurture all day long at work. Since I'm a little older than the junior women there, they come to me with all their issues, work-related and personal. The other day, I had to bring a girl down off the ledge! I mean not literally, but she was so over-whelmed with her workload that she was going to quit. I took her out for lunch, said I'd speak with her manager, and somehow saved the day. Then I came home to a call from my sister-in-law that my dad has to go to the doctor the next day and she can't take him, so I agree to do it even though it means rescheduling a dozen things at the office. Then my friend called with boyfriend issues and I helped her deal with those . . . I swear, all I want is a man who will pick the effing restaurant, buy me an effing drink, and let me lean back and enjoy. I just want a break from taking care of everything and have a man take care of me for a few hours."

"I agree," Wynn says. "I find that divorced men especially think we're their wives or assistants or something. It's like they've never had to make a social arrangement because some woman in their life was taking care of it for them. And they're looking for someone else to repeat that dynamic."

"And the funny thing is, we, as the women, are expected to be on our best behavior and look a certain way, you know?" Rachel says. "But the guys can't even plan a date. How's it going to be down the road if they don't even make the effort now? They don't seem excited to meet us, so why should we be excited to date them?"

"You know what gets me?" Wynn says. "When they hear I'm in fashion PR and say before the date, 'Don't get all fancy for me or anything. Let's keep it casual.'"

"Yes!" I say. "I hear that all the time and I'm not even in fash-ion. I met one guy, a divorced man in his midfifties, for dinner one evening last summer. He said something about my not getting all dressed up for the date, and since I'm so used to hearing that non-sense, I just let it go. It was summer and I wore a simple, pretty, cot-ton summer dress and wedge sandals. I would wear the same dress

> 'It's like being feminine is no longer something we should aspire to be,' I add. 'Putting on a pretty dress and shoes and doing my hair and makeup isn't a sign that I'm weak. There's a lot of power in femininity.'

out with a girlfriend. I hardly looked like I was going to a black-tie wedding. And the *very* first thing he said to me when we met was 'I told you not to get all dressed up.' And then he laughed in a condescending way like he believed that since I put an effort into how I present myself, I'm probably desperate for him.

"My date literally put me down for looking like a grown woman out on a date. I'm not sure how less dressed-up I could have been, barring a T-shirt and shorts. I want to be out with a man who wants to be out with a woman who's dressed like a woman out on a date."

"Oh, I agree," Rachel says. "You know that old adage: 'Dress for the job you want'? Well, I want a man who wants me to dress for the relationship I want. I want a sophisticated relationship. We are forty years old! When do we get to act like grown-ups without seeming like we are asking for too much?"

"We give our dates 110 percent," Wynn says. "We come home from work and get dressed *up* for the date. The men dress *down*. They give the date like 35 or 45 percent. The dynamic has changed."

Just then, two men walk by in suits and we gasp as if they were Brad Pitt and George Clooney.

"Man, what I would give to go on a date and see a man dressed like that," Wynn says. "But look, they aren't even on dates. It's a business dinner."

"Dating has gotten casual. Sex has gotten casual. Relationships have gotten casual, meaning you're not allowed to want something serious because then you're seen as desperate or something," Jacqueline says. "When do we get to be treated like grown women?"

"It's like being feminine is no longer something we should aspire to be," I add. "Putting on a pretty dress and shoes and doing my hair and makeup isn't a sign that I'm weak. There's a lot of power in femininity. And I have begun to tell men exactly how I want to be treated on dates. No, I won't meet you halfway. No, I won't just email you when I want to go out and if you're free, you let me know . . . "

"That actually happened?" Wynn asks.

"Yes! I was being set up with a guy and he said that he likes spontaneity so I should just email him next time I'm free and if he's free, he'll meet me somewhere. But, he said—and get a load of this—'If it's raining or windy, I may back out.'"

"What did you say to that?" Rachel asks.

"I emailed him back and said that I enjoy dating a man who enjoys dating a woman. I'm not emailing you for a date for you to turn it down because of the weather."

"Good for you!" Wynn says. "I love how he's more concerned about mussing up his hair than you are yours."

"So, we all agree that we want to date manly men who treat us like women. Where are these guys?" Rachel asks.

"They are hiding behind the idea that women want to be treated equally and apply it to courtship," Wynn suggests. "Don't get me wrong. I am very grateful for all the things feminism enabled for our generation. But as women began to act more like men and men began to act more like women, we began to meet in the middle and now have no desire for each other anymore. It's the price we paid."

"Well, at least we have each other," Rachel says, in her classic optimistic way.

We split the check when it arrives and then split off to go our separate ways. When it comes to our friendships, we'll always agree to meet in the middle.

LOVE IS RICH

I let my towel drop and look in the full-length mirror. Everything is in check. Hip bones are protruding just enough, abdomen is flat, thighs are thicker than I'd prefer, but this is nothing new. My breasts are not as perky as they were even five years ago, but at least they still look pretty good under a T-shirt. My arms are thin and slightly muscular. Overall, my confidence level is high, until I take a closer look at my face. I take a few timid steps to get closer to the mirror. I surprise myself with an audible gasp.

There it is: a line under my left eye that was never there before. A wrinkle is forming.

I'm compulsive about my daily SPF application. I'm diligent about night creams. I don't sit out in the sun other than to absorb a little extra vitamin D for a few minutes at the beach. I have never smoked a cigarette. I drink occasionally, socially, like any single New York woman who enjoys a cocktail with colleagues and friends. But now, as if overnight, here's a clear sign that I am aging.

I flop backward on the queen-size bed that sleeps one petite girl and cry. I put my hands back on my belly, which just moments ago I was proud of and feel its emptiness. I squeeze my breasts and wonder if they will ever serve a purpose other than to attract men. I feel powerless. It's not the wrinkle that concerns me; it's the visible proof that I'm aging out of my youth. Out of my fertility.

I look at the clock. It's getting late. I stand up, take another look in the mirror. *Stop*, I tell myself. *Just stop.*

To be single and forty-two in New York is at once exhilarating and depressing, empowering and debilitating. It's everything you've ever wanted it to be and nothing you'd ever imagined, all at the same time.

I wash my face and tap some expensive serum under my eyes. Then an SPF 30. Then concealer, foundation, eye shadow, liner, mascara, blush—on this day, I do it all without looking at my face too closely. I get dressed (a pleated skirt to counteract my depleted feeling), throw on some lip gloss, and head out the door.

I'm literally running to a breakfast meeting in Midtown to meet Stephanie Banks for the first time. Though I am right on time, Stephanie is already waiting, seated.

Stephanie is a well-known personality in New York City and the Hamptons. She is the founder and CEO of an advertising agency. Back at the office, she's got about twenty women—from interns to vice presidents, each one prettier and thinner than the next—working diligently on her behalf. Stephanie could have some business opportunities for me, so when I found out she wanted to meet me, I jumped at the chance. Besides, Stephanie is one of those advertising industry magnates who not only creates headlines, she is the headline.

"Nice to finally meet you," I say.

"Great to meet you, too," she replies, wide-and-smoky-eyed, with an air of surprising interest.

I am already enamored. Stephanie's rich, thick dark brown hair is remarkably smooth for a humid New York City midsummer day.

Did she get a blowout at 7:00 AM? Her grass-green, silk jersey dress is perfection. Her jewelry is stacked, thick, bold, and gold, like armor. But it is her ring that stands out. The diamond must be five carats, clear and bright. She wears it well.

"So you're the 'Auntie,'" she continues, referring to my company, Savvy Auntie. "I got your book and wanted to meet you. Clearly you've defined a niche for yourself. So you don't have kids, is that right? Do you want kids?"

Stephanie gets to the point, fast.

"Yes," I reply as the server pours much-needed coffee in my cup. "I do. I always wanted to have children, but I just haven't met the right guy." We haven't even ordered breakfast and the conversation has already turned to eggs. Somehow my fertility is always on the menu.

"How old are you?" Stephanie asks, all business.

"Forty-two," I say, hoping she knows that I get what that means as far as my fertility goes.

"So listen," Stephanie says, putting down the menu and getting down to brass tacks. "Get married and have children. That's the most important thing you can do. Otherwise, you'll regret it." The word "regret" is particularly regretful.

Stephanie is an ambitious, no-holds-barred businesswoman. Yet, family is evidently what's most important to her. It's important to me, too. I'm not sure who wants to convince whom of what at this point.

"Have children," she repeats.

Stephanie's BlackBerry buzzes and she pauses to look at the screen. "Sorry, I'm working with a new client while trying to get my Hamptons house ready for a party tomorrow night. They haven't delivered the chairs yet. It's driving me *insaaaaane.*" She responds to the message with well-manicured thumbs and puts the phone down.

Back to brass tacks.

"Listen, if you don't have kids, you'll regret it. Trust me. I know you're waiting for Mr. Prince Charming to sweep you off your feet . . . "

I shudder. "I'm just waiting for love," I interrupt.

"Love is overrated," Stephanie quips. "Look, I've been married to Thomas for over fifteen years. I mean I love him, he's my husband. But is it *maaaaad* love? No. Never was. I don't believe in that."

The waiter asks for my order. I'm feeling like toast.

"Want to hear my story?" Stephanie asks, as if there's a choice— although I must admit, I am immensely curious. "I came to New York this cocky kid from Connecticut, just out of school, looking for a job. Some rich guy I knew invited me to a party in the city. I was twenty-two. I got a lot of attention from the men there, all older, rich, and eager to meet the new girl. That's when I met Thomas. He offered to take me out to dinner to learn more about what I wanted to do with my career, and anyway, that first date turned into two, then it was months, then before I knew it, we were engaged."

Stephanie's BlackBerry is buzzing again. She ignores it. She's making this conversation her priority. I'm flattered and concerned, all at once.

"Look, I was still young, and out of all my friends, I wanted to be the first with a big rock on my finger. And so there you go. I got married, and a few years later, Sidney was born, then Sierra. Now we've got two amazing girls and a great life. Am I mad, mad, *maaaaad* for my husband? No. But we're happy. We have a *veeeeery* good life."

Since she is being so honest, I feel like being a little disarming myself. "But what about sex?" I ask. "I want to want to have sex with whomever I'm with. I can't imagine marrying someone I don't want to sleep with."

"Oh, sex is overrated," Stephanie balks as her BlackBerry buzzes again. "Sorry, it's about the chairs." She thumbs back a quick reply. "All that stuff goes away fast. In the end, you've got the kids. That's what's most important.

"Look," she goes on, "you're cute as a button. It's not too late. Go find a great guy and have some babies."

Here is my cue. "Do you have anyone to set me up with?" Stephanie has guest lists from here to East Hampton. Surely she knows one great available guy. At this point her BlackBerry is buzzing out of control. Stephanie pays our bill and grabs her Birkin in a motion to leave.

"Go to the Hamptons," she says with aplomb as she gets up. "There are a ton of great men there in the summer." Then she mentions some event I was not going to in the Hamptons that weekend. "You should rent a place and go to these events," she insists.

I was never the girl who went to the Hamptons to go to events to meet men. It felt inauthentic. But now I want to be that girl, regretting all the years I wasn't.

I walked uptown with a head filled with thoughts. Could I settle for a great guy for whom I felt some affection even if I didn't really want to go to bed with him? I'm OK with faking an orgasm once in a while, but faking wanting to be there in the first place? Not that I think Stephanie is faking love. She's just not making love a priority. And for whatever reason, Thomas is fine with that.

Good for them, I think to myself, wishing I could be like that. But I'm not.

I want the kind of love that allows me to give of myself in ways I didn't know I wanted to give, let alone could. I want to find the parts of me that loving another person brings out. I want to look at my partner in life and feel safe. I want to feel vulnerable and strong when he smiles at me. I want to share a knowing smile across a room with someone who knows me that well. Researchers say there are

> ❝ I want the kind of love that allows me to give of myself in ways I didn't know I wanted to give, let alone could. I want to find the parts of me that loving another person brings out. ❞

nineteen ways to smile, and I'm concerned I'll never know them all because I've never smiled at him.

I want the rhythm of the push and pull of a relationship. I want to pick up his prescriptions and his favorite coffee beans. I want him to text me our one-word, inside joke. I want him to refill my glass without asking. I want to be annoyed that he forgot to pick up the dry cleaning. I want him to take my love for granted. I want the downs to grow from, so I have the ups to appreciate.

Do I romanticize love? Yes. But shouldn't love be romantic?

I don't mean red-roses-and-caleche-rides-in-the-park kind of romantic or candy-on-Valentine's-Day romantic or fairy-tale-wedding romantic. I want the romance of everyday love that comes with bumps and bruises and unexpected surprises. I want to think about him when he's not with me. I want to think I see him walking up the street, realizing immediately he's out of town or on the other side of town, knowing it's my subconscious simply missing him.

I want to wake up at 3:00 AM and see him there lying next to me . . . I've left a place for him in my bed, you know. Years ago, I purchased a queen-size bed, but I've never slept on "his" side. I'm leaving space for him to come into my life. Sleeping on his side makes me feel as if I'm giving up on him ever showing up. Sometimes I think about how I'll never lie in that bed with my man, our legs crossed over each other under the sheets, and talk about how many children we want together. And I'll probably never be able to surprise someone with the news that the first is on its way. Once in a while, I look over at the empty side of the bed. *Just be there tonight,* I plead to no one. It's sometimes devastating to be so alone.

I'm heartbroken over a man I've never met because we haven't yet met. But my heartbreak isn't a crash. It's a murmur. It hums day in and day out. You won't notice it. I hide it well in my beautiful, glorious life of other things.

The day after breakfast with Stephanie, I meet with a billionaire hedge fund manager on behalf of a nonprofit organization to discuss a sizable donation. He's a wonderfully generous man. But like Stephanie, he seems to think that the real charity case we need to discuss is my single self.

I take the liberty of pouring myself some iced tea from his desk. He looks at me sideways, measuring my attractiveness.

"How old are you?" he asks. Somehow it's civil to ask a woman her age when you're considering setting her up.

"Forty-two," I say, and sit down without losing eye contact. I cross my legs, take a cold sip of tea, and hope my confidence convinces him that my age isn't something I'm afraid of. He is still looking at me sideways.

Then comes the question everyone wants an answer to, including me.

"Are you fecund?" the billionaire asks, using a word no one uses anymore, which only adds to the bluntness of his question.

"Am I *fertile?*" I repeat with a tone of shock in my voice.

He nods, expecting an answer.

"How would I know?" I say at a pitch a little louder than room temperature. I can feel my back straightening like the tail of a skunk ready to spray. "I don't know if I can have children," I say. "I haven't been trying."

He sticks out his lower lip in thought, straightens some papers. "What about Ronald?" the billionaire asks, not looking up.

I had been surprised to hear that Ronald works for the billionaire. He's someone I went out with once or twice, eighteen years ago, and we have kept in touch through mutual circles of friends. I'm not interested in dating Ronald. "Thank you," I say with my tail still up. "But Ronnie is not for me." I use Ronald's nickname to show we're familiar with each other.

"Why not?" The billionaire isn't going to let this go, even though the reason I've already given him should be enough.

"I've known Ronnie for many years," I point out. "I'm just not interested in dating him." I'm trying to be direct. The details are not important.

The billionaire is not giving up. "He's cut his hair, lost weight, and he's making a killing with me," he says, as if these facts should change how I feel.

"Thank you, but I'm not going to date Ronald," I repeat, going back to Ronnie's formal name to show I'm formally ending the discussion.

The billionaire picks up the phone and asks his assistant to tell Ronald to come into his office. "Wait, you'll see. He looks great," he insists.

Ronald comes in. He does look better than he's ever looked. The billionaire makes conversation that's about as awkward as when a Jewish mother introduces her son to a young lady she met at temple. I cringe, tail still up. I'm hearing Stephanie Banks in my head, warning me: *Love is overrated. Get married and have children. Or you'll regret it.* I smile with my mouth closed at Ronald, say it's nice to see him again, and add nothing further to the conversation.

"See," the billionaire says after Ronald has left the room. "He looks better than ever. What did I tell you?"

"Ronald is a lovely guy," I reply honestly. "But he's not for me."

"But *why?*" the billionaire says, exasperated. He just can't believe that a forty-two-year-old-possibly-no-longer-fecund woman is being so picky. "Listen to me, he's a good man. Get married."

"Look," I said pointedly. "I know how to get married. I deserve love. He deserves to be loved."

"Oh, love, *shmove,*" he says, dismissing me with a wave of the hand as if I'm a youngster with no idea what the real world is about. "Go out with him! Why not just go out with him?" It's now an order.

Forget what Stephanie told me. Forget babies. Forget regret! Forget it all! I think to myself, in frustration.

I finally spray. "Because I do not want to sleep with him! Is that reason enough? I do not want to marry and have babies with this man."

I would have said something much more off-color had I not been doing my best to bite my tongue in a business setting. There is a fine line to walk between sitting down for a meeting and standing up for yourself.

The billionaire pouts his lower lip again, nods his head.

No deal.

TWO WOMEN, ONE STORY

One would think that there would be a multitude of unique stories in a city like Manhattan. But if you listen closely enough, you'll notice that there are really only a few stories that happen again and again to millions of different people.

Take this story from not long ago. In a period of two days, I meet with two single women. Each a brunette, each named Sabrina. Each forty-one. Each never married. Each wants children. One works in human resources, the other in publishing. I'll call one Sabrina A and the other Sabrina B.

Here is their story:

Sabrina A: "I have such a story for you."

Sabrina B: "Are you ready for this one?"

"I am always ready for a good story," I say.

Sabrina A: "This guy contacted me on a dating site."

Sabrina B: "He said he was fifty-one, but when we met, I could tell he's probably in his late fifties."

Sabrina A: "But I gave it a shot. I'm really trying to be open-minded."

Sabrina B: "The first date was fine. We met for drinks."

Sabrina A: "And after the first drink, it was getting late and I was ready to end the date."

Sabrina B: "But then he ordered a second drink."

Sabrina A: "So I had to sit there, politely, as he sipped his Vodka Tonic."

Sabrina B: "It took him about an hour to finish his drink."

Sabrina A: "Here it was, now almost 11:00 PM, and much later than I expected or wanted to be out."

Sabrina B: "I crawled into bed the minute I got home, and he texted me at 12:30 AM to tell me he had a great time and ask me when I would like to go out again."

Sabrina A: "It was pretty aggressive, since I hadn't given him any hints like I couldn't wait for the next date. Could he not have at least waited until morning?"

Sabrina B: "I replied the next day that I'd see him again—because like I said, I'm trying to be open-minded."

Sabrina A: "And he texted back *immediately* with a plan."

Sabrina B: "Now you know I like a man with a plan."

Sabrina A: "I had mentioned I take Pilates." (Sabrina B, to be fair, had mentioned "a museum exhibit I wanted to see.")

Sabrina A and B: "He suggested we go to a Pilates class/the museum exhibit, then drinks, then dinner."

Sabrina A: "That is a lot . . . "

Sabrina B: " . . . for one date, I told him."

Sabrina A: "We settled on just dinner."

Sabrina B: "And I realized at dinner that while he is a lovely man, who clearly wants to get married and have children . . . "

Sabrina A: "I just couldn't see him anymore. There was simply no connection."

Sabrina B: "So when he texted for the next date, I replied with my regrets."

Sabrina A: "And he called me immediately!"

The women of the Otherhood are not planning to settle for anyone.

Sabrina B: "He would not take no for an answer."

Sabrina A: "He wasn't a lunatic or anything."

Sabrina B: "He was just really sad about it."

Sabrina A: "And I was feeling a little bad and even reconsidering . . ."

Sabrina B: " . . . until he said something that I just couldn't believe."

Sabrina A: "'You're forty-one. Don't you think it's time to settle for a nice guy like me?'"

Sabrina B: "'You're not getting younger,' he added, like I don't know how time works."

Sabrina A: "I told him he was a nice guy but that I wasn't interested in settling for him or any other man. He was flabbergasted."

Sabrina B: "Did he really think he could wake up in his late fifties and decide he was ready and that the next woman he met who was fifteen years younger than him would just marry him?"

Sabrina A: "I said thank you very much for the reminder, and hung up. I haven't spoken to him since."

And here is the only way the stories differ (besides the Pilates/museum thing). The following happened only to Sabrina B:

Sabrina B: "He asked me for my address because he wanted to send me a book. The next day, I received a FedEx package. It was a copy of Lori Gottlieb's *Marry Him: The Case for Marrying Mr. Good Enough.* The note read: *Read this book. I'll call you in a couple of days to discuss it. Lori Gottlieb is a smart woman.* He's texted and called a few times, but I haven't responded. I just don't have the heart to tell him that, as far as I know, Lori Gottlieb is still single. She never settled, and neither will I."

The women of the Otherhood are not planning to settle for anyone. Had we thought settling was something we could be satisfied with, we would have settled years ago, when we were more fertile. That's not to say that women who marry and become mothers at a young age have settled. It's just that women who want to be in love with the right partner before partnering for life are going to wait for him. And if he had arrived when she was twenty-five, great. Thirty-five? Good. Forty-five? Well, he arrived, and that's the important thing.

What the older men who waited for us to be ready to "settle" need to understand is that we have not been waiting to settle. We've been simply waiting for love.

HOW TO GET MARRIED

"He asked," Laura bluntly replies when I ask why she married John.

I stop walking so Laura can put her now-calm baby girl back in the stroller I'm pushing down Broadway. Her response catches me off guard and I can't help but giggle; Laura is hardly the type of woman who would be waiting by the phone for an engagement ring.

"No, seriously. I married John because he asked," she repeats. "You know me, I wasn't a huge dater. But I always wanted to get married and have children. And I went from one perfectly loving relationship to another, but none of my boyfriends proposed. Not even the guy I lived with for over a year when I moved to Detroit. And I moved to Michigan for him, by the way. And P.S., it wasn't me; he's still single at forty-four with no marital ambitions whatsoever."

Let me explain something before I go on. I don't normally ask women why they are married or unmarried, but as I speak to more and more women of the Otherhood, I can't help but notice something we all have in common: They don't delay falling in love, delay getting married, and rarely, once those things are in place, delay having children. Yet, it's assumed they all do. This "delay" myth has become so ubiquitous, in fact, the U.S. Census even referenced it in the title of a 2011 study about college-educated women having their first child later than ever: "Census Bureau Reports 'Delayer Boom' as More Educated Women Have Children Later." As if we all banded together and collectively decided to delay the very thing we know we cannot delay. As if we make these "delaying" decisions entirely on our own and not thanks to what men say they want. As if no man ever tells his girlfriend or wife, no matter how much older she's getting, "I'm not ready to have children. Let's wait." Boom indeed.

While college-educated women do tend to wait for marriage, or at least a live-in partner, before motherhood, no single-and-over-thirty-five woman I know who wants children is "delaying" having that child. In fact, most women I know who marry after thirty-five begin trying to have a baby immediately. At the bridal shower I once attended for a then-thirty-eight-year-old friend, the talk was about how she was expecting to have her girlfriends over again for a baby shower "this time next year!" Her timing was off by only three months.

"Anyway, when I moved back to New York City at thirty-four," Laura explains, "my single girlfriends here told me it was too hard to meet single men who were serious about dating and said I had to go online. With their persistence—online dating was so not my thing—I did. The first guy who contacted me on the dating site never asked me out. The second guy who contacted me was John. By our third date, I just knew he was the one. By our fourth month together, he proposed."

Laura and John got married when they were thirty-five and thirty-four, respectively. They waited one year before trying to conceive; although they knew it was a bit of a risk, fertility-wise, they also believed they should enjoy their first year of marriage just being mar-

> While college-educated women do tend to wait for marriage, or at least a live-in partner, before motherhood, no single-and-over-thirty-five woman I know who wants children is 'delaying' having that child.

ried, without worrying about trying to conceive. They got pregnant on their third try. I look down and smile at Laura's baby, Hope. I want to believe she is smiling back at me.

When women are childless due to singlehood, there's a "tsk tsk" reverberation to our so-called naïveté about our fertility.

"Naïve about my fertility?" asks Julie, thirty-eight, whose ex-husband decided he just didn't want to be married any more after two years of marriage. She was thirty-three when he broke the news—and her heart—just when she thought they'd start trying to have a child. "I get my period every month. I know how often I lose another egg!

"Yesterday, my twenty-six-year-old coworker said, 'You better get cracking if you want kids.' I wanted to say, 'Thanks for the advice to do something I can't do anything about.' It's frustrating to hear that I am not doing or haven't done all I could do to become a mother."

I've had my share of it, too. A commenter on a *Huffington Post* piece I wrote about circumstantial infertility—when you can't have children because you don't have a partner to have them with—called me a "femi-nazi career woman." It's a rather violent-sounding persona. Even if I *did* choose not to have children while enjoying my career, likening my choice to the Third Reich is draconian. The anger toward women, who do their civic duty by doing their best to earn a living and contributing to society through taxes and charity, before and after marriage, and often once they're mothers, is misplaced.

Of course there are some women for whom motherhood is not a priority or even an interest. But for the rest of us, there's this strange, underlying need to blame us for not becoming mothers by our midthirties—no matter how much we wanted to be mothers, no matter our frustrations and sadness over not being mothers—as if we brought it on ourselves, as if finding a man to marry is as easy as it seems to some.

"It's called 'blaming the victim,'" Dr. Robi Ludwig, a psychotherapist, explains to me over sushi later that night. "It's like when a crime victim is blamed for his or her victimization. It feels more comfortable for people to think that victims put themselves in a vulnerable position. We just don't like to be reminded of our own vulnerabilities, that life is not always within our control."

Yet, we know that we, the women of the Otherhood, don't sit back and passively wait for love to come. I've set out to ask some women in their midthirties how they are going about trying to find love.

I've organized a midweek, Midtown lunch with three professional women in their midthirties: Rory, age thirty-five; Mallory, age thirty-six; and Meredith, age thirty-five.

"I met a guy on Sunday," Meredith says right after we order, as though she couldn't wait to share the news. Mallory rolls her eyes.

"Meredith is always meeting new guys," Mallory explains.

"Not *always*," Meredith retorts, her prematurely Botox-ed brow hiding a furrow.

"Yes, you are," says Rory. "You are so good at that. Where did you meet this one?"

"The magazine area at Barnes & Noble in Union Square," she replies, as if she has done this before. "He was thumbing through *Fast Company* and I was pretending to flip through *New York* Magazine. I mean, I *was* flipping through the magazine, but I was more interested in meeting Mark."

"Do tell," eggs on Rory.

"He's thirty-eight, never married, totally cute. He works in finance. Turns out we have like fourteen Facebook friends in common but never met. We went out for a quick bite after talking in the magazine section for like forty-five minutes. He walked me home and kissed me good night! We're seeing each other again on Sunday night. I'm so excited."

I've met men at Barnes & Noble myself. The first was in the nonfiction best sellers section at the Barnes & Noble on Broadway and West 82nd Street. We went out twice but we had nothing more in common than a love of fresh, new nonfiction books. And in the late 1990s, I met a guy in the café. If I recall, he had a stack of travel books in front of him, and I was probably reading something by Seth Godin. Somehow we got to talking and later that week we talked some more at a nice restaurant on Second Avenue. He was a tall, thin attorney named Peter. Or was it Philip? Or Paul? (I remember it began with a *P* and went with his Park Avenue gray suit and thick, preppy, side-parted, sandy, wavy hair.) But to be fair, his name wasn't what was most memorable about him. It was his laugh. He laughed like a hyena. I had to stop saying funny things or, as he put it, "cute" things, because then he would laugh this god-awful laugh that I imagine caused the entire restaurant to look our way. I just couldn't see him again.

A couple of years later, I noticed PeterPhilipPaul in *The New York Times* Weddings section, his thick, wavy hair parted neatly, standing next to his smiling bride. Another petite brunette saw beyond his laugh. Maybe it was the thing she loved most about him. And for a moment that morning, I regretted not saying more funny things that night.

Meredith is especially good at being proactive at dating. "I mean, I won't go on a singles cruise or anything crazy like that because it sounds like one, long, awful singles event and you can't get off the boat! But yeah, I'll try just about anything. I did stop going to sports bars during some sort of playoff though. I swear, you could walk around in a bikini and those men are only interested in the game!"

Mallory, a thirty-six-year-old head of HR for a hedge fund whom Meredith invited along, agrees. "I tried the B&N thing a couple of weekends ago. Meredith is always trying to get me to be more proactive. And I'm not usually shy, but the whole thing feels so inauthentic, you know? So I go to Barnes & Noble and decide I'll sit in the café there and I take a few books with me, making sure one's not like a self-help book that will make some guy think I'm crazy or something and I look around and there are no seats left. So I go by the magazine section but there are these twentysomething women there picking up a boatload of wedding magazines like they didn't already plan their entire weddings after like four dates with their guys, and I put the books down and walked out."

"You have to try meditation, Mallory," Meredith says, then turns to me. "I keep telling her. She has all this negative energy about meeting men. You have to be positive.

"I've been seeing a psychic since college," she continues, "a medium to help me talk to my mom, who I hope has some wisdom from the afterlife, and I have a meditation coach. She told me to think of myself as a woman in love. So I make myself a really nice dinner and take long baths with bath oils and I buy myself little gifts now and again." Meredith holds up her right hand to show a diamond-encrusted cocktail ring she gave herself for her thirty-fifth birthday. "I was tired of waiting for my diamonds!" she says. "I love myself, so I bought this amazing ring for myself."

Meredith is thirty-five and an Ivy League–educated attorney. Looking at her, you'd never suspect she is a deeply spiritual woman. Her thick, layered brown hair is always blown out professionally, and today, her perfectly tailored sheath dress is accessorized with a classic pair of diamond stud earrings. She recently broke up with a man after about six months.

"He just wasn't flexible," she says. "I was expected to be the flexible one, as if everything I do in my life is a choice, and everything he does is not. I understand he has a young daughter and I totally respect that, but he lives in Long Island and would never come into the city to go to an event with me even when he didn't have her. And he refused to get a babysitter when he had Lucy over the weekend. I didn't expect him to sleep over in the city, because he had to go back to her, but come on, when he was married they got babysitters and went out Saturday nights. And then he'd be annoyed if I didn't want to go visit him and his daughter in Long Island on Sunday. I just didn't want to spend my Sundays taking his daughter to soccer or pottery or whatever. He would say, 'But you love kids. Why don't you want to spend time with Lucy?' If it was our kid, yeah, I'd love that he was so dedicated. And I would go sometimes, and it was fun, but seeing him was always on his terms, and that's what I was tired of. Basically I was frustrated by having a boyfriend only every second weekend no matter what was going in my life."

> 66 But the one thing I cannot control, the one thing that is most important to me, is finding love, getting married, and having kids! And my friends who are fortunate enough to have that make me feel like I've chosen this 'life of freedom' or whatever. 99

"It's not just men we're dating, though. I feel like being single and not a mom affects my friendships, too," Rory, a thirty-five-year-old attorney who works with Meredith says. "My closest girlfriend who got married at thirty-one rarely has time for me. And trust me, when she was single and on and off with the boyfriend who's now her husband, I was always there for her. But now she will only see me on her terms, and it's usually with a kid in tow.

"Why can't married moms value some adult time?" Rory continues. "I don't want to see you when you have your kids with you, sorry. We spend most of our time together doing what the kid wants and I end up spelling things so the kids won't understand what I'm talking about. And you know what she said to me when I asked her if just this once, because I really wanted to talk to her about something, if she could meet me for a drink after she put the kids to bed? She said no because she's too tired and it's not her fault if I work late. 'You made your choice,' she said."

"Choice?" Meredith said loudly. "Choice? What choice did you make? I hate when my mom friends say that to me, like I made a choice to be single. I can control what I do for a living and keeping in shape and where I live and all that. But the one thing I cannot control, the one thing that is most important to me, is finding love, getting married, and having kids! And my friends who are fortunate enough to have that make me feel like I've chosen this 'life of freedom' or whatever."

I know that feeling. Married parents, men and women, will see me come home on a Saturday night and ask me twenty questions about where I was and say things like "Looks like you had a good time!" And then, "I just like to live vicariously through you, that's all." Once, after another dud of a night in terms of meeting someone new, I replied, "I'm coming home alone. I would much rather have been home with my husband and kids, eating pizza and watching a movie."

"What gets me," Rory says, "is that they take their lives for granted. I want to say, 'Stop fantasizing about what you might be missing and start enjoying what you have!'"

"You know what's hard for me?" Mallory asks. "It's that being single always means it's two against one when I have a difference of opinion with my married friends. No one has my back."

Meredith: "I totally agree. The other night, my friend asks me right in front of her husband if I'm thinking about harvesting my eggs. I told them I'm not because to me it feels like throwing in the towel, you know? Like I've given up on meeting someone and so I'm freezing my eggs like an old maid or something. I know it doesn't really mean that, but that's how just the thought of it makes me feel."

"I agree 100 percent," says Mallory, toasting Meredith with her iced tea.

"And you know what my friend's husband said?" Meredith continues. "He talked to me like I'm twenty and he's my father or something and said, 'You're wrong. Do it. It doesn't matter what it costs'—yeah, because he's not paying for it!—'just do it.' He said that his sister didn't do it and now she's forty-three and pissed that she didn't. And then my friend adds that I don't want to regret it and if it were her, she would absolutely do it.

"And I'm wondering why I'm having a conversation like my womb is open for discussion with my friend and her husband.

Two against one and it's *my* fertility and a very personal, intimate decision!"

"I don't even like discussing this with my girlfriends," Mallory adds. "I have this one friend who is not proactive at all. She won't go online, she rarely goes out. She'd never go to Barnes & Noble or sit at a bar or do whatever to even try to meet someone. And she wants to talk about freezing our eggs. Talking about it really depresses me. I don't want to feel like I've given up."

I was thirty-seven when egg freezing became a topic of conversation among my girlfriends. It was 2006 and egg cryopreservation wasn't something on the tip of every thirtysomething woman's tongue yet, and it wasn't highly recommended because the technology wasn't where it needed to be to make the investment not just a disappointment. So the conversation would be more hypothetical than a real discussion. Today, it's part of normal conversation for women in their thirties and early forties. By the time the science became a more viable option, I was forty-two and not about to invest $12,000 when I didn't even know if I had eggs left to freeze.

"I don't just want a baby," Mallory adds. "I want the life. I want a husband. Even if I freeze my eggs, what would I do with them if I don't meet a guy?"

"I'm just tired of everyone having an opinion on my life," Meredith says. "Even a well-meaning partner at my firm asked me if I'm going to freeze my eggs! It's like because I'm single, it's an open invitation to comment on my life as if I'm on a reality show or something and everything I say or do is open for comment!

"Married people talk about my life like it's a walk in the park. They never consider what I might be going through, or even just basic issues like travel. One of the hardest things about being single is I can't find anyone to travel with. Everyone has their own schedule, budget, preferences, and I have all this vacation time accruing and no one to go away with. My married parent friends are like: 'You are so lucky, you can go travel whenever you want.' And I'm like, with whom?"

Rory pipes in. "You know what my friend said? He told me to just go by myself, like I don't know that's an option. I just don't want to spend all that money and go alone. I can't imagine being in Rome or Paris or even on a beach somewhere thinking about how romantic it is and not being with someone."

"That's why I don't even want to travel with girlfriends anymore," Mallory adds. "I went away with a few friends last summer and we'd get all dressed up at night and go out and have dinner together and go back to the hotel and get into our king-size beds in pairs like lesbians. And no offense to lesbians, but I don't enjoy waking up next to a woman."

"OK, OK, enough with this negativity," Meredith says. "Listen, my friend Diana just got engaged. She's forty-two! She's totally into the visualization thing and it worked for her. When she was moving in with her fiancé last week, she came upon love letters that she wrote to her 'future husband' in 2006. They were filled with her feelings for him. She also had a vision board with a picture of an engagement ring on it that looks so much like the one her fiancé gave her, the apartment they now live in, and words that described the man she wanted to meet! You know, attractive, fit, smart, chivalrous, and someone who wanted to be in a relationship, too. She said that every day she would envision this man and never lost faith, even when she was frustrated. And then one day, he walked right into her life. She totally believes she manifested all her dreams to come true. She's so inspiring!"

"So we're all supposed to start vision boards now?" Mallory says, a little cynically.

"I have an idea," Rory says. "We should each go to the magazine section of Barnes & Noble and pick up magazines for our vision boards. Even if the vision board thing doesn't work out, maybe we'll meet a guy."

"But you *have* to believe it will work," Meredith pleads. "Or it won't."

"Let's make a pact," Mallory offers. "We'll all focus on manifesting our husbands. It can't hurt, right?"

"Agreed!" Rory and Meredith say with enthusiasm.

"Me, too," I say. "It's never too late to believe in love, after all."

Not that I have ever really lost faith.

THE DATING BERMUDA TRIANGLE

I t's the very beginning of spring and things are heating up.

It's the natural change of the seasons, with optimism for love blossoming everywhere: in the steel buildings that tower over the city, in the rows of tulips outside the bodegas, on the crosstown buses that connect East and West Manhattan. The girls are hoping that by the time they get to the other side and the leaves begin to fall, they'll have already fallen in love.

Some of the single women of the Otherhood return to Match.com. Some cross Fifth Avenue like models on a runway, confidently striding in their new trench coats, bare legs, and platform heels, glancing at the men in suits passing them by. Some women get a quick blowout before cocktails at Harlow. Some send an email about a share house in the Hamptons. Some of us go shopping for a new spring dress. Spring arrives, and we fall into a comforting anticipation of what may come.

But there's been a misunderstanding, and the girls don't know it. Just as they take off into spring, some of these fabulous women will get caught in the Dating Bermuda Triangle, and it may take five years to find their way out. At least that's what the men have told me, now that I've been rediscovered.

> "He wanted me to know he's experienced in marriage, telling me he knows what makes marriage work, even though his didn't, and perhaps assuming that because I haven't been married before, I don't know what's important in a marriage. There is an irony to this misconception about single women; in fact, it's the reverse: If we didn't understand how challenging it is to be married, and all the valuable assets a marriage needs to survive, we probably would have married a long time ago."

It's just starting to rain when I meet David for the first time. I'm in one of my new dresses. "You'll have fun! Just go!" promised Simone, a mutual acquaintance, about the date. And it being spring, I had agreed.

David, my nice-looking date, is waiting for me when I walk into the restaurant. He introduces me to the older gentleman he met at the bar as he awaited my arrival. "You two are an attractive couple," the man offers, presumptuously.

At dinner, David repeats what the man said, as if it were prescient. "Does he know something we don't?" he says flirtatiously. I smile and tuck into the menu.

David is doing everything right. He is a nice guy, and he's invited me to a wonderful restaurant. And I'm enjoying myself. I do love a lovely date. But I'm not finding myself drawn to David. Still, I'm thinking, *you never know,* and I focus on enjoying the evening. It's spring after all.

But David is ahead of me.

"You knew the moment you walked in, didn't you?" David asks, referring to a mutual attraction I wasn't feeling.

"I did?" I reply, gently, hoping he won't take it as I meant it.

"I mean, I'm an OK-looking guy," he says with false modesty. "And we're having fun. When Simone told me about you, I was, you know, casual about it. It's just a date, right? But she did well," he says with a wink. He leans in and adds: "I'll have to call her tomorrow to thank her."

My date has done his homework. He looked me up online. He seems to have read my articles about my grief over my childlessness, and so he knows I'd always expected to have love, marriage, and children by now. And he wants to make something clear.

"You know, I didn't want to have more children, but I would consider it. If that's what you want. I mean, if you want to have kids, I would have kids."

It's a very generous and genuine thing to say. But it's especially bold coming on the first date. It has me on guard.

David is about ten years older than I am with two daughters soon to be graduating from high school. He's been divorced amicably for about four years. "We were friends, not lovers," he says of his ex-wife. "We're still good friends." He adds sweetly, "But I want to find someone I also will be in love with." Then he adds, squarely looking into my eyes: "Sex is an important part of marriage."

David did not expect me to sleep with him that night. He wanted me to know he's experienced in marriage, telling me he knows what makes marriage work, even though his didn't, and perhaps assuming that because I haven't been married before, I don't know what's important in a marriage. There is an irony to this misconception about single women; in fact, it's the reverse: If we didn't understand how challenging it is to be married, and all the valuable assets a marriage needs to survive, we probably would have married a long time ago.

I'm concerned David is planning our future while I'm still debating dessert choices.

Since I turned forty, dating has changed its course. Before then, men were more laid-back, and I would lean in. I wanted to be in a relationship, and on the rare occasion I met a man I wanted to be in a relationship with, I was focused on it. I wanted to land safely in a relationship. But I found few men wanted that, too.

I also remember when simply being a certain age made me less-than. Invisible. All I was to many men was a woman "desperate to get married" just by virtue of my age. I did indeed want to be married. I did without question want to have children. But I was never desperate. If I had been desperate, I would have married any man who'd have me. That was hardly the case. I did want to find love within a timeline that would enable me, biologically, to become a mother. But love was always the priority. Love was always my goal. Love always came first.

Still, discounting a woman as being just an age, not a woman, is part of the modern single man's dating dogma.

The first time I heard this, I was thirty-two. I met a cute European at a singles event. We talked for a while and somehow our ages came up. He was thirty-three and told me frankly that he doesn't date women over the age of thirty. He said he'd never know if they wanted him for him or for his sperm.

Years later, it had become a popular refrain. "I can't date women between the ages of thirty-five and forty," said a forty-year-old man I was interested in when I was thirty-five.

I was thirty-six when this same conversation happened as I sat invisibly between two male friends at a party, both of whom I had dated years earlier, each now forty-one. "I get that," the married one

> 66 Still, discounting a woman as being just an age, not a woman, is part of the modern single man's dating dogma. 99

of them said to the single one. "They're just desperate to get married." It wasn't even *his* experience, having married a woman who was thirty-three when he was thirty-five. But he chimed in to the manly man chorus anyway.

"I can't date women between the ages of thirty-five and forty," another man told me on our first date, after describing why his last relationship with a thirty-seven-year-old didn't work out, what with her wanting to get married and have children.

"I'm thirty-nine," I told him in return, not wanting to postpone the end of something I knew would probably end.

"You're different," he said immediately, as if I were.

"I don't date women ages thirty-eight to forty-two," said a divorced man with two young children whom I recently dated. "They're just desperate." *At least he upped his age range,* I thought to myself.

In fact, once I had emerged from the Dating Bermuda Triangle, somehow it became acceptable to share with me that dating women of a certain age was unacceptable. It was as if finding love before thirty-five made a woman up to standard. After that, she was assumed desperate.

It made me wonder if some people believe love is only for those who have found it.

Once I turned forty, I seemed to exit the Dating Bermuda Triangle. Now older men are relieved to know I'm no longer at an age where they feel the collective pressure by women about marriage and children. I am once again dateable.

> ❝ Once I turned forty, I seemed to exit the Dating Bermuda Triangle. Now older men are relieved to know I'm no longer at an age where they feel the collective pressure by women about marriage and children. I am once again dateable. ❞

But now, on the other side of the Dating Bermuda Triangle, the men wonder why I'm not pressuring them about marriage and children.

Back on my date with David, he saw he was not getting the response from me he expected, so he reminded me that other women, younger women, were desperate for him. "My ex-girlfriend is thirty-eight and within six months she put all this pressure on me. She wanted to know if I was going to marry her. Six months! I had to break up with her. It just felt so, you know, desperate."

I couldn't let it go. It had been building up for years. I tried to be gentle.

"Was this woman you dated truly desperate? Or was she telling you what you already knew, that her fertility has a hard stop that she's approaching? If you were not going to marry her or want to be with her and have a child with her, she simply needed to know. And so she very responsibly and courageously brought it up and asked you how you felt. And instead of respecting her for her maturity and her beautiful, natural desire to be a mother, you scoffed at her and labeled her as 'desperate.'"

My date looked down at his dessert plate. I knew he felt bad but I couldn't stop myself. There is something about the entitled male nonchalance about women's fertility that really upsets me.

"I know that men want to feel desired for a number of reasons, not just their sperm. But if this woman was still unmarried at thirty-eight—and my guess, because you're a great guy, is that she was also a fantastic woman—and looking for the right partner and was not desperate, as you called her, to settle for one she doesn't love, why would you suspect she hadn't fallen in love with you? Why don't you think she had met the man she felt would be a great husband and a great father?"

I continued, "Women over thirty-five who are losing their grip on their fertility are not desperate. They are hoping, praying, working at getting to the finish line as a mother before they can no longer have children. Had they been desperate, they would have married the wrong man a long time ago."

Awkwardly, David had wanted me to know that he was happy to date me even though I'm no longer in my thirties because I was no longer desperate. And somehow he thought it would make him more attractive to me to know other women were still desperate for him. Perhaps, somehow, he thought it would make me desperate for him, too.

David felt bad and apologized, and it earned him a second date. But halfway through our second attempt, David asked me where I thought "this" was going. "It seems to be going into the entrée," I said as the server brought our dinner to the table. "We're now officially one and a half dates in. I don't know where this is going, but that's what dating is for, right?"

My poor date. He was lovely and very generous. But he was at a loss as to why his charms were not working. He had entered his own Dating Bermuda Triangle where women sit back and the men lean in.

WHERE ARE
THE SUITABLE MEN?

I've made plans to meet Daniel, a platonic friend, for dinner at The General, a popular Asian restaurant in the Bowery, to ask his thoughts about the scarcity of suitable men. Daniel is a successful businessman in his early forties. He's one of those rare Jewish men who is super tall and, until recently, super single. He wears his salt-and-pepper curls trimmed neat, right up against his scalp. He has great taste and is always dressed in a beautiful suit and tie. Even on Sunday nights, he wears a sports jacket with jeans. Daniel is most definitely a suitable man.

"How was your date the other night?" Daniel asks, referring to my date with David. I consider Daniel a good friend and I'm not surprised he's remembered to ask about my date.

"Thanks for asking. Really nice guy, but we're not for each other," I say, not offering any further explanation because I don't want to sound critical of a kind and generous date.

"Hmmm . . . Seems like you don't meet too many men you are interested in," he says, perhaps as if it's my fault. "Any other prospects coming up?" he adds.

"Nope," I say flatly, but I can't help but feel defensive. Daniel seems to find new women to date much more often than I find a man to go out with.

I don't want to pick a fight with Daniel, but like a scab that's itching to be scratched, I ask him why he thinks there are so many more single women looking for love than there are men in New York City.

"There are no suitable men," Daniel says matter-of-factly. He takes a swig of his Vodka Soda as a period to his point. I guess I deserved a frank answer.

While Daniel and I have been friends for only a couple of years, I know how hard he's tried at relationships. He treats women well, always willing to indulge in a famed new lounge or restaurant. He's even been known to scout for good date places; he wants to find places he thinks women will enjoy for the ambiance and he will enjoy for the top-shelf liquor selection. He takes good care of his dates.

And in typical fashion, Daniel is about to take care of my dating problem.

"Here's the deal. I'll be honest with you," he says without a pause. "Single guys can be jerks. They either have no interest in dating anyone seriously and are just looking to sleep with you. Or they are looking for something serious but have no interest in dating a woman your age."

It's a sharp point.

"Sorry. It's just the truth," he says. "You should date guys in their fifties," he adds with another swig of his cocktail.

It's important to note that Daniel and I are the same age.

"Isn't your girlfriend in her midthirties?" I reply, one eyebrow cocked.

"Yes, but it's different for guys. We date younger. Karen is ten years younger than I am. But a forty-three-year-old woman . . . you

> **"** Unless a man is divorced with children and wants to be in a relationship with a woman he knows will be a good stepmother to his kids, men check out younger women. Much younger women. Women of the Otherhood become more than invisible to them. **"**

have to make concessions." And then Daniel says, "I think you should look for men who are fifty-three to fifty-nine."

It's not so much what Daniel says, it's the tone of voice he's using. It's as if he's telling me I have an incurable disease and the only way to survive is to date men at least ten years older than I am. I understand that if a man wakes up at fortysomething and realizes he wants children, he will look for a younger woman who has more time with her fertility, as troublesome as that is to admit. The problem is that men wake up at fortysomething suddenly ready for marriage, and the fortysomething women have now aged-out for them.

Ironically, there was a time when we dated only people our own age. High school, college, even in our early twenties, we dated men around our age. At some point, as men get older, they want younger women. First it's a year or two younger. Then it's a few years. Then, when they get to their late thirties, women in their twenties are their target.

Unless a man is divorced with children and wants to be in a relationship with a woman he knows will be a good stepmother to his kids, men check out younger women. Much younger women. Women of the Otherhood become more than invisible to them. Men become completely insensitive to us, as if our age is something we should understand is unattractive to them and therefore we should not be hurt by the things they say or do.

"I'm just being honest," Daniel repeats as I remain silent. He can tell I'm hurt, and somehow he believes his honesty should make me feel better.

I date men my age, even younger. Daniel is projecting his attraction for younger women on all men. But he's not entirely off.

The week before dinner with Daniel, I was at a TV show premiere chatting with Gary, a single forty-four-year-old attorney, and Wendy, a thirty-nine-year-old lifestyle personality. Wendy and I were suggesting men for each other, men we've dated who aren't a match for us but may be for the other. Women of the Otherhood are often trying to match each other up.

"He's a great guy but we never hit it off that way," she said. "I'll set you up with him!" It turned out her date and I had already gone out. In fact, Wendy and I have dated a few of the same men. These are the men we know are more serious about meeting someone and therefore actually date women around their own age.

We were running out of ideas when she spotted a tall fortysomething man with floppy brown hair and decided to pursue him. In a flash, she was gone, and Gary and I were still talking about dating. Gary doesn't attempt to suggest someone for me to meet. It's rare that a male friend will offer to introduce me to someone, so I'm not surprised. Nevertheless, I have an idea for Gary.

"I think you might like my friend Marcy," I said to him, thinking of a divorcée I know. But it was really just a test. The minute I told Gary her age, I knew he'd balk.

"Tell me about her," he said. I did. "And how old is she?" he asked on cue.

"Forty-two," I said, as if it's nothing.

"Not for me," he responded, as if she's nothing.

The ageists are all over Manhattan. Like Brandon, who recently married a woman he'd been dating for twenty-five years. Not the same woman. An exact replica of the women he'd been dating since college. All his girlfriends looked the same. They all had similar personalities. But Brandon waited for that girl and him to have a twenty-year age difference before finally proposing.

At dinner with Daniel, he contends, "It's not ageist for me to date younger women any more than it's ageist for you not to want to date men ten to fifteen years older than you."

"Daniel, you're not interested in dating women your own age!"

But my friend is distracted. A gorgeous woman is walking by and he's checking her out. "I'd date her. She's a hot fortysomething," he says cavalierly, as if any woman over forty would agree to date him simply because she's over forty.

"Maybe online dating isn't for you, where men search by age," he says, focusing back on our conversation. "You should go out and meet men at bars." As if I've never gone out to bars.

"I go out, Daniel," I say.

"Well, maybe you're not going to the right places," he says. "Go to sports bars."

"What women find is that unless you're actually into the sport, which I never am, it's awkward," I tell him. "The men know you are there to meet them and could care less. They are there for the game."

Daniel rolls his eyes.

"Don't roll your eyes!" I say. "Don't imply I am not doing enough."

"I'm not saying you're not doing enough. You're not doing enough of the right things," Daniel says.

"What would be the right thing to do?" I ask him.

"Go take a wine class or something!" he says, exasperated with me.

"That's absurd," says Martin Cohen, a strategic consultant and relationship coach, whose focus is on helping companies understand gender differences, when I meet with him later in the week to ask him about this very issue. "All you'll find in a wine class in New York City are women taking wine classes to meet men who don't show up."

Cohen is nationally recognized as the "gender balance guru." He has studied gender differences since the start of his decades-long career and is passionate about distinguishing what he calls the "power and possibility of who women really are." On a monthly basis, Cohen meets with single, or in a few cases, divorced, mostly childless, women in their midthirties and forties in New York City and South Florida. He's amazed at the women in his groups. Each woman, he says, is "particularly successful," and each one is feeling the so-called scarcity of men. And while the group is designed for networking, the conversation always comes back to dating and being endlessly single.

"This 'scarcity' issue is like a disease!" Cohen says passionately. "There is a scarcity in volume of men in these cities. There is scarcity in the kinds of men these women desire. And there is also a scarcity in places these men visit," he adds.

"This," he explains, "is why women begin to feel desperate. They are focused on finding a mate, falling in love, getting married, and having children. But lo and behold, *where are the men these women desire?* They are not at the singles events, they are not on singles cruises, they are not online.

"The men know they are the ones being sought out and are overwhelmed by the women who show up," Cohen continues. "There are men who can show up to meet women, but they don't. They hold that power. That's their secret. They are like boys in a candy store,"

> 'This,' he explains, 'is why women begin to feel desperate. They are focused on finding a mate, falling in love, getting married, and having children. But lo and behold, *where are the men these women desire?* They are not at the singles events, they are not on singles cruises, they are not online.'

he says. "And the women become sucked into the conversation of *where are the men.* The balance of power is absurd!"

Cohen gets solemn, adding, "Some women throw in the towel. They are so hurt by this trend that they become jaded, cynical, or settle in a mediocre relationship for comfort or security. And some women disengage and decide that finding a man is no longer a focus."

I think of many of my girlfriends, like me, are no longer interested in playing hide-and-seek with men who do not want to be found.

"And sadly," Cohen says, "some women fall into the trap. They are anxious to give men what they want and so they focus on sex. They are focused on their how their bodies look. But the women in my groups, and the women you are referring to, are *complete* women. You are secure. You are independent. You are not compromising. You are not codependent. And you won't fall for the tricks of a man's hidden agenda: sex and women who seem less powerful to them.

"You, and the women like you, know that the right men will connect to your integrity and your essence. Once the man sees you for who you are, you are able to offer your sweet surrender, your vulnerability, your femininity."

And then Cohen reveals the secret to how this paradigm can change. "When women give up on being the ones who seek out men, and become open to being the ones men seek out, everything shifts."

I take a deep breath. There is this blanket rule of blaming single women altogether for their circumstance. But the truth is, most men don't want to settle down, at least not until they are in their late thirties or forties. And women are told to pretend they don't want to be married because it will scare the men off. A woman is labeled "desperate" to be married if she admits she wants to be married until she meets a man who is ready to be married. It's a rather disingenuous way to live for both genders.

It somehow became unnatural for a woman to want to be married and have children. Women are walking on eggshells with men, as if even this hint of marriage might deem her "crazy" or "desperate." Even checking the box on an online dating site in your twenties or even early thirties saying you want to "get married" makes you seem as if you're coming on too strong. And yet, before you know it, you're deemed "too old" to marry.

I remember what it was like to be twenty-nine, unafraid of thirty. Not because I was courageous. But I wanted to fall in love and get married and so if it was thirty instead of twenty-nine, then that would be it. I remember saying aloud to a friend at my thirty-fourth birthday party, "This is it. I have one year to get married or I'll never be married. Once you're thirty-five, men turn the other way, like you're old news, or just old."

I no longer remember being eternally optimistic about love. Oh, I try. I get up and go out. And I ask friends and acquaintances, and total strangers, if they know someone for me. "I might," he says. Or "I'll keep you in mind!" she responds with enthusiasm that's not believable. Or they are blunt: "I don't know any men I would feel comfortable setting you up with," says Ray, the married father of three I meet at a Silicon Alley golf outing. "The men I know don't want to settle down. I don't know when they plan to grow up, but when they do, I'll keep you in mind."

I've attended singles events so unevenly weighted with women it felt as though I was at a women's empowerment group. One invitation-only event that specifically restricted the ratio of women to men had the same effect. Only two men actually showed up to meet twenty-five single women.

I've tried online dating until some of the men became abusive. "No wonder you're thirty-four and single," one man wrote after I did not respond to his message. "You're ugly. And you'll always be alone and you'll never have children." At least I knew that my intuition not to respond to his first message had been correct. Another man had "catfished" me—the term for when someone misrepresents themselves online. He was not a forty-year-old bachelor. He was a forty-year-old married man whose wife was expecting a baby. But mostly, once I was over thirty-eight, most of the men who were interested in meeting me online were about fifteen years older than me.

Online dating surely works for some; I even met a couple of men who are still friends of mine years later, although neither live in New York City. I tried alternative dating methods until they wore me down.

The challenge is that there are so many more single women than men in New York City. There are lots of women, including ambitious women who move to New York City to work, expecting to meet ambitious men. Only, the men don't follow. And so there are literally tens of thousands more women than men here. But instead of expecting more of the men, women are told to be less selective. We're not entitled to be so picky, I keep hearing. Most of the advice my friends and I hear begins with how women could stand to lower their expectations in order to be fulfilled.

A few months ago, I had a conversation with a married man about dating in New York. He got married at age forty.

"There just aren't enough age-appropriate, eligible men in New York City," I responded when he asked me why I wasn't dating anyone.

"Maybe you should date the short, fat, bald men you are overlooking," he said.

My heart sank. I realized he meant him, back when he was single. I didn't want to reveal to him that I have dated my share of short men, bald men, and overweight men and many variations thereof. I never turned down a man because he was any of those things. But all the men I dated who were in that group had something this man didn't have when I first met him when he was single. They had confidence. Confidence is one of the most appealing qualities of the men I date. It's not cockiness, which is confidence that is overplayed and probably masking insecurity. This man never asked me out.

The women I have spoken with may regret saying no to a suitor they did not believe suited them a long time ago, but most are happily not married to the men they thought they might marry at one time. The women of the Otherhood want to be married. They want to be mothers. But they don't want to settle for an average relationship.

And don't get these women wrong. It's not because they don't understand how hard relationships are, although they're told this often—usually in the way someone might make a point to a child about understanding more about X when they're grown. It's actually because women of the Otherhood do know how difficult relationships are that they don't want to settle for a relationship with someone they don't love. They know that with all the ups and downs, decisions and plans interrupted, for richer or poorer, through sickness and in health, for all the reasons couples break up (even the ones we all thought would make it) that if you don't have love, you have nothing to fight for.

Back at dinner with Daniel, he tells me, "I don't know what the right things for you to do are, but maybe you need to do something different. Maybe you need to work on yourself some more?"

Daniel knows I left corporate life to start my own business a few years ago, enabling me to do things I never thought I would do. I am an introspective woman. But Daniel is implying is that I'm not self-aware and that only when I know my "true" self will I attract the right man, or any man. And yet, there is no evidence that I am not focused on constantly developing my true self.

As mature adults, we should always be trying to understand our actions and motives. I pride myself on my personal growth, never expecting that a man or marriage would put me on my life's right path or save me from the challenges life brings. Rather, I rely on myself for that. Being ready for love means loving yourself. And at this very time in my life, despite not being in a relationship or being a mother, I have never been more in touch with myself or more proud of my personal growth.

I know Daniel means well; he wants to solve the problem because he knows I'm frustrated that I haven't met my life partner yet. Asking me to change my life again is his latest attempt. But at what point may a woman be deemed "enough"? It seems it takes finding a partner to prove to others that she is enough, and that she has tried enough things in order to meet her partner.

Meanwhile, Daniel says that I'm also not datable to men my age. So is it my age that I cannot control, or my lifestyle, which I have risked everything to improve, that is at fault? Which one is to blame? I don't think I am undatable because I am not good enough for a man to date. In fact, I think I'd be a really good partner for the right man. I think some men feel self-conscious about their limitations and so instead blame women for not catching them at the right time in their life.

Wynn's friend Mike was in love with a woman who was forty when he was forty-six. They dated for about ten months. Everyone thought this was it. Then one night, his friends asked him why Cathy didn't join them for dinner. "I broke up with her," he said matter-of-factly, with that air of cold superiority ageists thrive on. "I just couldn't end up with a woman who is forty. I want kids." Wynn, sitting across from him, said nothing.

I hear that story from Wynn at Forty Four, the Royalton Hotel bar in Midtown, a couple of weeks later. "Where are all the suitable men?" she asks over a glass of Merlot. She's quick to answer her own question. "They are in their late forties and all of a sudden desperate to be fathers. And I don't just mean to kids. I dated a guy recently who happened to look inside my closet as I was grabbing my jacket. He noticed two rows of neatly organized and pretty amazing shoes. He remarked that the shoes were pretty awesome, which they are. I immediately thought he appreciated good style. But then he said, and I quote, 'You've got expensive taste, baby. I could never afford you.' I explained that I didn't need him to afford me. I bought the shoes myself. 'Exactly,' he said. 'I want to take care of a woman. You don't need me to take care of you.' I never saw him again."

Wynn continues, "When men make me feel like I'm too old for love with an appropriately aged guy, I laugh to myself. I've never looked better or felt better in my life. So fuck 'em. Let them chase younger women who make them feel like their penis is bigger. All it does is make them look like big dicks. And it's not like they're all jumping into serious relationships to start having babies.

"And even Austin, the thirty-one-year-old I get together with once in a while just to have fun," Wynn goes on, "doesn't care that I'm forty, because he has no intentions of getting married any time soon. It's perfect."

It's not love. But it's life in the moment. The women of the Otherhood are not waiting for love to arrive on a silver platter; we're really enjoying and living the very best lives in the moment. We're leaving plenty of room for the main course when and if that arrives, but man, the appetizers can be pretty delicious, too.

FROM BOYS TO MEN

I'm wondering if I'm missing something, taking this whole "suitable" man thing too literally. I ask Jake, a guy I don't know well, to meet with me.

I walk into the pub and immediately spot Jake at the bar. He's already got a beer for himself, and he is chatting with the bartender whom he seems to know. As I walk over, he slides out a bar stool and welcomes me with a kiss on the cheek. I don't remember seeing him without a crowd of friends around him, and even though he's in jeans and a baseball cap, he's surprisingly, disarmingly, handsome. I notice his shirt is really stylish, modern, and sharp. And it fits him perfectly.

"You look nice," I say. And he blushes.

This is not a date. I had told Jake I wanted to talk to him for another male point of view. We are acquaintances and have never had a real conversation about anything other than the "great party!" we both attended. I wanted to speak with Jake because he's part of a group of guys around age forty who are very social, like frat boys who never really grew up. Wearing a suit for these guys—well, it's just not something they feel comfortable doing. I presumed he'd talk about the girls ten or fifteen years younger than him whom he dates. Or say something about not having any need to be a father any time soon.

On the other hand, despite his eternally causal demeanor, my intuition says there is something deeper about this guy. And so I was thrilled when Jake agreed to speak with me.

Jake is patient as I ask the bartender for beer recommendations. The beer menu is extensive, filled with artisanal beers I have never heard of, and I just can't settle for any old beer I can get at the 7-Eleven. But after three different tastes that fall flat, Jake gently pushes his glass toward me. "Try this," he says sweetly. And I like it.

I realize that Jake is shy. I admit, adorably so. We laugh about how it's a little strange that we've known each other for a few years but know very little about one another. We spend a while sharing how we grew up, moved to New York, and started our careers. I learn that Jake is a successful magazine publisher, not that he was showing off or bloating his career. It's just that he's been in magazine publishing since he graduated from college and has risen through the ranks, jumping from publisher to publisher, until he became one himself, and has done very well. But before we speak about him, he wants to know all about me.

He asks about my business. He wants to know how I was inspired to start it and how I began writing books. I had noticed he follows what I do via Facebook. He often comments or shares my work with his friends. It's felt very supportive.

We talk about our families, our mutual friends, and our appreciation for a good Manhattan bar that attracts an older clientele, not the college crowds we often find. And then we talk about how stylish New Yorkers are, as we look around the bar at the well-dressed crowd.

"I had to have this shirt made," he says of the one I had been admiring. "I can't find shirts like these in stores. And, well, I have actually been thinking about launching my own fashion brand, for men," he adds. "I have been looking into it for a couple of years. I just think it's hard to find the kind of stuff I like to wear. My cousin owns a number of clothing lines that are super successful on the West Coast and he's been really supportive and helpful showing me the ropes. I think this is my year to do it."

I cock my head and smile. "Really?" I say. "That sounds amazing. I can envision you doing that. You certainly have the style and management skills for it." I add enthusiastically, "And I think it really fits your personality."

"Thanks," he says. "I think so, too."

Again, I'm surprised by Jake. I didn't expect this of him.

"I am really impressed," I say.

"Yeah?" he says. I think he's touched.

"Well, I just thought . . . you give off the impression that you are this eternal frat boy," I say. "And you are sounding so mature and grown up," I add with a wink. I don't mean to be condescending, but Jake knows that he has this reputation.

"I know that's what people think of me, and I love being a kid, you know? But I am turning forty-two soon and I think that if not now, when am I going to do this?" He looks down at his beer. "It's my dream," he adds softly as he finishes it off.

But Jake's career ambitions are not going to be the most surprising thing about him tonight.

We order some snacks and another round of beers. We're just getting started.

"So what's your dating life like?" he asks, the beer keeping his shyness at bay. "You seem like the type of girl who always has dates. Do you date a lot?"

I'm caught off guard. I don't date more or less than the average woman. "When it rains, it pours," I say nonchalantly, trying to sound cool. "But there's always a drought now and again," I add, making sure he knows I'm available.

"I just think, I mean, you're beautiful and smart and you're doing your thing . . . I would just think that you get a lot of guys interested in you."

What a difference from what Daniel inferred that night at The General. I am beginning to wonder why Jake has never asked me out. *It must be the age thing,* I think to myself. "Well, I appreciate that," I say. "But I don't know that I live up to your expectation of my dating career," I say with a laugh.

"You want kids, right?" he asks, still shyly.

"Yes, I've always wanted kids. But I also always wanted love and that hasn't come yet, so here I am." I smile through a shrug.

"I don't want to tell you what you should do. But I'm just wondering if you've thought about having a baby on your own. I know a couple of women who decided to do that. And one of them met a guy while she was pregnant and now they are engaged and will raise the baby together," he says.

I'm intrigued that Jake is so up on this topic. "I know. But there are a number of reasons why I don't want to have a baby on my own," I say. "I really want to have a baby with the man I love."

"I get that. You can still have a kid," Jake says, with a warm confidence. I smile at his generosity.

And now comes the conversation I was really not expecting.

"I've been thinking about having a baby," he says. "You know, with coparenting," he adds, referring to the new trend of men and women having babies together with no intention of marrying or living together and every intention of raising the child together. "I know some women who want to have a kid and, like you, haven't met the right guy. I was thinking maybe this coparenting thing might be an interesting idea."

"You are thinking about having a baby with a friend?" I ask.

"Yeah. I've really looked into it. Ultimately, I decided not to do it. But I thought about it really carefully. But I am hoping I'll meet someone and, you know, in like three months, get pregnant, get engaged, and get married."

"In that order," I say, with irony in my voice.

"Yeah, look, I know this guy who met this girl and they both wanted to have a kid and they said 'why wait?' and they got pregnant right away and then got engaged. It was exactly three months from their first date to when they got married. That could happen."

I'm shocked. Not only is Jake considering coparenting, but he really wants to fall in love and get married and have a baby, in a short period of time.

"Well, are you meeting girls that you want to marry?" I ask. Now I'm curious about Jake's dating life.

"I go out and I meet, you know, girls who are, like, thirty-one or thirty-two, and I don't want to date someone that young."

I am shocked.

"Really? I thought you would prefer dating a woman ten years younger than you are," I say.

"If I dated a woman who is thirty-one, she will want to date for months, then move in together, then have a year-long engagement, then be married for a year, then get pregnant. I'll be a dad when I'm fifty! No. I want to date a woman our age."

I'm beginning to think Jake wants to date me.

"How come you've never asked me out?" I ask, two beers in.

Jake smiles but can't look at me. "I have never asked out any

> 'If I dated a woman who is thirty-one, she will want to date for months, then move in together, then have a year-long engagement, then be married for a year, then get pregnant. I'll be a dad when I'm fifty! No. I want to date a woman our age.'

of my past serious girlfriends," he admits. "They all asked me out first. I'm just shy. I'm not good at asking a girl out unless she lets me know that I should ask her out."

I'm half a beer away from kissing Jake right there and then to show him I want him to ask me out. I don't. But later, when he touches my hand to make a point, I touch his fingers in return. We linger there for a moment. And when he lets go, I ask: "Why did you let go?" And he holds my hand again. This is a date.

"I hope I'm being helpful for your book," he says.

Oh no, I think to myself. *I am not thinking about the book right now.* I'm out with a smart, handsome, successful man who wants to be married and have children. And he seems to like me even though I am two years older than him. I'm really so pleasantly surprised.

The bartender places down the check and Jake takes out his credit card. I had planned to pay since he was helping me for the book, so I go to stop him. But he says, shyly, "Well, it feels like a date."

So I say, "Well, I'll know for sure if you kiss me good night."

It was most definitely a date.

A couple of weeks later, Wynn asks how things are going with Jake. I had told her about the meeting that had become a date.

"He disappeared," I say, flatly.

"Ah, one of those," she says, knowingly.

Last year, Wynn had been seeing someone for about three or four months. They had planned a date for a Wednesday night but he texted her that morning to say he had to cancel. She was a little taken aback, as "canceling" a date felt a little harsh. She replied with an easy, breezy "Sure, let's reschedule for the weekend," thinking that perhaps he was feeling a little pressure, even though she had not put pressure on him in the least bit. And they always saw each other on the weekends. *Maybe he just needs a little time off,* she thought to herself. But she never heard from him again.

I asked her weeks later if she ever got an explanation from him. "Well, he's not dead," she said, a little morbidly. "We're still Facebook friends, and I can see he's alive and well."

"Why do they just disappear without an explanation?" I ask rhetorically. "A breakup, while hard, I can take. But a spontaneous combustion with no explanation is frustrating."

"I don't think about it," Wynn said. "It is what it is. He's not the first man to just disappear on me. He may not be the last. And no matter what I imagine might have been the reason, I'm probably wrong, so what's the point?"

I admire Wynn's stoicism. And she's right. The disappearing man is a common occurrence I hear about from friends again and again. And it's happened to me a few times, too. Jake not reconnecting with me is not surprising or disappointing. As Wynn says, it is what it is.

Back to our conversation about Jake, Wynn says: "Well, it sucks nevertheless. He seemed like he really wanted to meet someone and get married and have kids, and you seemed to like each other. Oh, Melanie, let's not spend another second trying to figure this out."

"I completely agree. Look, it was a fun night. And it's good to have a fun, good conversation and actually *want* to kiss a man good night. I'm honestly grateful just to have had that," I say sincerely.

After years of bemoaning a bad date or a disappointing result, I've learned to really enjoy dating again. It's rare to have great chemistry with someone on a date, and it's not uncommon to know that a date is not someone you will want to see again. And most dates are somewhere in between. The key is to be in the moment and to appreciate getting dressed up, doing my hair and makeup, slipping some cash, a lip gloss, and my keys into a slim clutch, and know that whatever comes of the date isn't what's important. It's important to live in the moment and know that I'm one date closer to meeting the one that will never end.

OLD-FASHIONED DATING

I'm waiting at the bar for Victoria to arrive—a friend I met through my good friend Gigi. Victoria is a successful film producer, probably about my age (although she never reveals her age), and like me, she is single and still looking for love. I'd suggested we meet at the Arlington Club, a new, old-school-style steakhouse on the Upper East Side. It has quickly become known as the hottest restaurant for well-heeled singles and divorcées in their late thirties, forties and fifties.

I arrive a few minutes early so I can do a little people-watching before Victoria gets here. I order the Arlington Club cocktail (*When in Rome,* I think) and turn back toward the room. As expected, the venue is filled with singles and divorcées: those of us who have yet to marry, and those who did and are now back on the scene after time spent with former spouses. I think to myself, *The more things change, the more they stay the same.*

The group is sophisticated, most of the men in après-work suits and many of the women seemingly coming from work in blazers, well-tailored skirts, and heels. Some look as though they've been planning their outfits for days. And others are in their nighttime Lululemon wear: black yoga pants and a leather jacket of sorts.

Women are tentatively checking out the competition and, of course, checking out the men, who are talking to each other about sports and business. "Hey, congrats on finally closing that effing deal, man," says one man to another with a handshake, while another man in their small circle offers him a manly shoulder pat.

In the deep corner between the bar and the window, two women are talking to three men. There are smiles and clinking tumblers. It seems they've just met.

A woman in a white blazer with a sleek ponytail and a glass of white wine is sitting alone at the bar. A man stands next to her and orders a drink. As he waits for his cocktail, he turns sideways toward the woman and starts to chat. He's handsome. She turns sideways toward him, smiles, and chats back. I refrain from shouting "BINGO!"

I turn around and notice a group of three women walk in tepidly. "Let's get a drink," says one, strategically nodding toward the bar with her well-coiffed head. And they do. As those three clear the doorway, a very tall, very blond woman who could take even a straight woman's breath away walks in. It's Victoria.

"Sorry I'm late," she says as she reaches for a hug, even though she's not late. "My timing has been off all day!"

"You're not late, Victoria," I say. "Your timing is perfect."

"Well, you were right," she says as the guy who "closed the effing deal" noticeably notices her. "This is definitely a scene."

At the bar, Victoria scans the cocktail menu and points to the list with a well-manicured nearly beige fingernail. "Do you think I should just order this One Night Stand drink and be done with it?" she asks with a laugh. She orders the Mojo Risin' instead, and it's a fitting choice. Victoria has a newfound confidence.

"Did I tell you I just closed on a loft in Soho?" Our friend Jacqueline had mentioned she had helped Victoria find an apartment to buy.

"Yes! Congratulations! I hear it's absolutely stunning," I say, having heard just that from Jacqueline.

"It's everything I ever wanted in an apartment, minus the husband and kids," she says, again with a laugh. "The only problem was that the entire thing was painted in this dark gray color so I lightened it up with a coat of ivory, and the wall that flanks the kitchen is now like a robin's egg blue. It's so pretty! See?"

Victoria shows me images of the loft on her phone. She's right. It's so airy and beautiful.

"You have to come by for drinks. I'll invite all the girls, Gigi, Wynn, Jacqueline—a whole group of fabulous single ladies!"

"Sounds great!" I say. And I mean it.

"I have something else to tell you," Victoria says in a loud whisper, putting her phone back into her clutch. "I froze my eggs."

"Really?" I say in a tone mixed with equal parts "good for you!" and envy.

"Yep," Victoria says. "It's been a couple of weeks since I did it, and I feel like I have a new sense of confidence about me. I mean, of course it's nothing I would tell a guy when I'm on a date or anything, but I just know in the back of my mind that I've done this and my little eggies are waiting for me when I find that special guy. I can't tell you the pressure it takes off my shoulders, or ovaries I should say! I feel a hundred pounds lighter."

Victoria is staging her life for today, and for tomorrow.

The hostess comes over to the bar to let us know our table is ready. We enter the dining room, which is intended to emote the feeling of a bygone era, when business was done over big steaks and Old-Fashioneds. The new, old-fashioned space is opulently designed in rich browns, golden tans, and elegant blacks. I immediately notice 1970s disco-era framed photos of New York City bigs on one wall, like designer Diane Von Furstenberg, pop artist Andy Warhol, and legendary Studio 54 insider Carmen D'Alessio. And, on the other side of the room, I spot Jeff Zucker, a current New York City big, framed by a bevy of eager young men laughing and chewing on steaks.

We can't get over the number of men in suits, groups of four or six together at a dinner that will surely be paid for with a corporate credit card. And like us, there are a few tables of women, "coupled" for the evening.

We sit down at our table, not too far from a couple on a date. Their table is overflowing with menu items, and their wine glasses are frequently refilled by the server. The man, nearing fifty years in age, blissfully overweight, is effervescent. You can tell he's feeling right at home and in his glory, but his pretty young date seems out of place. She looks to be in her early thirties and she is smiling at her older date acquiescently.

"Look at that guy," Victoria says. "I bet you he's either divorced and looking to start over again, or else he woke up a couple of weeks ago ready to get married and have kids, and so now he's on the prowl for pretty young things." We can both tell it's a setup gone wrong.

"I never go on blind dates," Victoria says, reading my mind. "It's just never been my thing. But I did go on my first—and last—a couple of months ago. I was set up by a woman I really admire. I did the math: She's fantastic, so the guy she wants to set me up with, he must be at least a little fantastic, right? But he was not *my* Mr. Fantastic.

"He was a good guy," she continues, "and so I went out with him a couple of times. On our third date, he presents me with a gold bracelet, the kind I would only wear on, say, some fantastic vacation to St. Barts where I play the role of the kept, Upper East Side wife." Victoria lowers her voice an octave and adds: "He might as well have given me a choker. I think he realized pretty quickly that while I appreciated the thought, the bracelet was not my style. I even offered to give it back to him, but he said I should exchange it for something I'd prefer. A couple of weeks later, after we'd stopped dating, I realized that the bracelet was probably a gift for his ex-wife—meaning, he wished that I was her. I went to exchange it for what I thought might be a new lipstick or two. Turns out, I could have purchased every lipstick in the beauty department!"

"Why?" I ask. "Was it a fancy brand or something? Was it paved in diamonds?"

"Melanie, Mr. Fantastic had given me a $10,000 bracelet! A *$10,000* bracelet! A gold bracelet with no diamonds or stones to make it seem like it was even close to being worth that much money. All I could think was, *Is that what he thought I wanted?* Why do these men assume all women want cliché, Park Avenue perks? Why do they all think we are the same woman—specifically the woman they divorced and wish they could marry all over again?"

In my experience, men who lead with their wallet think that their lavish lifestyle will win women over. They take us out to a very expensive restaurant for dinner, making sure we know it's an expensive restaurant. If they really want to impress, they send a car to pick us up. They say things like "I only eat in fine restaurants. What's the point of living in New York and eating mediocre food?" Or they'll arrive a few minutes late so that the maître d' can escort you to their "finest table" in a corner of the restaurant, where three handsome

> ❝ It's not that we don't appreciate Mr. Fantastic's generosity, but after you go out with a few Mr. Fantastics, you know the drill, and it all seems disingenuous. The attempt at making us feel special actually makes us feel the opposite. We're just another woman they are trying to impress with money. ❞

young servers will be taking care to make sure you have everything you need because "Mr. Fantastic called and he apologizes but he'll be a little late. He asked us to get you a cocktail while you wait." But I know this routine; Mr. Fantastic planned it just so I'll know that Mr. Fantastic can call and get the staff to read off the script he gives them. They know the script by heart because Mr. Fantastic does this little routine with all the women he takes to this restaurant.

It's not that we don't appreciate Mr. Fantastic's generosity, but after you go out with a few Mr. Fantastics, you know the drill, and it all seems disingenuous. The attempt at making us feel special actually makes us feel the opposite. We're just another woman they are trying to impress with money.

It's not hard to meet a man like this in Manhattan, especially the wealthy fortysomething or fiftysomething newly divorced man. *Money made me desirable the first time, why wouldn't it work the second time?* he thinks to himself.

It's not that I don't enjoy nice things and the comfort that comes with wealth. And I most definitely prefer a kind, generous date who enjoys treating me. But men who lead with their wallet because they assume that's what I would find *most* attractive about them—well, that's an assumption that I find unattractive. I want my date to get me on a whole other level, and I want to understand who he really is without the protection or façade of money. I want to feel a real connection with him, and him with me. Money can't buy that.

"The men I meet lately are divorced, sometimes for the second time," Victoria says. "And time after time, they want to meet their ex-wife all over again, even if they won't admit it. I always feel like I'm an experiment to see if they can do it right this time around. Or the divorced men are looking for the exact opposite of their ex, a sweet Betty to her spoiled-girl Veronica," Victoria punctuates her last point by fluffing up her blond locks, playing up the part of Archie's girl Betty. "But most of all, divorced men either want a much younger woman or, on the other hand, a woman who they assume is too old to have kids, because the men often already have kids and don't want any more kids," she says. "But now we can freeze our eggs and have kids later in life. So they should probably just focus on finding the right person, not on moving backward or moving forward. For just a moment, they should go on a date for the here and now."

And I agree. Victoria and I are a couple of new-fashioned, independent women who each want an old-fashioned romance with a modern, independent man. I admit it's a fine line, and perhaps a confusing one. Women want dates who on one hand treat us with old-fashioned courtship and, on the other hand, appreciate that we are modern, new-fashioned women. We appreciate when a man picks up the check, but we don't appreciate it when he thinks his wealth is why we are with him.

Women of the Otherhood fall in love with the man, not his money. And falling in love sometimes begins with a little old-fashioned courtship.

MARRIED MEN OF
MANHATTAN

There is one Saturday night in Manhattan that trumps all others. It's the one that occurs mid-May, just before the natives retreat to the edges of Long Island or New Jersey for the summer weekends, and it's a night that is just warm enough to go out without a jacket. The nightlife scene is replete with celebratory Manhattanites; the women are in their short Hervé Léger bandage dresses and open-toe sandals, and the men are in their glory.

The restaurants, bars, and clubs in the Meatpacking District overflow with older Manhattanites, not the outer-borough twenty-somethings who will take their spots come June. Tonight, a prominent group of hardworking, successful New Yorkers are letting loose at the rooftop lounge at Catch: one music industry executive, one jewelry designer, three hedge fund guys, four doctors, and Jacqueline—the successful, thirty-five-year-old real estate agent who invited me to join her. One of the financiers has reserved bottle service. The group is drinking vodka and champagne and trying to hear each other over the din of music.

It's the weekend, but like many New Yorkers, Jacqueline is networking. She's chatting with one of the hedge fund guys about his second marriage at forty-eight and expecting his first baby at fifty. "IVF," he says without our asking. "It's my second marriage and my wife's first and first kid, too. She was forty-five when we met," he adds. Jacqueline jumps right in with a property on the Upper East Side she thinks he'll be interested in: "You're probably looking for more room with a baby on the way. I've got a brand new listing, completely renovated three bedrooms, four baths, twelfth floor looking over Park Avenue . . . "

The jewelry designer and her boyfriend, one of the other hedge fund guys, join the conversation. They are interested in buying a home in the Hamptons. "I've got the perfect property for you," Jacqueline says. "It's in Bridge, right near the most expensive homes. It's a good deal because it needs to be completely gutted. If you can put another half million into the interior, maybe a few grand into the landscaping, you'll be fine for your first summer there . . ."

I start talking to one of the doctors, a surgeon, who looks to be in his early forties. He mentions he's engaged. "I'm getting married in two months," he says. "This is my bachelor party."

"A bachelor party two months before your wedding?" I ask, all of a sudden feeling like I've crashed a party.

"Yeah, well, we're all busy. Everyone leaves the island in the summer. I figured we'd get it in now," he says. He introduces me to Anthony, his best man and fellow surgeon, as well as the other doctors.

"That's our guy!" Anthony says. "Biting the bullet and fucking getting married!" he adds, as though both he and the groom-to-be were twenty years younger than they are.

It's about half an hour later when I notice Jacqueline deep in conversation with Dr. Anthony. I'm not surprised to see her so engaged. Blond, blue-eyed, fair-skinned, and brilliant Jacqueline is attracted to intelligent black men with dark skin, dark eyes, and bright smiles.

I also notice that the third hedge fund guy has his arm around the music industry executive's waist. The jewelry designer is laughing at something her boyfriend is saying. The doctors, minus Anthony, are conversing with the soon-to-be-married surgeon and some women they've just met. Everyone is settling in, and it's my cue to head home. I see no catch at Catch.

At 9:30 AM the next morning, I get a text from Jacqueline: *Had so much fun last night. I'm just getting home!*

Where were you? I ask, knowing the answer.

With Anthony. The doctor, she texts.

Ah! How was it? I ask, not really wanting to know the answer.

He is so my type! Had a great time! Jumping in the shower. TTYL!

But later that day, Jacqueline's euphoria has worn off. She calls.

"The doctor is married," she says with a disappointed tone. "And I had asked him while we were still at Catch if he was married. He said no. I asked him if he had a girlfriend. He said, 'Nothing significant at this time.' I asked him if he had ever been married. He said no. I asked him if he had ever thought about getting married. He said, 'I have, but it's never been right.' Finally I asked him if he had any children, you know, to cover all my bases. And again, he said no."

"So how did you find out he was married?" I ask.

"I Googled him. It was all there. Did he expect me not to figure this out? Any idiot can Google someone," she says.

"What did Google tell you?" I ask.

"Well, judging from his 2001 wedding blurb in *The New York Times* and a number of photos of him and his wife—one taken just last week at a charity function he had told me he was involved with—it is pretty clear he has not only a wife, but also three kids and a newly purchased $9.5 million home in Greenwich," she reports. "And get this. He called me this morning to see if we could get together today, and when I confronted him about being married and totally lying to me, you know what he said? He said he had been drunk and wasn't it fun?"

"What an asshole," I say. "What did you say to that?"

"I told him I had no intentions of wrecking a marriage, and I was not interested in ever hearing from him again, and I hung up," she says.

"I'm sorry, Jacqueline. It really sucks." I say, with nothing better to add.

"Thanks. I'm fine. I am disappointed. I don't mind a one-night stand. I'm a grown woman and I like sex. And we had great chemistry. When we were on the dance floor, it felt like no one else was in the room. I hadn't felt that way in a long time. Honestly, if he had been single and never called, it would have felt better. Now it just feels dirty because he didn't let me in on it. I can do a one-night stand. I can't do deception," she says. "I knew something was wrong when the groom-to-be walked into his hotel room at four thirty in the morning and Anthony threw the sheet over me. The groom was a little taken aback, and I thought he was just shocked there was a woman in the room. But now I realize it's because his best man was cheating on his wife!" she says.

"Oh, Jacqueline," I say. "These married men have no respect for single women. But if they have so little respect for their wives, I'm not sure we can expect much more from them."

This isn't the first I have heard about Jacqueline and run-ins with married men. She went on several dates with a man who said he was divorced, only to find out through an industry colleague that he was buying a three-bedroom on Riverside. "He's not only married,"

> "'Liars are good liars,' I say. 'He's lying to his wife, and the women he slept with before you, and the women he'll sleep with after you. He's gotten so good at lying that he thinks it's just another one of his great skills. He'll keep pushing the envelope, taking bigger risks, because with each coup, his ego fills up. He thinks he's invincible. But one day, he'll push too hard, and he'll fall.'"

she told me then. "He's expecting his second child any day now!" She met four other married men who took her out on dates, and she later found out each one was already married.

"That's why I asked Anthony all those questions. I didn't want to be fooled again. But he just blatantly lied to me!" she says.

"Liars are good liars," I say. "He's lying to his wife, and the women he slept with before you, and the women he'll sleep with after you. He's gotten so good at lying that he thinks it's just another one of his great skills. He'll keep pushing the envelope, taking bigger risks, because with each coup, his ego fills up. He thinks he's invincible. But one day, he'll push too hard, and he'll fall."

"You're right. I have to say the few married men I've slept with— not knowing they were married—were the most uninhibited lovers I have ever had. They are ready and willing to do anything to please me. I should have guessed Anthony was married when he said something like I was every fantasy he's ever had rolled up into one woman."

"That's the thing," I say. "They are focused on the fantasy and not on real life. I know there's a really good catch for you out there somewhere," I add.

> ❝ Oh, the cheating men of Manhattan, the breed of entitlement that has spread its virus to so many women I know. And I'm not immune either. I stopped using online dating sites when mostly married men would contact me. ❞

"Me, too," Jacqueline says. "I really believe it." And I can hear from her tone of voice she almost does.

Jacqueline isn't the first to get hooked by a married man fishing for a fantasy. James, the newly divorced man I went out with twice, told me his married buddies hang out at the bar at Lavo in Midtown to meet single women after work. "They just slip off their rings and pretend they're single," he said. James found it disgusting, thankfully. Too bad I didn't find it surprising.

Oh, the cheating men of Manhattan, the breed of entitlement that has spread its virus to so many women I know. And I'm not immune either. I stopped using online dating sites when mostly married men would contact me. I learned from experience that when a man quickly jumps off the site's chat function, or says he can't talk freely on the phone because he is separated but still living at home, it means he's married.

"It's been especially true once I turned forty," Alex, a woman I met through work, tells me about her experiences with married men. When she's been at conferences, she's had a couple of married male colleagues try to get her into bed. "They are unabashedly aggressive about it," she says. "They somehow think that because I'm forty-one, I have given up on a real relationship or never wanted one or who knows? And they assume I'd be very happy 'getting some' with them. The worst part is, you see them post photos of their wives on Facebook with a caption that reads something like 'To my best friend and the love of my life, Amy, on our tenth anniversary. I love you! Happy anniversary!' They don't even seem to be unhappily married! They just think that I'm a single woman over forty and so I'm relegated to having sex with married men—basically to getting whatever is available to me. It's incredibly insulting," she says. "I'd love to have sex with a married man," Alex adds. "The man *I'm* married to!"

I text Jacqueline later that night to see how she's doing.

Good! she replies. *Live and learn. But hey, listen, I can't chat. I'm on my way downtown to see Eddie.* (Eddie is someone Jacqueline has "playdates" with once in a while.) *I think he'll know how to make me feel better.*

SINGLE, AGAIN

I'm on a second date with James, the newly divorced, forty-four-year-old man who had mentioned his issue with his married friends at Lavo. He says he is ready to find love again. He was married at twenty-seven, very young for a Wall Street guy. "I thought it was the grown-up thing to do," he tells me. "We met in college and were living together and marriage was the next step." Two kids later, they realized their marriage was falling apart. "In retrospect," he explains, "we were so young. We just grew into our late thirties and forties wanting different things."

James is a nice guy who is wondering why a nice girl like me is still single. "I haven't met him yet," I say. "Or," I add, "I did and he wasn't interested in a meaningful relationship."

"My sister is like you," he says. James and I met through his sister, a forty-two-year-old woman I know. "She's great. She's dating an older man she's not that into, but he'd marry her in a second. He's really a catch. I wish she'd focus on that relationship. Instead, she's hanging out with a really young guy who she's never going to be serious with. I don't know why she's wasting her time with him."

"Oh, James, she's not wasting her time," I tell him. "She enjoys his company. And while you've had the pleasure of waking up with someone for nearly twenty years, she's been waking up alone for most of that time. She probably doesn't want to go to bed alone every night and wake up alone every day. She's forty-two. Why does she have to be alone every day just because this guy is not the man she'll live with the rest of her life? James, I don't want to sound too blunt, but she didn't marry the wrong person. You did. She can take care of her romantic decisions," I add.

"I never thought of it that way," James says sincerely.

"People only tell you what they want to tell you. She's telling you she's having this fun affair so that you'll not worry about her so much. She wants you to know that she's not always alone. She's dutifully dating the type of man you think she should date, but she's enjoying her life with a younger man, even if you don't approve of him," I say.

James thoughtfully drinks his wine. He had chosen a great wine bar for our date. *I wish I had stronger chemistry with him,* I think to myself.

"Maybe you'll have advice for me then," James says. "I was chatting with a newly separated, female friend of mine about getting back into the dating scene, since I'm a year or so ahead of her. Within minutes, she was bashing never-married women in their forties, saying that they put out negative energy and really don't want to find a guy. My friend is forty-five with two kids and thinks that she will have absolutely no problem finding a really nice, good-looking, successful guy in New York City. She thinks she'll be in a serious relationship within months, no problem. So how do I defend women like my sister and other really nice women I know, like you, who aren't married and don't have children?"

I know this newly separated, female friend James is talking about. I don't know this particular woman literally, but I know her

> **❝** The newly separated woman who got married in her twenties and who is now, fifteen or twenty years later, separated from her husband wants to believe that at the very least, *she* can get married. **❞**

type. One night a few years ago, Wynn and I got on the UrbanBaby.com forums to see what married mothers say about the single non-moms they know. The posts went something like this: "Women who aren't married by age thirty-five are pathetic," one woman wrote.

"They are enjoying their so-called freedom but will wake up one day old and childless and realize how truly pathetic they were," responded another.

Wynn and I laughed through the potshots. We know that *happily* married women don't spend time on these forums bashing single women. It's schadenfreude for the *unhappily* married moms, making themselves feel better about their discontented lives.

The newly separated woman who got married in her twenties and who is now, fifteen or twenty years later, separated from her husband wants to believe that at the very least, *she* can get married. She wants to believe that never-married women either don't want to be married or are not serious about marriage, so she can cancel them out as competition and up her own chances for finding a new mate. Certainly this is not true of all separated and divorced women. But I have encountered this type of single-again woman on a number of occasions.

I am ready to share my thoughts with James.

"First of all," I tell him, "this woman is not a friend. At the very least, she's not a loyal friend. If she were, she wouldn't disparage your sister to you, or to anyone. She's scanning the competition and is coming up with reasons why she'll be more attractive than women with no kids. To some men, she might be. To others, she won't. It's irrelevant; hopefully she'll find the right man for her. And the women she knows, or judges—same thing, hopefully they'll meet the right men for them. She's right about one thing: I am sure there are women in their forties who put out negative energy. But they aren't all single. Some are married. Some are blond. Some are gay. Some like to watch *Dancing with the Stars*. And some are divorced women with two kids."

I go on. "The desire to find and have love is part of the human condition, and it's not reserved for everyone but never-married women in their late thirties and forties. Never-married women never married the wrong guy. This woman did, not that she hadn't expected she'd be married to him the rest of her life. And the ability of the women of the Otherhood to be selective leads to better marriages once we do marry. Studies show that women who marry at age thirty-five or older are most likely to stay married.

"As far as your friend goes," I continue, "you might have this advice for her: Men like confident women. Confident women don't think anyone else is competition for meeting a great man. I honestly, truly, and sincerely hope she meets the love of her life very soon. I hope he's a great stepfather to her kids and that they have fantastic sex. If you want to defend your sister, which I completely understand and agree with, I would say something like 'My sister is an extraordinary woman. I hold her in the highest regard. She's got a smile that makes everyone else around her smile, humility that shines through despite her enormous talent and passion, she's a self-starter and creator, and she's the most loving and generous aunt to my children. Despite not having found love in her twenties or thirties, she's never settled for anything *but* love. To me, that's her greatest accomplishment. The courage to live her best life alone rather than live a mediocre life just to be married is something many others can learn from. She's not negative, and she truly wants to meet the right man. But I need not go on . . . you and I know she's not your competition. She's in a class all her own.'"

James is taking mental notes.

"Look, validating my ability to love and be loved is not something I need to spend energy on. Neither does your sister. It's honestly a waste of time. That's the only time I'll spend on a woman I don't know."

Ironically, I have my own encounter with a single-again friend a couple of weeks later when Lisa calls.

The thin, beautiful, daytime talk-show producer who is in her late forties is practically jingling over the phone in the way best friends do when they have exciting news. Only Lisa isn't my best friend. She's just really happily celebrating the end of her twenty-four-year marriage. She's newly separated.

Lisa got married in her early twenties to a man named George who is still very handsome. Together they had three equally gorgeous children, the youngest of whom recently left their classic four-bedroom Upper East Side apartment, bound for college. Lisa seems to be going through the classic empty-nest syndrome, now wanting to empty her nest of Papa Bird, too. She was perched on her tree branch looking at all the beautiful, perpetually-single singles, wanting to join the flock.

I've learned over time that those in their late forties and fifties who separate after their grown children leave home are their own class of single. They want to go back to where they left off before they got married, and for some that may mean spending time behaving as

I've learned over time that those in their late forties and fifties who separate after their grown children leave home are their own class of single.

if they are in their early twenties. The newly separated are expecting their lives will match up to the seemingly über-social lives of their ever-single girlfriends. To them, our lives are a Carrie-tale, as in Bradshaw, the fictional heroine of a lifestyle of Cosmopolitans, frequent dates, and filled social calendars.

Lisa and I met a year ago when our mutual friend, a New York City boldface name, introduced us at an opening party for the U.S. Open at a rooftop bar on the Upper West Side. With her back to her husband, Lisa confided in me that she was thinking about separating. "I see my friends who are divorced, and they say it's tough out there, but I don't know. I think it's time to fly the coop. You're single. Is it hard out there?"

The music was blaring. The roped-off section we were in—me, the boldface name, her family, her friends, her stylist, and a *Page Six* reporter—was tight. iPhones were texting, tweeting, and flashing their cameras as long-legged boldface names came and sat down next to us. It was a jungle out there.

Lisa wants to start over. I want to get started with love and marriage and hopefully children. Was I still waiting for a man to begin that chapter of my life while Lisa was ready to close that chapter? It is tough out here, but perhaps it's easier if you're starting over, not still trying to cross the finish line.

A year later, my iPhone buzzes. It's Lisa, who's recently moved into her first solo apartment. "I have someone to set you up with," she says, just assuming I'm single at the moment. I am. "Jeff's a great guy. Divorced, early fifties, good-looking, super successful, two grown kids and doesn't want any more children," she says quickly, as if the details don't matter. Then she wipes out my uterus with the ever-charming justification, "But that's OK because you say you're OK not having kids."

I did say that, but the context was that I would rather have love if I had to choose, but it's not my ideal situation. I want children. Sometimes, people can be so jarring with their comments. They don't know how much they hurt. She doesn't realize she hurt me, probably because I'm supposed to be "over" my childlessness by now. But I'm letting it go, giving Lisa the benefit of the doubt. Maybe this guy really is right for me. And I appreciate the setup.

Then she adds: "It's perfect because he's got two grown kids, so you are free to travel and do whatever you want. I would love that. If he weren't my best friend's brother-in-law, I'd go out with him myself. But that would be weird. He's like my family, too."

Spoiler alert: That is the least of how this whole setup gets weird.

"Fiftysomething is a little old for me," I say, hoping that I can get out of it because fiftysomething *is* a little old for me, no matter what the ageists want me to believe.

"He's a very young fifty-three. You would never know he was in his fifties. He's in great shape, and I *promise* you he looks like he's in his midforties." Lisa wasn't letting me out of it. "This is what we'll do," she goes on, not remotely taking no for an answer. "The three of us will meet for drinks so it's not awkward, and maybe he'll bring a friend so it'll be fun, and then if you like him, you can go out again."

Going on a blind date with a friend there is awkward. I start to realize that Lisa isn't setting me up. Lisa is adding another night to her newly single social calendar. I am simply a supporting character. She is a producer, after all, so it isn't a surprise that wardrobe, location, and script are also her call. And I let her do it because I am having one of those weeks where I am trying to be open to possibility. Everyone's advice is making me feel as though I'm not open enough. So what is one night out with Lisa, who I really like, and her best friend's brother-in-law, who looks as if he is in his midforties . . . and his friend? I feel my earlier quick response to age preferences might jeopardize my personal vow to not seem picky.

"I'm really not very picky," I say to try to make up for it. "I want three things. I want him to be smart . . . "

"He's really smart, you'll like that," she interjects.

" . . . Jewish . . . "

"Jeff's Jewish!"

" . . . and I want to want to have sex with him," I add, matter-of-factly.

"Melanie, that kind of funny one-liner isn't good on a date."

"Funny? That I want to want to have sex with the man I'm with?"

"Yes. I know you're really funny on camera, and I know you're a writer and you have those quick one-liners, but that just sounds like you wrote it," she scolds.

I didn't think it was a line or that it was funny. At the very least, it isn't my best work. After the call, I feel deflated. I call Daniel and ask if she's right.

"Sounds like Lisa's trying to make sure you don't outwit her on the date," he generously replies.

"But it's not her date," I reply, bewildered. "It's my date. I'm the one being set up. What is she being competitive about? And besides, that line wasn't funny. It was just matter-of-fact. I'm allowed to want to want to have sex with a man I'm dating."

Now let me be fair. Lisa has often told me I'm beautiful and funny. It is very nice of her to set me up. And I think she might feel that if she coaches me on the date, I'll seal the deal. But did I want to seal *this* deal? This man doesn't want more children, and while I've chosen love over children, he doesn't have small children I could at the very least shower with my maternal love. They are grown and I am "free to travel." But is that what I want? A travel partner?

"You guys will go to amazing places," Lisa encourages.

But I'm running my business. I am not semiretired from a successful career. I'm just starting out. I don't want to travel half the year.

"I know exactly what I want you to wear," she adds. "A flirty dress, like with boots or heels. He'll love that. That's what his ex-wife wears."

After a quick commercial break in my head to count to ten, I give her the benefit of the doubt. She's projecting how she wants the night to appear. If I sound and look like Jeff's ex-wife, he'll like me because I'm just like his ex-wife, only different (younger?). Lisa assumes that women in their early forties will date divorced men who don't want children because, well, what choice do we have? But Lisa is on the other side, wishing she could be me.

"You're so lucky you're forty-three," she says. "I'd do anything to be that young. It's hard to meet guys who want to date a forty-eight-year-old woman now. My ex-husband already found a girlfriend. Took him no time at all. My last setup was with a very wealthy guy. I met him at the restaurant he owns in South Hampton. But he was sixty-five if a day. And an old sixty-five. He was probably seventy. I made pleasant conversation but couldn't wait to get out of there. He called me a couple of days later. I managed to get out of it."

My iPhone vibrates a few days before the date. "I'm so excited!" Lisa exclaims as if this were her date. "Jeff is so excited, too, he's been texting me about the date all day! He saw your photo, and he thinks you're really cute, and he can't wait to meet you. His sister has been texting me, too, saying that if I get you guys married, I'm going to heaven!"

Married? Texting about the date all day? The empty-nesters are sounding like little ducklings, wet behind the ears.

"Lisa, don't you think that's moving a little fast? I don't even know if he spells 'Jeff' with a *J* or *G*."

"Well, he's a great guy. You're going to love him!" she says, fait accompli. Lisa is in preproduction. "Jeff is bringing his married business partner with him, who wants to see if I'd be right for his brother."

"Oh, Lisa, that's not kosher. I don't want to go on a double date with a married guy."

"He's not there to be with me. He's like a really religious Jew. He's there to see if I'm right for his brother."

"Religious men cheat on their wives, too, Lisa. And if he were so religious, he wouldn't be going out with us in the first place."

Lisa's showing her naïveté as a newly separated woman.

"Anyway, I have to move our date night," she says. "I can't make it Tuesday night now, so let's meet on Wednesday."

"Lisa, I have a business meeting that evening. I can't do it."

Lisa's voice starts to quiver. "Can't you move it?"

"It's a business meeting. No, I can't." I want to make it clear to Lisa that while I would love to meet someone, and I'd agree to whatever Central Casting asked, dating doesn't trump my earning a living. I am all I can count on.

"I'm just trying to do a nice thing and everyone thinks I'm so nice for doing this, and you're *single!* And I really need you to move your business meeting so this can happen!" Lisa is exhausting herself.

I've forgotten that this is Lisa's show. I regretfully acquiesce.

Lisa calls the day of the date, jingling again.

"I'm so nervous!" she says.

"Why are you nervous? I'm the one being set up." I, for the record, am not nervous. I stopped getting nervous about blind dates after my third one back in my early twenties.

"Well, the business partner is going to be there to check me out for his brother. It's so much pressure! I should have just let you guys meet for drinks by yourselves." As if she's even doing me a favor by coming on the date. "This is too much anxiety!"

I meet Lisa at a Lincoln Center area bar at 8:00 PM. Jeff, a nice-looking hedge fund guy, arrives shortly after, sits down at our intimate table, and starts talking to Lisa about the traffic on the way over. He doesn't acknowledge me. He is shy or uninterested. He looks small sitting on the high bar stool, and slightly wounded, either by the end of his marriage or else by the marriage itself.

Either way, it turns out Jeff isn't divorced. He's separated. He's been separated for a month. This is his first date since his marriage dissolved, and he's been living in a hotel in the suburbs not too far from the house he shared with his wife and his now-grown children. Lisa remarks that you can go to the restaurant at that hotel at night and see all the divorced dads eating dinner alone after work.

I feel bad for the sorry visual. Jeff sulks slightly.

"You guys talk!" Lisa chirps, watching us like a studio audience.

"It's hard to talk without feeling like you're watching us," Jeff says. I am grateful that he recognizes that this is not ideal. I like him for that. If only that.

Thankfully, Jeff's married business partner, a great-looking guy in his thirties, appears just then. With his confidence and personality and a smile full of brilliant white teeth, he practically makes Jeff disappear. Married Guy is clearly happy to be out, being his charismatic self, away from whatever is waiting for him at home.

I quickly learn that Married Guy and I have people in common. Members of his extended family have been *New York Post* scandal stories. I knew the stories. I knew some of the starring players. He and I were at the same weddings. Lisa feels excluded. This guy was there for her, albeit for his brother. I'm just happy that Married Guy wasn't there to pick up women for himself. But I'm not happy that his wife is probably trying to get their young children to bed at the same time. The night feels cheap. As the drinks keep coming, I abruptly get up to leave.

I'm out with two married men and a married woman, all of them out to be single again. I want to be home, married.

"You didn't like him," Lisa concludes when she calls first thing the next morning.

"He's a nice guy, but not for me. First of all, he's still married," I explain.

"He's not married. He's separated. He's like me."

"There is married. There is divorced. He is married. And he's green. I didn't realize I was his first date since he left his home. And Lisa . . . "

"He looks fifty-three, doesn't he?" she admits.

"Yes. He does."

Despite this show getting canceled after the pilot, Lisa wants to set me up again. This time, it's with her friend Helen, a woman in her late forties who is "single, no kids, like you. She's lonely, so you guys can go out for dinner together Sunday nights so you're not alone. You'll love her. Helen is beautiful and successful. We'll all go out together next week!"

I've never met Helen. I haven't called Lisa in a while. I'm separating, for now.

THE PRINCES AND
THE POSEURS

I ask Nora, a journalist, to meet with me. Just a couple of years ago, Nora was the poster child for being Single by Choice, a woman with no desire to ever be married. She was even featured in a magazine cover story about her choice, which received a lot of attention. But recently, Nora published a blog post, making a 180-degree turn from her previous position. She now wants to get married, or at least enjoy a committed, long-term partnership. I'm curious about why she's recently changed her mind.

"I adamantly believed I never wanted to be married," she says when we meet at the Met to see the *Impressionism, Fashion, and Modernity* exhibition. "I saw what marriage did to my parents. My mother felt trapped in a marriage she couldn't afford to leave, and when she finally did, my father felt abandoned by the woman he loved. I never wanted to feel trapped or abandoned, so I never let myself get that deeply involved with a guy.

"To me, marriage was an unrealistic goal," Nora adds. "I felt like love was ephemeral, so why would I ever commit myself to one man?"

We are admiring Gustave Caillebotte's *Paris Street; Rainy Day,* a painting of an elegant couple in the forefront, her arm tucked inside his, with the modernized Parisian boulevard behind them. Nora shares her new perspective. "But then I met Constantine and everything changed. He made me see that I was angry at my parents for not being able hold their marriage together, and at the same time, I had become exactly like them in my relationships. I'd leave first. A man has never left me, because just when it gets good, I leave so he can't leave me. I didn't believe in 'happily ever after,' so why would I pretend? But Constantine has this way of making me feel differently. He says, 'Look, there are no guarantees. I cannot promise you a happily ever after, and you can't promise me that, either. But I can promise you right here and right now.' I have to tell you, Melanie, it's the most romantic thing I've ever heard.

"Trust me, this is no fairy-tale relationship," she continues. "Neither of us is perfect. Constantine is a bit of a slob. He's no Rockefeller, but he's really ambitious. He takes good care of me emotionally, in his own way, and there's comfort in that, you know? I still do not believe in Prince Charming. But I am getting more comfortable with romance. I'm daring to be in love!"

"I don't believe in Prince Charming, either," I say. "And I'm tired of people accusing me of being too romantic and not realistic enough about the man I ultimately want to be with."

After the exhibition, we order wine and cheese at the Met's Great Hall Balcony Bar. We're still discussing the so-called Prince Charming myth. "What is with this 'Prince Charming' thing, anyway?" I ask. "First of all, Prince Charming always seemed a little effeminate to me. I don't need a tall blond man in tights and tails. I don't need a man on a horse."

Nora agrees. "I mean, is Prince Charming really the kind of man who seems like he knows how to have great sex? Because he doesn't seem like it to me. He seems like a great-looking guy who got lucky

> ❝ I have always been romantic, but I've never lived in a fantasy world. I've always lived in reality and want a man who lives there, too. I know the difference between fantasy and reality. ❞

being born into royalty. I'm not attracted to lucky. I'm attracted to hard work. Hard work is much more fuck-able than luck-able. The man I'm with is not Prince Charming. Constantine wouldn't even be friends with Prince Charming!"

I know some believe I'm still single because I'm waiting for a mythical figure I never found compelling. How would that even be possible: That the same woman who managed to get to forty-three, single and self-sufficient, is somehow waiting for, or even desiring, a fairy-tale figure? I'm not looking for a man who will save me. I don't need saving. But I do long for a man who is chivalrous. I would like to meet a man who will bring out the best in me and encourage me and support me in my endeavors. I have always been romantic, but I've never lived in a fantasy world. I've always lived in reality and want a man who lives there, too. I know the difference between fantasy and reality.

The cameras flash repeatedly as Sonja Tremont Morgan and I pose for photos in front of a step-and-repeat at her *Social Life Magazine* cover party. I had become friends with Sonja, a star of Bravo's *Real Housewives of New York City,* earlier in the year over dinner after a celebrity-studded runway show at New York Fashion Week at Lincoln Center. Sonja is the mother of a beautiful daughter and the ex-wife of a legendary banker. Despite having one foot in *reality*, she's firmly planted in reality. These days, her reality is about living life with passion. Sonja, ever the socialite, loves to throw a party. "This is Melanie Notkin," Sonja announces to the cameras as if they care. "She's a best-selling author." The cameras keep flashing. "She's a big supporter of mine," she adds in vain, to no one who's interested. Sonja knows I will do what I promise, I will be helpful and honest and sincere, and I will always show up to support her, as she does for me. When you're a New York City celebrity, you get a lot of people who pretend to be your friend, pretend to want to help you, pretend to care. These are the poseurs.

There are always poseurs at celebrity parties. For instance, the young girls who know the guys who are sponsoring the event who come in their best dresses to catch a glimpse of the famous. They pretend to want to sleep with the men who invite them, like little lambs to the party. But they are also unabashed and unashamed. They come in clans, with long hair and big, shy, awkward smiles. The benefit to being over age thirty-five in New York City is that you don't look like the young girl who recently moved to New York City, thick with naïveté. And I suppose the benefit of being younger is that you are thick with naïveté.

There are a number of fanciful people in the room. There are the Housewives, and husbands and boyfriends of Housewives. There are older, tall, drunk gay men in red shirts and pointed shoes. There are pretty, young gay men who pay no attention to them. There are a few straight men who come out to meet the young girls, like the thrice-divorced, very wealthy fifty-nine-year old physician "personality" holding the hand of a girl who can't be older than twenty-four with long blond hair cascading down her back. There's Devorah, the editor in chief of *Social Life Magazine*. We exchange kisses on both

> ❝ The whole thing is a little out of the ordinary. It's a Manhattan night at its glamorous best. But I'm having trouble figuring out what's real. *Who's real?* I wonder as the Bravo production cameras are rolling. ❞

cheeks, remark something kind about how we look in our party attire, and quickly run out of things to say.

The whole thing is a little out of the ordinary. It's a Manhattan night at its glamorous best. But I'm having trouble figuring out what's real. *Who's real?* I wonder as the Bravo production cameras are rolling.

"Let me get a photo of you," says a man with a camera and wink. He's paparazzi and I'm wondering why he's not hiding behind a bush. I pose. *Flash*. I take one with Todd, the man who works with celebrities to do good. *Flash flash*. One with Prince Lorenzo, from the reality series *The Bachelor. Flash flash flash*. The prince's handler, a tall, blond PR woman in black, who brought along a young blond starlet no one recognizes, beckons the paparazzo to take one of her aspiring client. He takes one last photo of me, sideways. *Flash*. After half a glass of Ramona Singer Pinot Grigio, I find the bathroom. It's remarkably stark. There's no lock. I realize the beautiful apartment we're in is staged for sale. No one lives here. Even the penthouse is a poseur.

I look around the room for someone to help me. I spot Harrison Black, the thirty-nine-year-old, single, successful entrepreneur who is a bit of a boldface name himself. Harrison Black is always referred to by his first and last name, as if he's Mr. New York. But even though we're meeting now for only the first time, he seems quiet and

> 66 Sometimes, posing about love can be as intriguing as love itself. It's a dance, hoping neither of you will take it too far. 99

unassuming. I immediately forgive that he's the one who brought the gaggle of girls. I call Harrison Black over in my best impression of a woman in despair. Would he guard the door?

"With honor, m'lady." he says in a gallant reply fitting the moment.

Once I'm done, we start talking. He's charming. And he's bored of the young girls he brought with him. Or they have no interest in talking to him more than they have to. This knight in shining silver tie offers to get me another glass of reality show wine. It's the kind of story you tell the grandchildren, or at the very least is the introduction to your wedding story in *The New York Times* Weddings section. *They met at a socialite's party when he courteously guarded the bathroom door for her . . .* But there's no romance. I'll happily fake it for the evening. He's faking it, too. He's not interested in me. And I'm not interested in him. But we're both interested in pretending to be.

Sometimes, posing about love can be as intriguing as love itself. It's a dance, hoping neither of you will take it too far. I ask about his business. He asks about mine. We laugh at some joke he's made. It's going swell. But then he's interrupted by one of his girls. The gaggle is looking for the next party. He's the captain; he has to go. We bid adieu.

I find another bachelor, the handsome prince. We talk delightfully until the blond woman pulls him away to get in front of one last photographer. The fifty-nine-year-old physician asks for my card as he's leaving, coat on. The production crew packs up. The House-wives go back to their houses. Sonja, the effervescent hostess, says thank you and good night to the gay men who surround her. The night is over, in a flash.

Midnight. My chariot is about to turn back into a pumpkin. I head home, back to my own reality, a small, well-lived-in one-bedroom apartment. I pretend to be happy about it.

No one believes in Prince Charming. But for a night, we can all indulge in an enchanted evening.

RACHEL MEETS HARRISON BLACK

"May I offer you a condom?" Rachel asks, as if she's passing out pigs in a blanket.

Harrison Black laughs. It's their first date since meeting a few weeks earlier when I had invited them both out for drinks with friends, and Rachel, who was feeling all empowered earlier in the night, feels vulnerable now.

"Why are you laughing?" Rachel asks in a whisper, even though she knows it's because she just handled their awkward sex moment like cocktail hour at a wedding.

"You've been watching too much TV," Harrison Black replies, still on top of her.

"I'm clean, are you clean?" she asks, ignoring him.

Harrison Black rolls off of her.

"Look, I just don't want to deal with any issues," Rachel says. "Just the time sitting at the gyno and the bills . . . A condom is, like, a buck-fifty," she says. She knows she is not going to win this argument.

"I was checked last month, and I don't have any STDs," he says. "And it's not about the money."

"Good. I just don't want to deal with distractions right now," Rachel says. Rachel has a distrust of younger women, the women Harrison Black is most likely to be sleeping with. It makes her feel old.

"Aren't you on the pill?" Harrison Black asks with an air of entitlement.

Rachel thinks to herself, *Why is it that men expect women to swallow hormones on a daily basis so they don't have to bother covering up?* "No, why would I be on the pill?" she asks him.

"I don't get it when girls aren't on the pill," Harrison Black says to himself.

"Despite what men think, the pill actually completely changes your chemistry," Rachel tells him. "Why would I be on the pill when I frankly don't have a ton of sex? And besides," she adds, as a way to reassure them both, "I'm not ovulating." Rachel would like to be a mother, but not to Harrison Black's baby. He's a good guy, just not the right guy.

"What does that mean?" Harrison Black asks.

Rachel's happy it's dark so that he can't see her roll her eyes. "It means I'm not at the part of my cycle when I can get pregnant," she explains, wondering why grown men know so little about a woman's cycle other than those four or five days that prove she still has one.

"Plus, I'm thirty-nine. I'm probably not getting pregnant so easily," she adds. She says this thinking it will relieve him but now she also feels bad herself. *Fuck it. This is a turn-off. Come on, Harrison Black. Let's do this already.*

Rachel reaches down between his legs and says, "I want to feel you in me," hinting that she'd prefer he didn't wear a condom either, which is really what this whole conversation is about: He doesn't want to wear a condom. "It's been such a long time since I've felt someone in me," she adds out loud, surprising even herself.

> **"** Sex is easy but a connection is hard to find. And sex without a connection to the man she's sleeping with doesn't feel good. Sure, it may feel good in the moment, but the next day, it feels empty. **"**

"I'm sorry to hear that," Harrison Black replies tenderly as he turns toward her. Somehow, it turns her on.

Harrison Black is on top again. Rachel yields.

"Why are you smiling?" Harrison Black asks a little later.

"Because that was really, really good," Rachel says.

Harrison Black gives her a kiss on the forehead, says it was good for him, too, and they both fall asleep.

Rachel and Harrison Black are both thirty-nine, neither ever married. Yet, somehow, even though Rachel wants to have sex just as bad as he does, there's always a sense that she's being "used" while he's just having fun.

It's been months since the last time she had sex with anyone else, not because she can't find someone who'd want to sleep with her, but because she's not interested in just "having sex." Sex is easy but a connection is hard to find. And sex without a connection to the man she's sleeping with doesn't feel good. Sure, it may feel good in the moment, but the next day, it feels empty.

Rachel has made the exception with Harrison Black. "He was the perfect date, a perfect gentleman," she tells me later over dinner, a dinner we arranged specifically so she could tell me about the date. "He made reservations at the Lion, which was so lovely, and he looked so handsome in a blazer, nice shirt, and dark jeans. After dinner, he took me to this restaurant bar he loves, and we talked there

> 'Yeah, he wants to meet a girl who's like thirty, thirty-two, and get married and have kids. It felt a little like he was picking out a pair of jeans. And then he said that if the marriage didn't work out, they'd just get divorced—like he was returning a pair of jeans that never fit quite right.'

for another couple of hours. We had a great conversation about our backgrounds, our families, our careers—he's such an impressive entrepreneur!" she adds.

"Sounds like you like him," I say.

"Look, I know we're not going to end up together. Like you, I want to end up with a Jewish guy and Harrison Black isn't Jewish, plus he told me he doesn't want to be with a woman as old as he is. And we're the exact same age."

"Well, the wanting to date a young woman is unfortunately not surprising," I say.

"Yeah, he wants to meet a girl who's like thirty, thirty-two, and get married and have kids. It felt a little like he was picking out a new pair of jeans. And then he said that if the marriage didn't work out, they'd just get divorced—like he was returning a pair of jeans that never fit quite right."

"Doesn't he want to go into a marriage that he expects will work?" I ask Rachel.

"Yeah, I mean, that's the idea, he said. But then he went on about how half of all marriages don't work, so he knows what to expect. He'd be happy just having a couple of kids in the end."

"Sounds like he's been thinking about this a lot," I say.

"You know," Rachel says, "a successful, thirty-nine-year-old man can say stuff like that and it will probably end up coming true for him. I asked him how his search is going for this ideal thirty-year-old who wants to get married and have kids with him. He told me he hasn't found her yet but that's OK with him because he doesn't want to have kids for at least another two years. Don't you admire his flexibility?" Rachel says sarcastically.

I laugh.

"Men over thirty-five don't have to worry about their fertility lifespan like we do. I envy and kind of resent it at the same time," Rachel adds.

Rachel explains that, nevertheless, it was nice just to wake up next to someone. Even though she's not falling in love with Harrison Black, she likes that he stayed for a little while in the morning and had coffee with her and chatted about music and the news before he left.

"So you had fun?" I ask Rachel.

"I really did. I regret not making him wear a condom, though," she admits. "I know he doesn't have an STD but what if I get HPV? That's what I'm worried about."

I know Rachel well enough to know that she does not have a lot of sex. And I'm happy she was able to enjoy some intimacy.

"Listen," I say, calmly. "Condoms don't even protect you from HPV. It's a virus that can be caught by genital touch, the place where the condom ends and he still touches you. Literally half of the adult population gets HPV at one time or another. And if even you get HPV, it often goes away on its own in a couple of years. And if it doesn't, the type of HPV that leads to cervical cancer is very rare. I'm not saying to ignore it, but please don't be overly concerned that you are headed toward that fate, or that you even have HPV in the first place!"

"But what if I do? I mean, I don't want to take any chances!"

"Rachel, go see your gynecologist and get a pap smear to get tested. I don't want you to feel burdened by this," I say.

"I will," Rachel says. "But I just hope she doesn't think I'm a slut if it turns out I have it."

"If your doctor implies that you are overly sexual because at age thirty-nine you had sex twice this year, switch doctors," I say.

"You're right," Rachel says.

"Please let go of that stigma that just because you're single people are going to think you're slutty or being used by men. You're not either," I confirm.

Just then, as if on cue, Rachel receives a text from Harrison Black.

"Aw, he texted: *Had a fun night, R. You're really cool. See you soon,*" she reads.

Rachel replies: "*Me too, HB. And you're cool too. See you soon.*"

"Will you?" I ask.

"Why not?" Rachel says with a shrug. "We're friends now. And I had a lot of fun last night. And even if he's not the one I'll end up with forever, I'm learning to enjoy myself right now."

"Speaking of enjoying ourselves right now," I say, "want to share the molten chocolate cake for dessert?"

"Absolutely!" Rachel says.

And it was really, really good.

SEX IN THE OTHERHOOD

I didn't really know what I was getting myself into. The woman on the phone recommended Lukas. Devin, my usual guy, was unavailable. On a whim, I said yes. Sometimes, you have to be daring.

Lukas Tralmer is the kind of handsome that holds you still like a strong wind pushing you against the wall, only I was seated, and his hands were in my hair, tugging this way and that. Occasionally, he'd shake his head in disapproval. I wasn't going to argue.

"Have you been using a paddle brush?" he asks in his German accent as he gently tugs my hair again, accusing me of something I've never done. Blushing, I shake my head.

"I'm going to have to teach you some things," he says in a way that is both alarming and disarming at the same time. I nod my head. *I'd like that,* I think.

Lukas pulls something cold and metal out of the drawer. "Do you trust me?" he asks in a way that means he'll stop if I say no. I don't want him to stop. I'm ready for this. I swallow hard.

"Do it," I say, so he knows I trust him.

Lukas tenderly pushes my head down. He snips. He flips my head back and snips again. Then to one side, *snip snip snip.* And the other,

> **In my late thirties, I had become at once more liberated about my sexual encounters, less concerned about what they meant or what they should have meant, and more focused on being human.**

snip snip snip. And once more. And again. He's not even looking at me. I know exactly what he's focused on. And I don't interrupt.

After a while of this (I don't know how much time has passed) he sprays whipped mousse onto his palm. "This much," he says. "No more."

Yes sir, I think.

He glides his fingers through my hair, and then roughly shakes it out.

The heat from the hair dryer makes me sweat.

When Lukas is done, he stands back to inspect his work. "You like it?" he says, asking me for input for the very first time since we've met. That's what I liked the most. I wanted him to take charge. Be decisive. And he was.

"It's exactly what I needed," I say, snapping into a shy smile.

Ted Gibson, the celebrity hair stylist, walks over to say hello. "I see you've met Lukas," he says, dimples wide.

"Ted, he's amazing!" I say a little too breathlessly. It doesn't matter that Lukas's hairstyle for me is more morning-after bedhead than I had expected. I feel fabulous.

It was, after all, the best "sex" I had had in a while.

In my late thirties, I had become at once more liberated about my sexual encounters, less concerned about what they meant or what they should have meant, and more focused on being human.

And on the other hand, I wasn't having a lot of these encounters. The bottom line is that, like Rachel, I just prefer to be intimate with someone I feel a strong connection with. Sometimes there are months in between. Sometimes it's a year or more. But when it happens, it's great sex. I'm present. I'm enjoying myself, and I'm enjoying the man I'm with. I am self-aware but not self-conscious. I've let him initiate, courting me, treating me well, making me feel like a woman. That's what works for me. I lean back from everything else going on in my life at that moment and let him lead the dance.

After I leave the Ted Gibson salon on Fifth Avenue, I head next door to Eataly to meet Mia, a thirty-three-year-old makeup artist, and Rory, the thirty-five-year-old attorney I met through Meredith, to talk about sex and dating in your thirties.

Rory reports she is having more sex than ever. "And it's better, too," she adds. Rory is the type of petite and adorable that makes her appear ageless.

"I'm not a slut or anything," she quickly appends, because women who have sex unfortunately feel compelled to apologize for having sex. "I'm not having a ton of sex," Rory reveals. "But I'm having more of it than I have ever had. I've learned that the trick is not to overthink what it means, or what he means. I have to say, that is really what makes sex so much better."

Rory is at a turning point. She's beginning to live the life she wants, not the life that society expects of her. And yet, her reflections on her sexual emancipation seem less coming-of-age and more about deciding to enjoy the party she never expected to be invited to.

"When I turned thirty-five, I started to give myself permission to take pleasure in my singlehood. I was tired of having to worry about whether the guy was serious about dating me or dating in general. Or if I was being 'slutty.'" Rory puts the last word in air quotes. "I just wanted to finally enjoy being a woman."

"I agree," says Mia. "I have no qualms about having sex with a guy I like. I was in a relationship for years, and I'm now free to do whatever I want. It's great!"

Rory swipes her long, honey-colored bangs across her forehead. "Well, I haven't even had a serious relationship in five years. And I never thought I'd be this age and not a mom, let alone not married. So I decided that if I'm going to live life in the single lane, I'm not going to feel bad about sex anymore."

As we're talking, a text lights up Rory's iPhone, and she looks down at it. "Look at this," she says, showing us the text: *I want a massage baby.* And, quickly, another: *No massage baby?* A couple more followed.

"Four texts about his stupid massage since we sat down together, like, twenty minutes ago. Yesterday, he sent me a photo of his 'thing.'" Rory rolls her eyes but she doesn't seem completely turned off by it.

"Was it big?" Mia asks, with a wink.

Rory shrugs. "I guess. I don't know. It kind of creeped me out to be honest. Men don't get that they are the visual ones. I'd rather he send me a witty text or something smart. He wanted me to send him a pic of my naked boobs in return."

"Ah yes, the boob pic. Almost a requirement with guys these days," Mia says—from experience, it seems. "Did you send it to him?"

"*Nooooo . . .* " Rory says. "I'm not sending a photo of my naked boobs to any guy. It's just not my thing."

This is the point where I'm supposed to say something like "You deserve better than these guys." It's become a clichéd refrain, one we say to each other with every story about a guy gone wrong. We know we deserve better. But loneliness can be so powerful at times that we acquiesce to anything that will help us feel less lonely for a moment. And when loneliness goes on for years and years, it's easy to want a break from it.

Still, I wonder if having "sex like men"—compartmentalizing sex as a physical thing and not an emotional one—can leave someone feeling even lonelier?

Rory is about to respond to the text when I stop her. "He can wait for a response from you. Enjoy him if that's what you want, but not always on his terms." I have no doubt she'll reply to "massage guy" before she goes to sleep tonight. But I want Rory to have a little power. Relationships, even purely sexual ones, shouldn't be all struggle and no power. Rory nods knowingly and turns off her phone.

"I'm telling you," Mia says, "now that I've let go of what sex is supposed to mean and instead just have sex when I want to . . . like, I have so let go of the idea that you can't have sex with a man on the first date. That's just stupid."

I have to agree with Mia on that. I know too many happily married women who had sex with their then-future husband on the first date. If you feel that rare, immediate, and deep connection with someone and it organically gets physical, the relationship won't be over because you had sex with him on the first date.

A man I once dated told me, "There's no greater turn-off than a woman who says 'I never do this' as you're fooling around on the first date. By the time a woman is in her thirties, she's in fact probably done it. And we guys don't care. We want her not to care, too." I hadn't cared. And he and I were both happy to wake up in each other's arms the following morning and many mornings following. But I also knew his emotional limitations as our short dating life continued.

> 66 Regardless of whether women feel free to do as we please, there's still a stigma to having sex on the first date, or even before the fourth date, as if it means we're slutty and too easy—or worse, that we're destroying the chances that the man we choose to sleep with will ever want to get serious with us. 99

Regardless of whether women feel free to do as we please, there's still a stigma to having sex on the first date, or even before the fourth date, as if it means we're slutty and too easy—or worse, that we're destroying the chances that the man we choose to sleep with will ever want to get serious with us.

The scolding refrain from people, usually married people, goes like this: "You slept with him? On the first/second/third date? Well, you just threw that relationship out the window!" But a woman in her thirties who's at her sexual peak, with greater confidence than she's ever had, who wants to have sex on the first date or whatever date (or even when it's not a date) should just be able to have sex. It just may not come without its own consequences.

In my opinion, if a woman has sex because she likes a man, not because she wants him to like her, she'll be better off. Sex only helps develop deeper emotions when there are some emotions there to begin with.

Alex, an industry colleague, is beginning to see sex differently, too. "I grew up in a really traditional Catholic family and I learned that sex for women is about losing something that was once yours. I learned that one day I would *lose* my virginity and *give* it to a man. I was *giving* him my body. I was *giving* him my sex. I didn't want to be in a relationship because I didn't want to have to give anything of mine away. I was in my early twenties when I lost my virginity but I immediately felt trapped by that boy. It wasn't his fault. He really liked me. It was mine. It was like I was giving him all of me, and I didn't want any part of that.

"I was so guarded around men," Alex admits. "I'd sabotage every relationship, because I wanted to prove to him that he wasn't taking anything from me. I recently started to soften up when I realized that sex is much better when I *want* to give it and want to *accept* what he gives me."

I have learned from many single women that this shift toward sexual self-empowerment often begins in the midthirties, as they come to understand that sex without meaning—a "hookup"—isn't satisfying. When you're in a relationship, even if it's a relationship you know won't lead to marriage or anything close, sexual partners learn more about each other and their needs. We become less shy and more intimate with each other as trust and comfort grows. We learn how to satisfy each other on multiple levels. And the woman, who is less likely than her male partner to have an orgasm from vaginal sex, is freer to tell her partner what she needs to orgasm, even if she may be too embarrassed to share it with anyone else.

Women begin to get tired of trying to be semivirginal, apologizing for having sex with a man too soon to everyone including the man, and become women who realize they enjoy sex and intimacy too much to want to feel ashamed about it. But unlike the four cosmopolitan women we watched on TV in the 1990s, the ones who taught us how to have a "male" attitude about sex, today's women don't want to prove they can have sex like men, that is, sex that doesn't require or result in an emotional connection. I find that most women today want to have sex like women. They want meaningful sex where there's a real connection with the guy. It's not that sex equals a lifelong commitment, but it means you can both enjoy some moments of emotional and physical intimacy.

It's not about when or how often we have sex, but *how* we have sex. What is having sex like a woman? In my book, it's knowing how to tell your partner what you need and wanting to be satisfied by sex. Then, leaning back, literally and/or figuratively, and enjoying sex. Even if you're giving your partner what he wants, when he wants it, it's on your terms.

I've noticed that men feel the same way about sex after thirty-five, too. Craig is someone I met through a married woman who offered to set me up with her husband's best friend.

"They think I'm a player," he said at a local bar the night we met, referring to the friends who set us up. "I'm forty-three and I've never married, but I've tried. Until about six months ago, I was almost engaged to a woman I was with for a year. She has a son, and I didn't care, because I want kids. And he's a great kid. I even bought a ring. But she started to act weird when I wanted to see my friends, like she didn't approve. I can't spend every Sunday doing what she wants me to do. I had to break up with her. But I would have married her."

I sympathize with his "player" label. His best friend's wife had mentioned to me that he might be a player, but I took that with a grain of salt. In the world of Otherhood, single men over thirty-five are considered players and single women over thirty-five are called career women. We all earn our respective badges, even if they're inaccurate.

"'Player' implies I'm having sex with random women and leaving before morning comes. I don't have sex like that. I don't want sex like that. I want meaningful sex. The kind you have when you like someone and it means something, you know?"

> **"** The same married friends who warn that if a single woman has sex with a man too soon, he won't want to be with her, also have this fantasy about all the sex these single women must be having simply because they are free to have it. **"**

I know.

"My married buddies, especially the unhappily married ones, think I'm out having sex all the time, because that's what they want to be doing. One of my buddies says that if he were single, he'd be banging a different girl every night. I explained to him that that's not what happens. No one wants that. We *want* to want to be there in the morning."

The same married friends who warn that if a single woman has sex with a man too soon, he won't want to be with her, also have this fantasy about all the sex these single women must be having simply because they are free to have it. In some married women's minds, single women are having a lot of erotic, hold-me-down-and-tie-me-up sex with handsome men we meet online, in bars, or wherever their fantasies take us.

"A married girlfriend of mine was in town recently and all she wanted to talk about was my dating life," says Rachel when the subject comes up again over cocktails at the Mandarin Oriental Lobby Lounge. Rachel and I are doing a belated-birthday celebration for our now-thirty-seven-year-old friend Vanessa, along with our friend, Dr. Logan Levkoff, a sexologist and sex educator, and our friend Jacqueline. "She was very interested in hearing about all the sex she assumes I'm having," continues Rachel.

"Look, I don't know your friend," Logan, a married mom, says. "But her assuming that you're having a lot of sex is basically a sort of cliché way for people to manage aspects of *their* lives that are not being fulfilled. They wonder if their lives might be better off if they were single, like the women in *Sex and the City* and *Fifty Shades of Grey*. Single women aren't all into BDSM just because they can be."

"Yeah," says Rachel. "I'm really not interested in meeting men just to have sex. It doesn't make me feel dirty or anything, but the experience just isn't satisfying to me. I'm not going to say I've never had a one-night stand, but they are few and far between in the twenty-plus years I've been having sex."

"The truth is," Logan says, "married and partnered people have much more sex than singles do."

"I'm not surprised," says Jacqueline, rolling her eyes. "I find it ironic that we are thought of as these quote-unquote 'liberated' women having quote-unquote 'sex like men' with nary a care in the world—and yet we also have to feel apologetic for having sex when we actually do have sex, as if we are victims of men who are taking advantage of us. It honestly makes me dizzy just thinking about it. Which is why I don't think about it very much."

Me either. But I have to share this one story . . .

In the late winter of 2012, I was invited to an event for moms (as I sometimes am for work), and while we were all waiting for the guest speaker, the conversation turned to the best-selling book series all the women were reading, *Fifty Shades of Grey*.

The runaway best seller had been immediately dubbed "mommy porn" when it was released, as if single women don't enjoy, or don't need to enjoy, erotica. In fact, I had read it, too.

Stacy, a married mom of two, was a little shy, but because *Fifty Shades of Grey* was the only thing anyone was discussing at this event, talking about sex with women she'd just met was suddenly de rigueur for her. Stacy was ready to indulge her curiosity. She had questions about some of the adult toys mentioned in the trilogy. Specifically, she wanted to talk about the vaginal balls. The topic immediately piqued everybody's interest; we were all equally curious. Then, Stacy turned to me and asked, "Well, you must use these all the time, right? What are they like?"

I blushed. I have never used vaginal balls, or most of the toys mentioned in *Fifty Shades*. But Stacy assumed that because I've long been single, I must've had—and I must be continuing to have—a lot of experimental sex using a wide range of toys.

I quickly corrected the misconception. "I've never used them and I don't think I have the kind of sex life you think I have. I date, and I have relationships, but to get to a point where I trust my man with sexual exploration . . . well, that hasn't happened in a long time. In fact, I imagine married couples are more likely to experiment."

One of the other mother moms confessed to having Googled the balls. "I was tempted to buy them but didn't," she admitted. *If I were in a relationship, especially a marriage, I'd buy them in a second,* I thought to myself. I admit to having a real fantasy about how to keep sexual fantasy alive when I'm settled into a long-term relationship.

Back at the Mandarin, Jacqueline suggests, "Let's talk about the sex we *are* having."

"Well, I just broke up with Gavin, so I guess I won't be having sex for a while," says Vanessa, surprising us all.

"What?" says Jacqueline. "I thought you guys were doing great. It's been over a year! What the hell happened?"

"It was my birthday present," Vanessa says, "I didn't expect an

> 'Intimacy is a difficult thing for some men to talk about because they haven't really been taught how to have those conversations.'

engagement ring or anything, but he gives me this fancy box, and I honestly thought it was going to be a piece of jewelry or something, and that's not at all what it was."

"What was it?" Rachel asks.

"It was a vibrator! A $250 vibrator! How scared do you have to be of intimacy to give your girlfriend of over a year a fucking vibrator for her birthday?"

I find myself losing focus. I realize I'm enthralled by the mystery of what could possibly make a vibrator worth $250. Vanessa snaps me back to attention when she exclaims, "What better way to tell your girlfriend to literally go fuck herself!"

Before we all get on the "Gavin's the worst boyfriend ever" bandwagon, Logan speaks up. "I don't know that I would take it that way, Vanessa. I see it differently." The rest of us are looking at Logan with disbelief.

She continues, "Studies by vibrator companies show that almost as many men use vibrators as women."

"On themselves?" Rachel asks.

"Well, they might, but . . . Vanessa, Gavin probably wasn't saying to use the vibrator without him. But that's sometimes a hard conversation for men to have. A luxury vibrator is a pretty extraordinary gift. I really think he meant it for your pleasure."

Vanessa looks confused. "But it was a sex gift. I was expecting a gift that showed his love for me," Vanessa says, a little sadly.

Logan responds, "He may have fantasies, but he doesn't know how to broach the subject with you. Intimacy is a difficult thing for some men to talk about because they haven't really been taught how to have those conversations. Maybe the luxury vibrator was a way of telling you he wants to get closer to you, to be more intimate with you, not leave you to pleasure yourself."

Vanessa now looks relieved. "I just don't want to be with someone who gives me a vibrator for my thirty-seventh birthday. I want to be with someone who appreciates me as a whole person, not just his lover," she admits.

"I understand that, Vanessa," Logan says. "Consider going back to the table with Gavin and saying, 'This is not who I am. I am vulnerable, and I am in love with you.'"

"He knows I love him," Vanessa says.

"I know," Logan says. "But give him the opportunity to get vulnerable with you, too. Show him the way. Women are often better at that than men."

"I'll talk to him about it," Vanessa says. "But for now, let's change the subject. I don't want Gavin and his vibrator to take over this night." ·

I ask Rachel about Harrison Black. I'm curious about how it's going.

"Harrison Black is a great guy," Rachel says. "He does all the right things, even walking on the outside of the sidewalk like a true gentleman. I like that he knows that's what a gentleman does. And it makes me feel protected, even if the gesture came from back in the old days when men were protecting women from sewage streaming down the gutters or something like that."

"I agree!" I say, "I love it when a man purposely walks on the outside. It makes me feel like a lady, even if I'm in shorts and a T-shirt."

"Exactly," Rachel confirms. "And Harrison Black would never dream of letting me pay or not taking me out before, you know, taking me home, but the thing is, it's just sex. Neither of us sees this going further than that. In the end, I want to marry a Jewish guy, and he wants someone ten years younger than me. But when we're together, we play the roles of a true courtship. Before and after we end up in bed, we talk about meaningful things. We have a solid friendship. And that connection makes the sex more fun. And he always calls me the next day to check in, mostly because I've asked him to, but he listened and he does it. It's really sweet.

"It would honestly make me so happy if he found the right woman," she continues. "In the meantime, I'm going to have sex. Every girl needs a little intimacy now and again. This is the perfect type of sex to have, platonic but meaningful."

The interesting thing about Rachel—and my friend Wynn, who's sleeping with thirty-one-year-old Austin, no strings attached—is that both have just one sexual partner. Even though they can have sex with whomever they want (after all, they are not married or in a monogamous relationship), they choose to have sex with just one person for a period of time.

After three years of seeing Eddie, a thirty-year-old trust fund baby, for casual hookups, Jacqueline has also recently taken a new approach to sex. It was fun at first. Eddie lives in a large TriBeCa loft and always had a nice bottle of champagne chilling in the fridge when she arrived. But they've been doing this for a while and sex with Eddie was getting boring. He's not very adept at communicating with her emotionally. And his ability in bed? Well, according to her, it's mostly all about Eddie. Jacqueline played along at first, but at some point, she had to take charge if she wanted him to know how best to take care of her, and it just wasn't working for her.

"Everything changed when I got a call from Eddie at 1:00 AM on a Saturday night," Jacqueline explains. "I was home that night, reading, taking a long bath, and drinking a really nice glass of wine." (Jacqueline had learned from our mutual friend, Meredith, that treating herself the way she wanted her future partner to treat her may help manifest that type of man into her life.) Eddie making a bootie call at 1:00 AM made it clear: He was probably not that man.

"I'm not sure if it was the erotica I was reading, or the fun I was having in the bath by myself, but I was inspired to change the dynamic," she says. "I had been convincing myself I was a modern, liberated woman, and that sex with Eddie, no strings attached, was great. If Eddie didn't care if it led anywhere, why should I? But I was fooling myself. The sex was average, and the next morning, even though he was always sweet with me, I would feel dissatisfied with Eddie, the sex, and most of all, myself. Even though I would agree to meet Eddie, doing it whenever it pleased him and *however* it pleased him made me feel used.

"Here," Jacqueline says as she reaches for her phone. "I want you guys to read the exact conversation I had with Eddie that night. I didn't pick up the phone when he called, and instead, I texted this to him an hour later. It changed everything."

Jacqueline: *I don't wait for men to call me at 1:00 AM on a Saturday night to go see them for sex. What's with you? Why would you think that I'd be OK with that? I find it insulting. Disappointed.*

Eddie: *Disappointed?? Imagine how I felt when you didn't answer my call!*

Jacqueline: *Disrespectful. I won't do this anymore, Eddie. The end.*

"And then what happened?" I ask Jacqueline. "Did he come crawling back?"

"Eddie called again and this time I picked up the phone," Jacqueline says, smiling. "Eddie told me some things that really shocked me. It seems the minute I was brave enough to tell him how I really felt, it moved him to do the same."

"Oh, good," I say.

"Eddie told me how he thinks when I get mad at him, it means I don't like him. And then he added as proof the fact that I post about my good dates on Facebook. He said it taunts him! I had to explain to Eddie that what *we* do isn't *dating*. He's never actually asked me out. I told him there's a difference between asking me to come over and actually asking me out on a date. Asking me to come over makes me feel cheap, or like I'm not desirable, or like I have no value to men in a meaningful way. I admitted that I really did hope for more, but knowing that he's four or five years younger than I am, and well, filthy rich and can attract a much younger, prettier, taller, skinnier, whatever woman he wants . . . "

Jacqueline is a beautiful, successful woman. But I understand that when a man only wants sex, on his terms, from you, that means he's also dating other women. And it can feel like *those* are the women he wants to be seen out with in public. It wears on a woman.

She continues, "I was brutally honest with Eddie. I really figured that, at that point, I had nothing to lose. I explained that I want more from the men I date, and I deserve more. So if a gentleman decides to be a gentleman and ask me out on a date, I'm going to go. And I'm not going to be shy about sharing how the date made me feel on my Facebook page if I want to."

Jacqueline says, "I explained to Eddie that he's never done with me the things he knows I love to do. But then he told me that he likes spending time with me, and that it's not just about the sex. So I said that he should show his affection for me more freely and treat me like a lady, because that's what turns me on. Not bootie calls. He got all flirty again at that, so I said something like, I appreciate your desire for me, but that's all about *you*. If it's all about you, when is it about me? He asked me to tell him what I need. So I said that I would love it if *he* would be the guy to ask me out and to treat me the way I want to be treated."

"How did he react to that?" Logan asks.

"Eddie told me, and I wasn't surprised, that he is incredibly shy, and he doesn't like to go out to big social events and stuff. But then he promised to take me to a nice place and that I will have his undivided attention."

"Well, that's good," Rachel says.

"And then I took a deep breath and said that I'd be really happy to have more than what we have right now. He said something about baby steps and told me how much just my voice turns him on. I said, 'Eddie, it's good to know my voice turns you on. But you need to learn what turns me on if this is going to go any further.'"

"Taking the reins! Go, Jacqueline!" I say.

"You have no idea, girls," she says. "I then told him exactly how many times I need to come before he can even think about coming himself." I'm blushing as she's speaking. Jacqueline is hardcore in control. "It really turned Eddie on," she reports, nearly blushing herself.

"Anyway," Jacqueline says as she looks at her watch. "I have to get up so early tomorrow. I really should go."

"Wait, what happened since this big talk?" I ask.

Jacqueline shrugs with a smile. "Seems he's falling a little bit in love with me," she says. "We've gone on two dates since that call, and we have another one tomorrow night. And the sex, well the sex is kind of explosive. As in, the best sex I've ever had."

"Do you think you're heading toward a relationship?" Rachel asks very curiously.

"Well," Jacqueline says, "Meredith's whole 'treat yourself as you want him to treat you' thing might be working after all. Eddie is enjoying being challenged to make me happy, and I'm challenging him to learn how to connect with me on a deeper level. And it's like seeing him mature right before my eyes. He admitted to me that his dad would put him down when he would get emotional, you know, that whole big-boys-don't-cry stupidity that raises boys to be men afraid of being emotional?

"Look," she continues, "I'm not sure Eddie is the one for me in the end, but that's what dating is for. And now that we're actually dating, and learning more about each other on a whole other level, he's definitely impressing me. So let's see where it goes. All I know is that sex is much better not just because he's learning how to satisfy me, but because it's become more meaningful since we connect in other ways. I feel satisfied on many levels, and that's a good thing."

WAS IT CHOICE OR CHANCE?

Celia and Sam got married. The bride, thirty-six, had recently become a more observant Jew, attracted to the family values, warm traditions . . . and the men. *These guys want to be married and have children like I do,* she thought to herself. And so she chose to live a more observant lifestyle. And Sam, observant and over forty, was ready to get married.

I'm at a penthouse event space a few days after the nuptials to celebrate with Celia and Sam. The chic room is filled with chic, brown-haired women and chic, brown-haired men. The food lining the buffet is traditional brown Jewish fare: brisket, beef, and chicken in an appealing brown sauce, along with mashed potatoes and potatoes cooked another way that also look remarkably like mashed potatoes. On a separate table, a bowl of salad greens and a large platter of crudités are placed, observing the faux American Jewish dietary restriction of not mixing healthy vegetables with fatty foods. I scoop some brisket onto my plate and make my way over to some friends.

Abby, a lawyer, has broken up with a really nice guy. They are still friends. She bought an apartment, and she's really happy at her new job as an in-house corporate attorney. She chose to leave the partner track at a top Midtown law firm for better hours at her new job and, potentially, better dating.

Joe, another attorney, is half proud and half in disbelief that his son is moving away to attend college. Joe's been divorced for fifteen years, and now he's really on his own. He's trying to decide what to do next.

Liz is married, two kids. She's nonchalant about the whole "married mom" thing, believing she's simply lucky that she met Nate by chance on a singles trip a decade ago. Marriage and motherhood were never a badge she wore with superiority, but rather a badge she wears like people wear any part of their lifestyle.

"We're all good," she says effortlessly when I ask about the family. "Nate's good, the kids are good, I'm good, work is good. Life is good."

And I know by her mild temperament, she's telling the truth. That's good.

I'm sipping the seltzer and cranberry Nate offered me when Audrey waves me over. Audrey is married to Simon, a somewhat reserved hedge fund manager. Audrey is very outspoken and a reporter for a Hollywood gossip website. They met on JDate and married two years ago. They're both over forty and the perfect yin and yang together.

"I *tohhhhtally* get what you write about," Audrey says as Simon makes a beeline for the beef, knowing we're about to talk girl-talk. "I was forty-one when I met Simon. I know what it's like to feel like it may never happen. I can *still* feel it!" Audrey is a card-carrying member of the Otherhood. "And I have so many *faaaaabulous* friends who are still there," she adds. "Isn't it amazing that the most *faaaaaabulous* women are the last to marry?" I nod as Audrey continues. "My friend Shelly is forty-two and thinking about moving. She hasn't met a guy and she isn't happy at work anyway. Michelle is forty-four and single and, oh my God, she's so *amaaaaazing*. You

> ❝ To me, when you tell a woman she's made 'choices,' it implies that she made the wrong choices, the choices that led her away from falling in love, marriage, and children. ❞

have to meet her. And I have a friend who is forty-six and single but you know . . . " Audrey shrugs. "She made her choices, right?"

Audrey has me until the "choices" point. To me, when you tell a woman she's made "choices," it implies that she made the wrong choices, the choices that led her away from falling in love, marriage, and children. But falling in love is never a choice, whether one wants to meet someone to fall in love with or whether one falls in love with the most inappropriate person.

A piece I wrote for *The Huffington Post* that same week went viral. It's about how people make snap judgments regarding what I've "done wrong," or about what could possibly be "wrong with me," to explain why I haven't married. In the article, I list a number of assumptions people have about my singleness:

She's not picky enough and made bad choices.

She made a choice.

She never made a choice.

And yet a married dad I've known for almost twenty years (most of which he spent single) sent me a message in response to my piece: *I don't think any of those things. You made choices just like the rest of us.*

There you go, that "choices" comment again. It's frustrating. It implies I made the wrong choices, deliberately, when all my choices toward love, marriage, and children were made with the best intentions. They simply didn't result in love, marriage, and children. I never chose not to fall in love. Then again, I also never chose to marry the wrong man. I didn't choose career over love. After all, I have to earn a living. What were my choices? Did I stumble upon late-age singlehood by misfortune? Or did I somehow make choices that I knew would lead me here? Or could lead me here? Did I even really have choices, or was everything moving toward a predestined fate?

I think it's a balance of things I can control and things I cannot control, like a no-fault accident. Still, I want to figure this out. Was it my destiny to be single and childless at this age? Or was my fate the result of my choices, no matter how well-intentioned they were? I had always chosen love over everything, but somehow I wound up with nothing. Now, the uncertainty makes me feel restless. I'm thinking about this when I arrive at Alison's apartment later that week.

Alison, dressed in legs-up-to-there skinny jeans, is mixing drinks in the kitchen. A freezer door slams shut, ice cubes drop into glasses, and a blender is turned on. Laughter is loud and strong, and I know I'm walking in on something exciting. I can't tell what it is exactly, but I know I've entered the room at the exact moment the story reaches a head because just then, Mia throws her head back and raises her arms in a commanding *"Ohhh! Yes!"*

Alison wipes up the mess she's made preparing our drinks while Mia continues to giggle softly. The two women light up the room, and I remember why I'm so happy to be their friend. I've caught Alison off-guard.

"Oh my God! You're here!" Alison greets me with a wide smile. "I'm so happy to see you! Go sit down. I'll bring the cocktails over in a minute!"

The other women are already seated in the other room. I see a pop of an iPhone flash, a flash of a bare shoulder from an errant neckline on a silk blouse, big smiles as I enter and take a seat between Claire and Catherine. There's nothing like the pure joy of the girls all together on a weeknight to let off some steam and reenergize.

Alison, the hostess, is forty, divorced, no kids, a catalog model and an actor who appears in national commercials you've probably seen. Mia, thirty-three, is a makeup artist for TV and film and recently ended a long-term relationship that wasn't right. It was *her* choice, but still, "it *felt* like a divorce," she says as she walks into the room and places her cocktail on the table.

Both Alison and Mia are tall, blond, talented beauties you can't take your eyes off of. And both women are dating Jewish men.

"Listen up!" Alison says to the room as we each take a cocktail from her tray. "My agent called yesterday. He wants me to audition for a movie cast as, get this, the 'shiksa goddess'! Am I made for that role or *what?* I'm certainly playing that role pretty well now. I'm a natural!"

Alison is madly in love with Gabriel. Gabriel is divorced from Marla, a Jewish woman he had married when they were both twenty-seven. Now forty-one, three kids and two cars later, Gabriel is in love with Alison. And I can't really blame him.

They met exactly when Alison's friend, Paula the psychic, said they would. "Before the end of the month, you're going to meet the man you'll marry," Paula had said at Alison's annual reading. Alison, who's known Paula for years and always believed her, didn't believe her.

"I'm dating a cute guy now," Alison conceded, "but I don't think he's husband material."

Paula agreed. "It's not him, Ali. It's someone from your past. You'll meet him again. And this time, it's right."

"And sure enough," Alison reveals to her guests, "I met Gabriel on the last day of the month! We had met ten years ago at our mutual friend's wedding when he was married and I was engaged. Literally the day after I met with Paula, our mutual friend set us up to have coffee. We did. And now . . . I think he's the one! Can you believe my fate? I'm Gabriel's shiksa goddess!"

I don't like the term "shiksa," the Yiddish word for a non-Jewish woman. And the expression "shiksa goddess" is especially jarring. It's reserved for the women some Jewish girls fear the most—the tall, usually blond, statuesque, Christian beauty—that is, the unattainable women some Jewish men desire the most: Uma Thurman, Ivanka Trump (who converted to Judaism before she married her orthodox boyfriend), or just about any model . . . like Alison.

I admit to myself that Ali is right; she *is* made for the role. And as much as I adore her, I'm also thinking her relationship with Gabriel means there's one less eligible Jewish guy for the Jewish girls. And many Jewish women prefer to marry within the faith. We carry the Jewish babies and the Jewish guilt.

Mia, who has recently started dating Mitchell, a Jewish man I happen to know, agrees with Alison's assessment of the casting potential. "It's *perrrrfect* for you!" she exclaims, lifting her tumbler to toast the news.

"Shiksa?" asks Claire, a successful Internet entrepreneur who moved to New York just a couple of years ago from Texas. "What's a shiksa?"

"It's a woman like *meeeee*," Alison sings. "A totally non-Jewish girl who gets the Jewish boy!" And then she leans in toward Claire and gently adds: "If you have the choice, date a Jewish guy. I'm telling you right now, they make the best boyfriends."

And I suppose they might.

Claire tells the story about a man she met on eHarmony who didn't make a move on their first date but sent her a text the following week saying he'd like to tie her up and have sex with her on their second date. She chose not to see him again. Catherine is dating a man out of town whom she adores, but she knows it can't go on like this forever. They'll need to make a choice.

And Mia is also considering her options. She's dating a number of men, not just Mitchell. There's a photographer, a model, a violinist, and a funny-looking hedge fund guy she's oddly attracted to. "But Mitchell is the one with the best personality," she explains endearingly. "Jewish guys always have the best personalities," she adds, looking at me for a knowing nod. "But you know, who knows?" she says with a coy smile and a shrug. Mia is newly single, absolutely stunning, and has a lot of choices. And for the first time that night, I admit to myself that I'm envious.

I'm Jewish. I've always felt a certain deep connection to my traditions and a sense of pride—and obligation—for continuing many millennia of Jews. When I was only five years old, I pleaded with my parents to enroll me in Jewish day school so I could learn Jewish things, whatever those things might be from a five-year-old's perspective. I grew up the only one of my Jewish friends to eschew pepperoni pizza for plain, or a hamburger for a fish burger, an almost-kosher diet whenever we went out to eat.

When I was nineteen, my mother died, and I soon upped the ante on my already traditional lifestyle. Like Celia the bride, but many years earlier, I turned to Orthodox Judaism for a sense of family the community provided and what I expected to be a promise of my own family in the future. The Jewish boy who wore a yarmulke on a date to the movies comforted me; I could have a modern life in a traditional home. And those boys were supposed to want to marry, too. They were supposed to want a family. And being a religious girl, they should have wanted me, too.

In my early twenties, I moved to New York City from Montreal knowing that there would be a greater selection of modern orthodox men—the term that describes Jews who live the modern everyday American life while also maintaining their religious observances. I worked for Jewish organizations and opened my small Upper West Side apartment to large crowds of single Jewish men and women for Shabbat dinners. I went to synagogue every Saturday morning, in my best temple-appropriate dresses, hoping I'd meet a guy who would intrigue me.

Those Saturdays bled into other Saturdays, into months of Saturdays and years of Saturdays, and quickly into nearly a decade of Saturdays, when I finally began to wonder if what the older people in my life had warned me about was true. Was I limiting myself out of chances for marriage and children by dating only men I thought had similar family values? Were my good intentions failing?

I first began to think twice when I was in my late twenties, although it took a few more years to fully disengage myself from the idea of getting engaged to an observant man. I was newly broken-hearted. It wasn't a healthy broken heart, the kind that happens to most of us at least once in a lifetime and we learn from it in time to meet a more appropriate partner.

I'd classify the heartbreak as desperate, which is probably why it was so painful. When you're part of a community limited in size, and the one man (the *only* man) you are into is the one your friends love for you, too, the one who challenges you intellectually and whose sense of humor leads to the most fun you have yet experienced, the very same one who you hadn't been attracted to at first—albeit because of all the red flags you saw him waving—but the one your friends say is perfect for you, you think the two of you are meant to be. And one Friday night, after my Sabbath candles were lit and our friends gathered for Shabbat dinner, like night to day, that was it, and I fell hard. I ignored the little red flags I saw and waved one big white flag instead. Him. I surrendered to him. And that, I thought, would be it.

What a love affair it was. Within a couple of short weeks of our first date, we shared "I love you"s and I felt safe; I had met the man I would marry! And we would continue to live in this safe place of common friends, common history, common values, and a common belief system.

Until the one day, just a few months after I let go and let him in, when we were reading the newspaper on my loveseat and he told me the news: "I need to take my 'I love you' back," he said.

He wasn't sure how he felt anymore, he explained. And the less sure he became, the more sure I became that he *was* the one. My safe love turned into desperate love, and having never been in love like this before, I held on even more tightly to a man who wanted to be let loose.

And so one night he came over to tell me it was over, and I cried. I cried deep, hard, guttural, end-of-my-world kind of tears, for days.

The Breakup wasn't just a breakup with this man, a man I thank now. He did the right thing; we were not meant to be married. But the breakup was an earthquake, a fissure in my world separating me from what I knew was the possibility of marriage and children, and what I realized was probably never going to come easy for me. Was he the last man I'd love in that world? I couldn't accept that to be true, and so I kept on believing.

I had stuck my stake in the ground, making my life in Modern Orthodox Judaism, and I was naïve to think that the promise of a traditional life was reciprocal. I'd give up Saturday shopping for marriage and children, roast chicken, and the handmade wood-and-bottle-cap Hanukkah menorahs my kids would make in kindergarten. I believed I was truly making the right choice. The best choice. And for most of my time in that world, the only choice for me. What would be if it wasn't to be?

We think by age twenty-seven that we are adults, but we are still holding the narcissism of our childhood close. Our worlds are bigger, but they still feel small to us. We have yet to see our lives as ever changing, ever growing, ever moving from people to places to people to places to new worlds and beyond. We are terribly shortsighted and unwavering in our idea that our lives will remain looking exactly the way they are or the way we imagine they should be, plus a higher income, a few kids, and of course, the one we love.

A couple of years after The Breakup, still single, still observant, and still stubbornly loyal to my traditions, I was invited to meet a renowned spiritual woman who had been delivered to New York City from Israel by some well-meaning rabbis. They believed she might be able to offer insight and prayer for the woes of the community. My woe was singlehood, and among the dozen or so women in the synagogue rabbi's living room on our day to meet her, I was not alone.

I understand Hebrew, but this woman's Hebrew was of an ancient tongue, as if it was spoken in the language of the Dead Sea Scrolls. It was difficult for me to understand. All I understood from our very brief meeting was that she wanted me to come back the next day with some photos of myself. Special prayers would need to be said at a spiritual site in the Holy Land, the photos left there. I was the only one who was asked to bring photos. It was concerning, and I didn't know whether to feel special or like a special case in need of extra prayer. I was hoping for the former but suspected it was the latter.

The next day, photos in tow, I went to see the *rabbanite,* as she was called. She looked at my photos carefully, as if the three-dimensional version standing right in front of her was not sufficient. She looked up at me, a crease in her forehead appeared, and she shook her head as if she was about to deliver bad news. Instead, she delivered more uncertainty. The rabbi standing next to her translated: "It's very hard for you, she says," he said.

"Very hard," she repeated in English with an accent I can only describe as prophetic.

"The *rabbanite* will pray for you," the rabbi soothed.

And I wondered: *When it came to my finally finding love and marriage, was it not in my own hands? Were there other forces that had a hand in my fate? Was I wrong to think it was all up to me?* At a time when I was my most religious, I wanted the least to believe I was not in control of my fate. As I look back, I seemed to have been stuck in a quagmire of doing what I thought was best with regard to whom I dated, not doing what might have been best for me.

"You're limiting yourself," chimed-in my therapist. After The Breakup, I went to sit in front of this man every Tuesday afternoon at 3:00 PM like clockwork for years. I could feel time ticking away every week. "You're not like these guys," he said, again and again, never really explaining why. "Go date some other Jewish guys—not the religious ones." I retorted with some response about existential connections and my true beliefs, and as he might have predicted, nothing changed. Once I was in my thirties, I was no longer feeling eligible among that Orthodox Jew crew. I had aged out. But my naïveté hadn't. And so on Sunday, I'd buy a new dress for temple the following Saturday. I kept trying.

But by my mid to late thirties, the pattern got to me, finally. *Groundhog Day,* I thought to myself when I awoke one Saturday morning. *I can't do this again.* And I didn't, ever again.

I still choose to date Jewish men exclusively; the responsibility

> 66 I reminded myself that I had no regrets, but I did wonder if my well-intentioned choice to date only orthodox guys in my twenties and well into my thirties was a bet on the wrong brisket. Had I carved my dating life into thin, lean slices against the grain? Or, I wondered, had I done the very best I could in spite of a fate that would be what it would be, no matter my choices? 99

to marry a Jew looms large like a decree from my foremothers and forefathers, not to mention my own late mother and her late father. I reminded myself that I had no regrets, but I did wonder if my well-intentioned choice to date only orthodox guys in my twenties and well into my thirties was a bet on the wrong brisket. Had I carved my dating life into thin, lean slices against the grain? Or, I wondered, had I done the very best I could in spite of a fate that would be what it would be, no matter my choices?

I was reminded of that very thought a few months later. I was having drinks with Teresa, a woman I had recently met. This much I knew about her: She's thirty-nine, single, in marketing, and she appeared in a reality show before reality shows were the only thing on television. I also knew that she's Catholic, suffered a near-death experience before she should have been old enough to recall that she had, and as a result, she says she's apparently somewhat psychic. It appeared there were more psychic women in Manhattan than I realized.

The bartender was pouring a second round of merlot for the two single women at his bar that rainy night when Teresa, who had seemed distracted for a few minutes, touched my arm. "Did you have a very religious Jewish grandfather who passed away?" she asked out of the blue.

When you're caught off-guard in Manhattan, the first thing to remember is that magnificent discoveries rarely happen here on purpose. The city is filled with surprises waiting around the corner every day. Perhaps it's that we're rarely caught off-guard merely because we're so often caught off-guard. So even though I felt I was possibly about to hear from my grandfather who died four decades earlier, I decided to stay calm and collected. Calm. Cool. Ready. The restaurant froze in an amber-lit hush. The bartender, just in front of us seconds ago, had disappeared out of view. I could hear a Parisian song playing in the background. And Teresa was looking over my shoulder.

"My Baba," I said. "My mother's father. He died when I was a baby, but I know he was a very religious man," I added to confirm Teresa's description.

"He's been walking back and forth along the bar for like twenty minutes," she said, relieved to know whom he belonged to. There was of course no religious, Jewish man walking back and forth along the bar of this nonkosher upscale French restaurant just off Madison Avenue. It was a ghost. Or should I say "spirit"? Either way, he seemed to have something important to say, and I was listening to Teresa who was listening to my Baba, the religious ghost spirit.

"I thought he might belong to you," Teresa said. "He's showing me a . . . what is that big certificate a Jewish bride and groom get at their wedding? It's all in Hebrew. I can't read it."

"The *ketubah*," I answer as if I'm teaching Jewish Weddings 101 and not in the midst of a psychic revelation.

"Yes, that's it," she confirmed. "Your grandfather is pointing at your name in Hebrew. He wants you to know it's there."

Get right to the punch line, why don't you, Baba . . . Take that rabbanite! I immediately thought.

I tried to stay blasé, but there were tears in my eyes. I hadn't thought about my Baba very often. I didn't remember him. I didn't feel a connection with him. Well, I hadn't. Things were about to change.

"Don't cry," Teresa said, probably experienced at having made people cry before in a similar way. I made myself stop because I didn't want Teresa to stop. She went back to Baba. "He says that he understands why you no longer keep the Sabbath," she said. I was deeply intrigued and potentially blushing. Teresa wouldn't know about my religious observance—and how in heavens did Baba know? "But he does want you to go back to lighting the Sabbath candles," she added. "And he says to talk to him when you do. And to your mother, too. They are both there, listening. Pray for what you want."

As I got into a cab after drinks with Teresa, I was finding it easier to believe that my late grandfather was in the bar with me than it was to believe there was a future *ketubah* with my name on it. Still, I've been lighting the Sabbath candles every Friday night since that fateful evening. As far as I see it, I don't have a choice.

I get a text a couple of weeks after the apartment gathering from the hostess, Alison. She didn't get the part in the movie after all. But she got the man. The shiksa goddess and the Jewish boy are engaged. They'll be married next spring.

WHAT CHOICE DO WE HAVE?

I need to get out of the city. Or, at least, get off this island. It's common for the habitual Manhattanite to leave the city simply to come back and declare our undying, unconditional love for our home. We all know the truth: In order to know for sure we're in the right place, we have to step away from it and look back at it more objectively.

I'm getting together with my friend, Andrea Syrtash—the popular relationship expert, television host, and author of several books on dating, marriage, and relationships—for a walk along the Brooklyn Heights Promenade, one of the most romantic spots in Brooklyn. The fresh perspective is making me think of love and about choice versus chance as Andrea and I look out toward Manhattan.

"Isn't Manhattan just incredibly beautiful?" I ask rhetorically. "Look at all those stunning buildings filled with ambition and dreams, hard work and determination." It's a brisk, sunny September day, not a cloud in the sky, and Andrea and I take a pause before we continue. It's difficult to look at the southern tip of Manhattan, even over a decade later, without remembering another brisk, sunny day and what we lost—who we lost. Seeing the city from this vantage point makes me realize how fortunate I am, perhaps even how selfish I am, to even debate choice versus chance.

A couple in their midthirties walks by us, arm in arm, as a group of women and men in their late twenties walks by from the other direction. A young mother stops a few feet away from us, holding her young daughter's hand. Andrea sees me notice the little girl, her long wavy brown hair waving freely in the air as her mother zips up her red quilted jacket. My friend puts her hand on my back with a touch of compassion.

But it's not the child I haven't had that I am thinking about. I'm thinking of a friend who was killed on September 11th at age thirty-two, not yet married, not yet a mother. Some had said it was fortunate that she did not leave children and a husband behind to mourn her. But I was always saddened by the fact that she never had the opportunity to get married or experience motherhood. That fateful day still gives me perspective on life. While I may not be where I expected to be at this age, I got here, safe and sound. I smile appreciatively at Andrea, who can tell I've been elsewhere for a moment.

"It's hard to believe that in all those buildings, in all those windows, under that big, bright sky, I haven't found him yet," I say.

"Melanie, I get it," Andrea offers. "I speak to so many spectacular, educated, accomplished women who have trouble finding men they are interested in dating. And there is this huge misconception out there. Society, friends, siblings, even parents somehow pity these amazing women and think of them as those poor girls who can't get a date, as if they have no choice but to be single."

I shake my head in knowing frustration.

Andrea continues, "What these people don't realize about a woman like this is that being single is a choice she's made. It isn't her choice

> 66 The single women of the Otherhood know they are not *Waiting for Godot*. They are not waiting in vain for life to present itself to them with meaning. They choose. They choose to wait for the love they're meant to have, the love that will add more meaning to their lives. 99

to remain single. We all know she wants to be in love with the right man," Andrea says. "But it's the choice of these talented, attractive women to wait for that man to come into her life, or she into his. She isn't single because no one has picked her yet. She isn't waiting to be chosen."

She isn't waiting to be chosen. Andrea is right. The single women of the Otherhood know they are not *Waiting for Godot*. They are not waiting in vain for life to present itself to them with meaning. They choose. They choose to wait for the love they're meant to have, the love that will add more meaning to their lives. Others may say a single woman in her midthirties, and certainly by her forties, has been looking too long, or that she has too many distractions like her career or her passions. And some may say that she is looking in vain for someone who does not exist and that her life will pass her by if she doesn't choose to settle.

But the women of the Otherhood know they are preparing themselves, filling life with things that are meaningful, that give life purpose. They are actively choosing to live life to the fullest. Their true existence and meaning are not dependent on how or when they are united with love. They know that on their journey of self-actualization, they will come upon the love that we are meant to have. They believe that their future partner will recognize them because they are the love that he was meant to have. They will choose one another.

Andrea asks, "Do you remember that line in *Jerry Maguire* where Tom Cruise says to Dorothy, the Renée Zellweger character, 'You complete me?'"

"Yes. Who doesn't remember that line?" I say.

"Exactly. It's been embedded in our culture. But it gives the wrong message, saying that we should look for partners who complete us as if we are not whole people to begin with.

"The single women you and I know are full women," she continues. "Whatever it is—their careers, their nieces and nephews, their friends and family, their homes and hobbies, their travel and cultural interests—whatever it is that makes them feel fulfilled, these women are not half filled, waiting for someone to complete the other half." Andrea pauses pensively for a moment, and then goes on: "And the reason why society looks at these fabulous women with pity, I think, is because they assume single women are unhappy and unfulfilled. But I have to tell you, the single women I speak with are very happy. Yes, of course most of them want a man in their life, but that's icing on the cake for them. And we know that women who marry later are less likely to divorce, in part because they are so fulfilled before they enter marriage. It is because they are whole already."

Andrea is giving me the outside perspective I was hoping for.

"Their choice is to wait for the right guy," she confirms. "But on the flip side, they also have to make some proactive choices if finding love is indeed a priority."

"Most of the women I speak to or have known for many years make finding love a priority," I say, somewhat defensively. "I think people judge single women for not doing enough to meet a man be-

> 'The single women you and I know are full women,' she continues. 'Whatever it is—their careers, their nieces and nephews, their friends and family, their homes and hobbies, their travel and cultural interests—whatever it is that makes them feel fulfilled, these women are not half filled, waiting for someone to complete the other half.'

cause they mistakenly believe that if they were doing enough, they would have found him already."

Andrea responds, "I don't mean that single women should make finding love a full-time job. But it means making hard choices and saying no to things sometimes if they make it harder to find love."

"Like what?" I ask.

"I know dating, even finding men you actually want to date, is hard. But sometimes I see women with negative attitudes about it. And that energy shows. So my advice would be to say no to being pessimistic about love. I hear women say that there are quote-unquote 'no' men out there. Or they say that it's 'impossible' to meet someone. Those words are extreme. We know that's not true. We have to believe it."

I'm reminded of something my friend Sloane said to me about dating conversations she has had with her single girlfriends who are all in their midthirties. "I just had to pull myself out of the perpetual negativity," she told me. "It was overwhelming for me to hear, ad nauseum. What is the ROI on negativity? Nothing. So I pulled myself out of it and just stopped getting together with them."

"But let's be honest," I say to Andrea. "We can't go out every night and be active in online dating and going to every singles event.

It's exhausting. Plus, we've been looking for love, some of us, for over twenty years. Like you said, we have so many other things in our lives. We can't spend all of our time proactively looking for love. That just feels desperate. And to your point, we're not desperate women waiting for life to begin once we're finally in the right relationship. I know some women just take a break from all of it," I add. "I did that when I was forty. For about six months I didn't accept what seemed like a mismatched blind date or attend many social events just in case there might be a man to meet there. A married mom friend of mine kept reminding me of my biological clock, but I just couldn't go on another going-nowhere kind of date for a while. I felt time was better spent recalibrating. I didn't have the heart for another disappointment. I just didn't."

"I understand," Andrea says.

"I'm not saying I didn't go out at all or that I turned down a man I met if I thought he was interesting. It wasn't an all-or-nothing kind of thing. I needed to step back so I could step forward. And after a few months of reenergizing myself, I was back in the game," I add.

"Look, a healthy, happy life is a balanced life," Andrea says. "And no one should be living in an extreme in any direction. Looking for love shouldn't take up all your energy, but neither should it be the last thing on a woman's list if she's made love a priority. You're right. People who think in terms of 'all-or-nothing' will end up with nothing. Extremes don't work. When you are balanced, you will attract quality people into your life."

"I'm not even sure it was a conscious choice that I made," I add. "I just didn't have the emotional energy for it. I didn't have the heart to say yes to something I knew would just be disappointing. But that was two or three years ago. I honestly love dating now. Even the bad dates are fun in some way. I still don't agree to dates with someone I don't have an attraction to on any level, but if I'm set up with someone who is wonderful but I just don't have a connection with him, I usually still have a great time. Taking that break reminded me why dating can be fun!"

Andrea is smiling.

"But what about the men?" I ask. "Do you find the single guys you speak with are looking for love, too?"

"Yes, I do," Andrea says. She mentions a common friend who felt he had too many choices among the groups of women he met in New York City. He moved back home to Vancouver to take a step back and not be distracted by all the choices he had so that he could focus on finding love. "There are definitely endless options for men in New York City," Andrea says. "But I find that when a circle of male friends begin to get engaged, a single man within that circle begins to think about settling down. Or, some just decide that they've had enough of dating and want to nest."

I look toward my city again, at all the buildings, the windows, and the possibilities.

"It's getting late. I should head back to the city," I say. It's time to go home.

I get back into the city to meet my friend Sloane at the Union Square Greenmarket. I step out of the subway and spot her immediately. She's in her requisite aviators and cargo pants, standing in front of her natural habitat: bushels of leafy greens.

"*Hiiii!*" she says, as she greets me. "Isn't this amazing? Look at all this kale, chard, and chicory! I'm in heaven, seriously. Pure heaven."

It's not that Sloane is a super health nut. She's just trying to make smart, healthy choices, like all the women I know.

"I love kale," I say, as I pick up a head of kale and wonder how many people could be fed by its enormousness.

"I eat kale chips like candy!" Sloane says. "I think I'm going to make a huge salad for the weekend," she adds with childlike excitement as she moves to another table to check out the endless rows of handsome heirloom tomatoes. I haven't seen Sloane this cheerful in a while. After a brief marriage that ended amicably, Sloane, now thirty-five, is back in the dating game. She's noticed that things have changed.

"I wish I had a man to share all this with," she says with a smile that quickly disappears as she examines a bushel of cherry-pink radishes. "Do I really want radishes? Sometimes I think they are just too good-looking not to get." She shakes her head. "No, I'm getting what I really need," deciding it's a no-radish day.

"Speaking of good-looking, any good dates lately?" I ask with a wink. Not that I have a positive answer to that question myself.

"Not really," she says. "I went out with this guy I met and liked online two or three weeks ago, but I never heard from him again. It's so odd. You think you both had a great time because you have all this stuff in common and you have fun. You're both laughing, his body language speaks volumes, and he is totally charming. He kisses you good night before making sure you get into a cab . . . and then BAM!, you never hear from him again. I checked his profile the next day, and he'd logged in right after our date. That was a blow. Dating is so much harder in my thirties than it was in my twenties. I thought it would be better, like the guys would have matured a little. But it seems it got worse, not better."

We pay and keep walking around the market.

"When I met Adam," Sloane says, "I was twenty-eight and he was thirty-one. We got married when I was thirty-two, and the marriage was over the week I turned thirty-four. Honestly, I thought I'd be *livin' la vida loca* in some high-rise on the Upper West Side by now, strolling on Columbus Avenue with two or three kids in tow. But I think Adam and I knew we were making a mistake before we even got married. I'm not even sure why we chose to go through with it. It's not that we didn't love each other. We're just two very different people. He's so sweet and laid-back and I'm a bit of a warrior, always looking to heat things up. By the way," she says, lifting her sunglasses up into her hair, "I still love Adam. I just couldn't imagine having kids with him and spending the rest of our lives parenting together. Anyway, he already has a serious girlfriend and they're living together. I'm sincerely so happy for him. It's just . . . I'm making enough salad for an army, and I have no one to share it with."

"He's living with someone already?" I ask. "That was quick."

"Adam is a good man. He wants to be married. I bet you, had I just let things lie, we'd still be married, and I'd have at least one of those babies by now. He told me when we were thinking about ending things that it's life—love fades, he said. But that cut like a knife. I knew then that he was no longer in love with me. I want my husband to be in love with me and only me. I had to walk away. But he's a great guy with a ton of girls to choose from. His girlfriend is twenty-nine.

"I really didn't imagine dating in my midthirties would be this hard," she goes on. "I want to fall in love again, forever this time. And I want kids. I really did everything right. I got an education, a decent career, I have a nice apartment in Chelsea, I have good friends, and you know I am completely, madly in love with my nephew," she says.

"So I thought I'd focus on dating the way I focus on everything else in my life—by making it a priority," she says. "But when I told my friend Derek, whom I've known since I moved to New York City fifteen years ago, that I want to meet someone and get married again and have kids, he told me straight out that I sounded desperate and men don't like desperate women. I was so shocked by that response. At what age is it acceptable to admit you want love and children?"

I think to myself, *There are choices that are acceptable for women to make, like our education, career, where we live, etc. These choices are seen as empowered choices. But there are choices that are not acceptable, like a woman showing that she wants a deep relationship and children. These choices can make a woman look vulnerable, weak, and somehow desperate . . .*

"Have you seen this Tinder app?" Sloane asks as she pulls out her iPhone. "Derek showed it to me. You sign up through Facebook, and it tells you who is in your area and you can check to see if there are people you want to meet. He told me how he and his guy friends go on it looking for twentysomething women to meet because you can search by age range. There are hundreds of girls on it in his area, and he looks at their photos and clicks 'yay' or 'nay' and then onto the next. He literally went through, like, thirty girls in a few seconds and nixed all but one. I told him I thought it was disgusting, and you know what he said? 'Manhattan is a candy store for the successful single guy. So many choices.'"

I couldn't help but see that some men are empowered by all their possible choices. They don't seem to feel weak and vulnerable. They continue to have power.

"They have so many choices and easy access to them," Sloane says. "They can get dates with younger women on an app, on dating sites. They can text a girl they are already hooking up with to come over, and if she says no, they'll try another, and if none of those options work out in the moment, they have access to a gazillion porn sites online. Derek told me there is so much porn online he's actually taking a break from it, because he's beginning to realize that he is never satisfied with the women he's actually dating. He's always looking for the next, next, next thing. *Urrrrgh!*" Sloane is getting riled up, and I understand. She is doing her best to try to make healthier choices, and her male friends are like little boys in a candy store who want it all.

While the choices women have regarding dating are more limited, the choices we have for our fertility are opening up. I'm not convinced it's entirely a good thing. Over a late lunch at The Coffee Shop across the street from the Greenmarket, Sloane and I quickly get to the topic of fertility.

"A couple of my girlfriends are freezing their eggs," Sloane says. "One put her end-of-year bonus toward it and another, who was saving up for an apartment, used some of that money. I honestly have no idea how my friend Sari found the money to do it." Sloane shrugs and looks at the menu, thoughtfully.

"What are you deciding on?" I ask.

She puts the menu down and says: "I'm not freezing my eggs."

"I meant for lunch," I say with a wink.

"Oh! Well, I've decided on the Greek salad for lunch and hope for my fertility," Sloane says with a laugh. "I just feel like freezing my eggs is like throwing in the towel on meeting someone and having it happen the way I imagined it would. I can't even think about it. It just upsets me."

I have heard the same response from other women in their thirties.

"But then my friends who have done it or are working on freezing their eggs tell me I'm crazy and that it's great insurance. It's funny. Even just six or seven years ago, no one was talking about freezing their eggs. The science wasn't even where it needed to be.

Is waiting for love, knowing there's a chance I may never be a mother, an acceptable choice? 〞

And now, if I don't make this choice, I'm being an irresponsible woman, or worse, a naïve woman. To be honest, sometimes I wish egg freezing wasn't even a choice. I know so many women are able to have children because of it and that's a miracle and awesome and everything. But while I know the technology is supposed to be empowering for women, I also think it takes away the power for other women to just move on when the right partner hasn't come in time."

"I completely understand," I say. And I do.

"Look, it's not like I don't think about it. But first of all, it's a lot of money. And even if we put that aside for a second, for me, having a baby is about having a loving family. I don't think I would consider having a baby on my own. The man I end up with is part of the baby equation for me. So yes, on the one hand if I freeze my eggs, I've invested in the choice to wait until the right man comes into my life and have a baby with him even if I'm forty-five when that happens. But what if that doesn't happen? Is waiting for love, knowing there's a chance I may never be a mother, an acceptable choice?"

When the server comes, Sloane changes her mind on the Greek salad and orders a burger and fries. "Fuck it," she says after the server takes our order and leaves. "Sometimes, I just want to make a bad choice and enjoy it, damn it!"

We look at our bags brimming with bushels of kale and both laugh out loud.

"You know what they say," Sloane says. "The road to hell is paved with good intentions."

A DATE WITH DESTINY

I call Wynn to hear about her date with Michael, a forty-one-year-old divorced dad of two. A mutual friend of theirs set it up.

"Michael is a great guy. He's so smart, so accomplished, and he sounds like he's a really dedicated father. He made reservations at a really nice restaurant and was wearing a suit, which I found lovely. It was a very grown-up date."

"Well, that's good to hear," I say, enthusiastically.

"The conversation was really good. We talked for hours. Turns out we have a lot in common," Wynn says.

"Sounds like you had a really good date!" I say, again, more enthusiastically.

"Well, yes, until he mentioned that he doesn't want more children. I wasn't prepared to hear that on this first date—even though, as you know, I would consider not having children if I fell madly in love with a man who didn't want or couldn't have them."

"Oh. That's not good," I say, disappointed for my friend.

"Yeah. Well, turns out, his ex-wife wasn't really dedicated to raising the children, so he basically was raising their kids himself, plus he was the sole breadwinner. He doesn't want to go through that again. And I told him that I completely get it, but since we were being honest with each other, I felt like I could tell him that he should consider first focusing on finding love, and if he finds the right, loving partner he was meant to have, maybe then he'd feel differently about having children with her. I told him that if he met a woman who was a constant support, not only to him and his career but his kids, too, maybe he'd find the emotional strength to reconsider fatherhood."

"That was pretty insightful of you," I say. "How did he respond?"

"He was grateful. I don't think he had looked at it that way before, and I think he realized that I might have a point. I also think he was interested in hearing it because, at forty-one, he doesn't really know who to date. He says that a woman in her thirties probably still wants children. He was actually considering waiting until he was fifty before starting to date again, just so he could be sure not to meet someone who wanted to have children. Can you believe that?" Wynn asks.

"That doesn't seem like a realistic idea," I say. "Anyway, didn't the friend who set you up with him let you guys know about the kid thing?"

"Well, you would think so, but no," Wynn says. "Maybe my friend just assumed I can't have children or something, I don't know, or that I don't want children because I didn't settle with someone just to have kids. Who knows? Anyway, I'm thinking that maybe I should see a professional matchmaker? You know, someone who actually sets people up with people who want or don't want the same things."

I have personally met several fabulous, dedicated, successful matchmakers in New York City who truly love what they do. And some of these women have become friends of mine. So, after my discussion with Wynn, I ask Amy Laurent, a thirty-six-year-old matchmaker, relationship expert, and author, who was recently the costar of Bravo's *Miss Advised,* to have dinner with me. I am curious about what a single matchmaker makes of the Otherhood.

66 'First of all, men can smell panic a mile away and run in the other direction. But even more so, making a huge life decision because you're in a panic is not going to have good results. People make bad decisions when they are not emotionally balanced.' 99

We meet at the Atlantic Grill on the Upper East Side and find a table near the bar. Amy's charisma is infectious. She loves life and loves what she does for a living. What I admire most about Amy is how she is focused on taking care of her health and well-being. She's always at the gym or finding some new way to keep active and healthy. And she takes care of me, too, by texting images of her latest supplement regimen or telling me what she's done to get her equilibrium back after an unusually stressful day, and then encouraging me to do the same. Amy is a nurturer, not just of herself, but of her friends, too, and her clients.

I'm sharing my admiration with her over chopped salad. As it turns out, remaining calm is something Amy thinks of as a necessity for business and her personal life.

"Women who come to me in a clear panic, who want to find a partner so they can have a baby right away because their clock is ticking—well, I'll be honest, I hesitate to work with those women," Amy says. "First of all, men can smell panic a mile away and run in the other direction. But even more so, making a huge life decision because you're in a panic is not going to have good results. People make bad decisions when they are not emotionally balanced."

"What about the men?" I ask. "Do they get anxious about becoming fathers before they're fifty, or whatever their age limit is?"

"Yes," Amy says. "I see men who are in their midforties or fifties who have never married and decide they are ready to start a family. But they don't want to date a woman who is over thirty-five. Most women who are in their early thirties are not interested in dating men who are fifty. And that's where I come in and say to the men, 'Look, I know you have this list on paper and these parameters, but let me use my creativity to set you up with someone I think you'll really connect with.' I explain to them that that is the beauty of my matchmaking. My job is to make a chance meeting happen."

I'm inspired by this idea. We think of matchmakers as people who take a list of criteria and then try to match two people who are looking for those things. In my experience, most people think of a matchmaker more or less like a headhunter. But Amy's a believer in creating opportunities for two people who may not have otherwise met.

"I tell my clients that life can change in a day," says Amy. "You have to have faith in that. And then I ask them to have faith in me, so I can go beyond what they think they want and what I think they need. I ask them to bend a little on their age requirements, up or down. I remind them that their laundry list hasn't worked for them so far, so give me the flexibility to do what I do best. Usually, if they let me do my job, they find that I'm right."

"And what about you?" I ask. "Are you feeling the pressure of being thirty-six and single? Does it bother you that the men in their late forties say they would not date a woman your age?"

"It's not an easy thing to hear, but I can't show that. I just brush it off and carry on with finding the client an appropriate match," Amy says. "Look, I definitely want to have children," she adds. "But I won't go to extremes to become a mother. Like, honestly, the idea of freezing my eggs really creeps me out. It's just doesn't feel natural to me. And if it doesn't happen the way I expect it to happen, and I don't become a mother, then I'll come to terms with it. I'm not the kind of woman who wonders if her life will have purpose if she doesn't have kids. I don't believe that if I never become a mom, I'll never be a full person. That's just not me. I choose love first. And I will never settle. I believe things in life unfold the way they do for a reason," Amy says. "Everyone has to find their path and I have complete faith that I'm headed in the right direction."

The server brings our main courses when Amy sees something she does not approve of. "Look at that couple on a date over there," Amy says, pointing with her eyes. "She's pulling out her wallet! She should not be doing that. Oh good, look, he refused to take her money. Good guy!"

"Dating has really changed for this generation, hasn't it?" I say.

Amy agrees. "Everyone is confused," she says. "We are independent women, and men don't want to insult us by assuming we want them to court us, and then there are some women who feel like they are supposed to offer to pay or whatever. I'm very traditional, though. The dynamics of the times we live in have changed, but the science hasn't. Men want to date feminine women and women want to date masculine men.

"I coach my clients on how to date. I tell the men to be men and the women to be women. Take this couple on their date. If she were my client, I would tell her not to pick up her purse. I would recommend she fill the awkward moment when the check comes by gently touching his hand and thanking him for dinner. I would tell her to say she had a really nice time and that she appreciates it. She should make a really sincere gesture, not a quick 'thanks,' as she pops into a cab at the end of the date. That's all a man really wants, you know, to feel appreciated."

> Today there is a new classification of women that never existed before. No one really understands them. They are not what people used to refer to as spinsters who remained single and childless. They are really fabulous women who have great careers and don't need to settle for a man to support them, or maybe they were in long-term relationships that didn't work out. 🙶

I tell Amy how the number-one complaint from my single girl-friends is that men so often can't plan a date.

"Oh, some men have become lazy about dating. I see it all the time," Amy responds, getting back to the idea of balance. "I coach my female clients to be strong and independent, but to be feminine on dates. I coach my male clients to be gentlemen and to court the women they are dating. We all need to come to peace with the fact that we are all trying to find a new balance when it comes to dating."

Inspired by my conversation with Amy, I call Samantha Daniels, another top New York City matchmaker, TV personality and producer, author, and owner of Samantha's Table, a matchmaking service. I want to know her thoughts on modern dating.

"It's definitely a new world," Samantha says. "Today there is a new classification of women that never existed before. No one really understands them. They are not what people used to refer to as spinsters who remained single and childless. They are really fabulous women who have great careers and don't need to settle for a man to support them, or maybe they were in long-term relationships that didn't work out. There are lots of reasons, but in the end, things have changed, and I think everyone is a little bit confused."

Samantha agrees with Amy on what men want. She says, "I think women, no matter how strong and independent they are, should enjoy being women, even 'girly girls,' on dates. Men want to date women, not women with masculine energy."

"And what do women want?" I ask.

"Women want a man who makes them feel like he cares about her, makes her feel safe, and, eventually, loved. I tell my male clients to take the time to plan a nice date. I'm telling you, men have gotten lazy about that stuff, and younger women are allowing men to be bad daters, and the men will be bad if they can get away with it."

But Samantha sees that women can focus on something important on their end, too.

"I think that women sometimes have this fantasy about what they imagined their lives should be and, lo and behold, now they're in their late thirties or forties and it's not even close. I want women to be true to themselves. It all comes down to whether or not they want to be on a journey to find the right partner, or if they want to focus on their age and biological clock. I see that in men, too, by the way. They wake up one day in their forties thinking about their age and wondering how they got there without having built a nuclear family life."

"And are they looking for a younger woman at that point?" I ask.

"Some are, yes. They want a big family and want me to match them with younger women who can offer them that. But when these men go too young, they realize that it's challenging. They don't have the same cultural references. It becomes awkward at work functions. And the men realize that some young women aren't really interested in marrying them, they like the nice gifts the older man offers them.

Eventually, those men come back to me asking for someone whom they have things in common with and with whom they share similar backgrounds, and age becomes secondary."

Samantha continues, "But I also have male clients who, even though they always thought they'd be fathers, are now fortysomething and are on the fence. They would prefer to meet someone and have kids, but for them, it's about love. These men tell me that it's more important for them to find a true partner and then decide together if they want to have children. If she's a little older, they'll figure out what to do. These are men who are on a journey. They want a real connection that leads to love and marriage."

"So those men are out there?" I ask.

"Yes," Samantha says. "And they are most attracted to women who are on life's journey themselves. They are attracted to women who also know that marriage is more than just two people meeting and getting married. Marriage is really hard. You have to have a solid, meaningful partnership. It's not about a list of criteria. It's about a deep connection. Men and women who are authentic about who they are and who are ready to go on life's journey together will fare best. And these men and women are out there," Samantha says.

I close my eyes and touch my heart as I hear these words over the phone. I am equally surprised and relieved to learn that Samantha has clients who feel this way and who are able to articulate it to her. It makes me believe that there is a man out there for me who will appreciate how I've worked on becoming the very best me I can be, and how I continue to work on myself, growing and exploring new ways to reach my potential, while learning how to live in the moment and enjoy the life I have. There are men who, like me, are waiting for the right love, who believe, as I do, that love comes first. It's remarkably heartening.

And finally, I speak with effervescent Lori Zaslow, the co-founder of Project Soulmate, another New York City matchmaking service, and the former star of another Bravo network show, *Love Broker*. And Lori agrees, "There are some really great men out there. And women have to believe that and think that way. The mind is a muscle, and the bottom line is that you have to actively believe in love and in yourself. You can manifest your love. You really can."

All three of my matchmaker girlfriends are actively considering matches for me. I think I'll give matchmaking a chance. I really do believe in love.

MY LAST CHANCE

If you're single, of a certain age, and living in Manhattan, New Year's Eve is an ill-timed reminder that you're single, of a certain age, and living in one of the most romantic cities in the world with little chance for romance by the end of the year or the start of the next. For us, midnight on New Year's Eve can be the loneliest time of the year. It marks another year without love, or the right love, or lost love. But it's also a night of celebration. And so we muster all the hope we can that the next year will bring the right love our way.

I'm a born romantic. I believe there's always a slight chance for romance. So when the invitation to a New Year's Eve party finally comes the last week of the year, I gladly accept. I may not have a date, but I'll have holiday spirit.

The invitation calls for "retro black tie" dress and hints at a magical, musical night at the hosts' home, an Upper West Side brownstone. Not knowing the couple and their circles of friends that well, there's actually a possibility I might meet someone new. Even if he and I merely make for a timely, short-term romance that begins and ends on this last night of the year, it will be enough.

> It's New Year's Eve and I have a choice: Regret the love that didn't come this year, or be optimistic that love will come in the next. I choose optimism. Living in the past is no way to live. I choose what's ahead.

New Year's Eve turns out to be a mild winter night, and my outlook on the evening is likewise getting warmer. I've just curled and teased my hair, added a sparkled barrette to hold one side of my mane back while the other falls below my shoulders. I'm wearing a black sequined jumpsuit—my ode to the late Donna Summer, queen of disco. I'm retro 1979 and hoping for a last dance, a last chance, for romance tonight.

I enter my friends' brownstone humming. I look around the room—bow ties and updos coupled off. The guests are retro-swing, not swingers; I've walked into a prewar speakeasy, not Studio 54. I realize that I'm out of place and out of pace with everyone else. My timing is off. I should *not* be in my early forties and single, never married. It's clear.

I was always a romantic about New Year's Eve. I remember convincing my parents to allow me to stay up and watch Dick Clark on television. I'd wear a pretty dress and my pretty shoes, a pretty barrette in my hair. I recall New Year's Eve 1979: I was nine years old, Donna Summer's "Last Dance" was my favorite song, and I just knew that by the time I was an adult, I'd dance the last dance of the year with my future adoring husband. The song stayed with me, and the dream of being in love on New Year's Eve did, too. The possibility of not being a married mother by the time I was my married mother's age was not something I could even imagine.

But here I am. It's New Year's Eve and I have a choice: Regret the love that didn't come this year, or be optimistic that love will come in the next. I choose optimism. Living in the past is no way to live. I choose what's ahead.

I smile when I spot Janis, the hostess, a tall, elegant brunette my age. She greets me in her era-perfect gown, a pair of diamond earrings (a recent gift from her husband, Spencer) dangling from her ears. "I love Donna Summer!" she exclaims immediately, and I know she's trying to help me feel as though I belong. Her mother walks over to welcome me and to show me a video of her granddaughter drumming on a drum set she received for Christmas. Her family was in tune and in step.

In my head, I chastise myself for my choice of outfit—*Always needing to be the belle of the disco ball, aren't you?*—as I busy myself at the bar by asking for a glass of champagne. The bartender has run out of flutes and pours my bubbly into a wineglass. "I hope this will do?" he asks as he hands it to me.

"It's still champagne," I reply with a smile and wish him a happy New Year.

I leave the bar, glass more than half full, and I spot a potentially single man by the food. I go over and chat with him, figuring I don't know too many of the guests, so why not ingratiate myself to a man in a tuxedo? But after a few awkward exchanges, he says he wants to refresh his drink. He asks if I'd like one, too. My glass is half empty now.

"I'll be back," he says. But I'm not expecting his return. I walk over to the parlor where the guests are singing along while Spencer plays the piano.

"Any requests?" Spencer asks the guests who are flipping through books of sheet music, two by two. Those standing around the piano have already sung along to every show tune and jazz hit I know and a few I don't. But I want to play along. I yell over the crowd, "Donna Summer! 'Last Dance!'" and raise my nearly empty glass. There are only a few minutes left before the ball drops but I'm slightly optimistic we can get the song in.

"It's not very New Year's Eve-y" Spencer replies, not realizing he's just killed my last chance to fit in, my last chance for a last dance tonight. I smile graciously, knock my last drop of champagne out of my glass, and privately toast myself for having the courage to try.

Instead, the host plays Eric Clapton's "Wonderful Tonight." I sing along... But as I do, my eyes tear up.

. . . And then she asks me
"Do I look all right?"
And I say "Yes, you look wonderful tonight."
. . . I feel wonderful because I see
The love light in your eyes
And the wonder of it all
Is that you just don't realize
How much I love you
. . . As I turn out the light,
I say, "My darling, you were wonderful tonight" . . .

As I sing along, I think to myself, *Why doesn't anyone think I am wonderful tonight? Why can't I meet one man who loves me no matter what I'm wearing or how offbeat I am? Why can't I ever find the right man at the right time? Why didn't the dream that New-Year's-Eve-1979 me had come true by this New Year's Eve?*

The 1940s guests turn toward the large flat-screen TV with just one minute to go before the countdown begins.

Standing beside me, Rick holds Vicki's hand as she rubs her pregnant tummy with the other. They are expecting their second

66 Few moments feel more vulnerable than being the only single woman in the room as the clock strikes midnight on New Year's Eve. You feel out of place, out of pace with the life you were supposed to have . . . the life that did not happen again this year. 99

baby. I see Celia and Sam, my newlywed friends, looking at each other as though it's their wedding all over again. The host and hostess are standing next to one another by the piano, their arms around each other. And all the men are thinking about their women: *She looks wonderful tonight . . .*

Few moments feel more vulnerable than being the only single woman in the room as the clock strikes midnight on New Year's Eve. You feel out of place, out of pace with the life you were supposed to have . . . the life that did not happen again this year.

"Ten . . . nine . . . eight . . . "

It feels like everyone's in on it, like a couples' conspiracy of happiness . . . Can they tell by looking at me that I'm still that nine-year-old in her party shoes and barrette waiting to be her mother's age so she'll finally be married and in love?

"Seven . . . six . . . five . . . "

I'm mouthing the countdown, silently, too choked up to speak . . . *Time is going by so fast . . .*

"Four . . . three . . . two . . . "

Well, that's it then, isn't it? New Year's Eve and I'm all alone. It's the very last second of the year and I'm about to enter next year as a party of . . .

"One!!"

"Happy New Year," I manage in a whisper, quieted even more by the exclamations of all the lovers in the room.

About ten or fifteen more seconds pass as I stand there, like a black sequined penguin standing alone in the desert. Then, with great generosity, Rick gives me a kiss on the cheek. I look at Vicki, thanking her with a smile for lending me her husband's affection for a second. She smiles back. After all, Vicki and Rick married when she was thirty-eight. She's knows what it's like to be single on New Year's Eve.

I accept another full glass of champagne from a server passing by. I remind myself, *There's always this year.*

THE VOWS WE MAKE

Sometimes the first snow comes late in winter.

I'm climbing the steps up and out of the Chambers Street subway station on a dark, snowy, winter night in TriBeCa. The sidewalks are covered in a thin layer of slippery snow, so I carefully and skillfully walk up Hudson Street in my warm boots. It's not my first Manhattan winter.

I pass a young married couple, their little baby girl snuggled into her stroller. Three twentysomething blonds walk by me, shivering in their tights and impractical yet pretty boots. A strikingly handsome young African American man throws a gray wool scarf around his neck. It seems as if the first snow is made for beautiful young people.

As much as we know snow will come, and no matter how late in the season it arrives, the first snow is still here sooner than we expected. And yet, we are ready to fall in love with it, in it, and with all the romance around it.

I came downtown to meet Gigi who came uptown from Brooklyn. The waitstaff at Restaurant Marc Forgione is young and good-looking, and Gigi, a sought-after interior decorator, and I are fortunate enough to have two attractive servers vying for our attention. Tucker is the younger one with a mop of dark brown curls and a sweet, innocent smile offering warm cheer. Patrick is a little older, sly, more direct with his eyes, and a lot sexier. We tell Patrick we'd like a warm, wintery cocktail to start. It's clear he knows exactly what these young fortysomething ladies need.

It doesn't take long before Gigi and I are talking about dating. "Any good dates lately?" she asks.

"I haven't met anyone recently," I admit. "You know, when it rains, it pours."

Gigi is thinking about dating on a whole other level. "I don't know if I told you, but I'm no longer dating. I'm not looking for it. I'm not asking for it. I don't want it. I'm serious. I am no longer dating."

As I listen, I'm noticing how beautiful Gigi is. It's not a classic beauty; it's a deeper beauty. She shines with charisma and confidence and a touch of vulnerability. She speaks with certainty but not arrogance. Gigi is just the type of woman any man would be lucky to know, let alone date, let alone fall in love with.

"I'm tired of what dating does to me," she says as Tucker serves the entrées. I find myself envious of his youth. "I'm focusing on other things," she continues. "I have other projects. I have other goals. I'm just not interested in anything else."

I understand. Everyone takes a break from dating. But Gigi is quitting dating like someone quits smoking. She says she's done and I believe her.

"Marriage and children would have been great back in my twenties and thirties," she explains. "But now love and children aren't things I need to focus on. I don't want to feel like I have to stop what I'm doing with my life now that I'm still alone in my forties. This is my life now and I'm going to live it as I see fit. I'm living a life other than marriage."

Gigi has put a lot of thought into this. I admire her resilience, and at the same time, I realize I've been feeling the same way lately.

> 'Marriage and children would have been great back in my twenties and thirties,' she explains. 'But now love and children aren't things I need to focus on. I don't want to feel like I have to stop what I'm doing with my life now that I'm still alone in my forties. This is my life now and I'm going to live it as I see fit. I'm living a life other than marriage.'

As I get older, I find myself much less concerned with the immediacy of meeting someone. I'm comforted by the fact that my life is more extraordinary than I had ever imagined it might be. There is something about being in my forties, and accepting that my expectations of a traditional life of marriage and kids never happened, that enables me to see how despite that, I'm OK. I'm more than OK. I'm actually happy. I've learned that our imaginations always seem better than our lives. But if we reflect inward, our lives are probably better than we ever imagined. I'm also finding that Gigi and I aren't the only ones feeling this way.

Later that week, I'm with Wynn to celebrate a feature about her in *Women's Wear Daily,* in an Upper West Side wine bar. Wynn takes a moment and glances at the tables filled with women out with women looking for men. There are no men in suits at the wine bar. No men at all, in fact, except for one young male server.

"Maybe I'll never be married," she says with aloof stoicism. "I'm OK with that. I've got a great apartment, a great reputation in my industry, and I've got a lifestyle I can afford. So what if I never marry? Kids? I'm getting tired. Do I really want to run after kids at this point?"

But I know, given the choice, she absolutely would. But then, she doesn't have the choice.

I've caught myself admitting that I am no longer attached to the idea of "marriage." Being at an age where motherhood is no longer a given, why not give in to what a life partnership looks like?

"I don't even know if I need to find the 'love of my life,'" Wynn adds. "I'm fine with being with the right person at the right time, no matter how long that time lasts. It could be weeks, months, decades, who knows? Maybe I'll get married at fifty," she ponders. "Whenever it comes, it comes."

Like Gigi, Wynn is not speaking in sour grapes. She really believes her life is fantastic, and she's so relieved she hasn't settled.

"I have a childhood friend who married at age nineteen," Wynn says. "And amazingly, she's blissfully happy. And I know people who got married in their twenties who aren't. Some people get married. Some don't. I really just think it's all luck.

"There are women for whom marriage and children is their primary life goal," she adds. "And they get married. I'm not saying they are in love, but for them, that's not where happiness comes from. That wasn't their goal."

And then Wynn says: "I vowed to myself never to settle. It was never in me to do that. And so, marriage and motherhood hasn't happened for me. And you know what, I am realizing that's truly OK."

Eric Klinenberg, author of *Going Solo* and professor of sociology and director of the Institute for Public Knowledge at New York University, isn't surprised to hear this when we meet near his office so I can share Gigi's and Wynn's—and my—new revelations on marriage. I want his take on this relatively new trend of women living alone, longer than they had expected to years earlier.

"The women you are referring to, the ones who may not have expected to remain single into their late thirties and older, would like to be with someone, just not anyone," Klinenberg says. "These women choose to live alone over other options. And they are willing to remain alone until the right option presents itself."

"There's always a trade-off," Wynn says. "Some women settle because they really want to be married. For others, like you and me, it's about being in love, about a partner who adds something to our lives. There are so many components that go into a connection: You have to have chemistry, similar values, lifestyles, expectations, etc. That's not so easy to find."

"Look, Melanie, let's face it. If you wanted to find a man to marry you, you could find a man to marry you," Klinenberg says, not flirtatiously, but generously. "You, and the women you are speaking of, are not looking to a relationship to solve your problems. You're not unhappy. And you're certainly not desperate. There are those who might say you are setting your expectations too high, that you should settle for the nice guy," Klinenberg says, "but that's not something you are willing to do, nor should you. And you're not the ones who are Single by Choice, who choose never to have a partner, preferring solitude. Very few people aspire to live alone."

"In the meantime," Wynn says, "I love spending time with my friends and my nieces, and I love my job. And I'm enjoying the younger man in my life. He's great fun. I don't romanticize romance," she adds. "That fantasy, if it ever existed for me, is over."

"That's right," Klinenberg says. "Once women are less focused on their biological clock, they do a great job at making and maintaining relationships, with friends as well as family members, so even if they're single, they're less likely to be alone. They don't run a big risk of feeling isolated."

I'm relieved to hear that, although not surprised. Still, I don't want to live my life alone. I do hope I will still meet the love of my life. But then I'm reminded of something Wynn had said at the wine bar: "Life doesn't happen on a specific timeline. A wedding is not a bar mitzvah. You can plan that at age twenty-eight, you'll marry the love of your life, and if you fail, it's like you've broken with society. It will happen when it happens, and until then . . . "

"Until then," I said, "I'm not the wrong wife in the wrong life."

A couple of days later, I'm reading *The New York Times* Sunday Styles section and come across the stories of two couples in love.

In "Vows" it reads: *She's 97. He's 86. And they're getting married. "I like him very much. I love him. So we're going to be married,"* explained the bride, in a very matter of fact manner.

And in "Modern Love," *Eve marries Sam when she's 70 and he's 80.* Eve writes: *"He and I often told each other, 'We are so lucky.' And we were. Young love, even for old people, can be surprisingly bountiful."*

I know it to be true. A few weeks earlier, my then seventy-nine-year-old father had called. "It's the twentieth anniversary of our first date!" he said, referring to his second wife. He sounded elated. "I met my bride twenty years ago tonight!" And while it was lovely to hear that my father and his second wife have been together for two decades, it made me happier that they are in love, as though it's their wedding day. Twenty years together, and he still calls my stepmom his "bride."

And when I visited my father and stepmother at their retirement village in Florida to celebrate my father's eightieth birthday just a few weeks later, I couldn't get over the couples who came to share the occasion with him. Each one was more youthful than the next in their golden age. The women were all spectacularly attractive in slim slacks or sundresses, and the men in their polo shirts and jeans kissed their brides on the cheek or wrapped an arm around their waists. The women pulled iPad Minis from their clutches to share photos of their children and grandchildren, and the men talked about their next fifty-mile cycling adventure.

These septuagenarians and octogenarians take great care of their health and well-being. Retirement was solely the end of their careers and the extraordinary beginning of a vibrant third trimester of life. It strengthened my belief that my right love, no matter when he comes, even if he comes in my golden age, is ahead of me and not behind me. I won't give up on love. And I won't give up on life and all the other things it offers me or, better yet, that I offer myself.

WOMEN AND CAREERS

It's almost February, and everyone is getting desperate for a love story.

Late on a Tuesday night, the producer for a national evening news show emails me. The city that never sleeps is now the city that never ceases working.

"We're doing a story on women who are childless by choice. Are you available?" he writes.

I'm not childless by choice. But the assumption is that because I'm childless and in my early forties, I must be. I ask him to give me a call. I can't explain this over email; there are just too many myths to debunk. It's time for the story of the Otherhood to come out.

I let him speak first. "Every year, the Sunday before Valentine's Day, we produce a segment on love. This year, it's about why people let children get in the way of their love life." He doesn't know that my non–love life got in the way of my having children.

"I'm not childless by choice," I say. "I just haven't met the right man and I've always dreamed of having a family, not just a child. I want to have babies with a husband I adore. And I'm not alone." I tell him about the Otherhood.

> 66 Marrying a spouse you've picked, who's also picked you, seems like something most modern American couples do. I'm not sure I understand why on earth someone would *not* be somewhat selective about his or her life partner. 99

He doesn't sound convinced. It just doesn't ring true to him. I can't blame him; the Otherhood has kept itself under the hood. Deciding against single motherhood, or confessing that you actually want to be in love with the father of your future children, has somehow become the unpopular point of view.

"I have to ask," the producer says, "and please, don't take this the wrong way, but I'm looking at your photos online right now . . . you're really cute." Pause. "Are you just picky?"

Marrying a spouse you've picked, who's also picked you, seems like something most modern American couples do. I'm not sure I understand why on earth someone would *not* be somewhat selective about his or her life partner. I don't answer directly; instead, I go into recent history.

"We expected to have the social, economic, and political equality our mothers didn't, and naturally, the husbands and children they did. We never thought that somehow, we'd never have love and a family. But now, we're here, in our thirties and forties, wondering how we got here and living our lives unplanned," I say.

"Hmmm," he says, considering this story.

"You must know women like this," I persist. "They are your sisters, friends, certainly coworkers." I can detect even over the phone that that last part raises an eyebrow.

"Yes, I work with a number of women like that. You know, they are in their late thirties and forties and forgot to get married and have kids."

Biting my tongue.

"They have one big story to produce and think that when that one is done, they'll focus on marriage and children. And then another big story comes, and another . . . and before you know it, well, you know," he says, assuming he'll find sympathy on the other end of the phone, "they are married to their careers."

"Oh, no," I reply. "You are buying into that 'career woman' myth that women who remain single by a certain age are somehow naïve about their singlehood, their fertility, and their own pursuit of love. These coworkers you're referring to, they are not married to their jobs. They are committed to waiting for the right partner. In the meantime, they are not sitting at home waiting for him to ring the doorbell. They are out pursuing their potential. In fact, these women, the women who remain single, are not the 'old maids' or 'spinsters' of decades ago—the ones who were not as desirable to men. These women are in fact among the most fabulous women in America. They are among the best educated. They are among the most put-together women: healthy, attractive, independent, and self-sufficient. How is it possible that on the one hand, these women are among the most successful women we know, and yet on the other hand, they are assumed to be naïve about their fertility and their pursuits for love and marriage? They know."

"So you want to be a mother, right?" he asks to confirm he understands.

"Yes, I do. And I want you to know something else about these women. They may not be mothers, at least not yet, or by choice, but they are leveraging their maternal love onto their nieces and nephews and all the children in their lives. There is no obligation to love other people's children. Loving these children is a gift.

"The women of the Otherhood are a modern love story," I add. "It's not the love they expected, but it's the love that's needed now. Instead of assuming they are coldhearted women who don't understand what marriage and motherhood means, assume they definitely do. They deserve to be loved. They deserve to love. And whomever they end up with deserves to be loved. They are brave and loving and giving and patient. And whether or not they want to have children of their own one day, they want love and to be loved."

I think I've surprised the producer. Pleasantly so. We make plans to film the following week, but as these things often happen in television, the story was bumped. Alas, the Otherhood would still be waiting its turn for the spotlight.

The problem with the term "career woman" is that it's anachronistic; it's from a generation ago, when a woman who worked was an outlier, a rebel, a feminist. It's really not relevant to today, when half of the modern workforce is made up of women: single, married, divorced, widowed, and everything in between. Having an income, whether it's a one-earner or dual-earner household, is no longer a choice for most North American women. It's a necessity.

Yet even the Boston University Department of Economics couldn't resist the title "Are Career Women Good for Marriage?" for a 2008 report. The authors explained that by "career women," they meant any woman, married or single, who works. Which only begs the question: Why are there no "career men"?

And while there are certainly women who are child-free by choice (and sometimes that choice is made in order to have more

> " The problem with the term 'career woman' is that it's anachronistic; it's from a generation ago, when a woman who worked was an outlier, a rebel, a feminist. It's really not relevant to today, when half of the modern workforce is made up of women: single, married, divorced, widowed, and everything in between. "

career freedom), most of the women I know want children. They also want to pay the rent, live comfortably, and pursue careers that inspire and enlighten them.

"I hate it when people call me a 'career woman' because they think I've put my career ahead of becoming a mother," blasts Wynn, who is in a particularly frustrated mood on the phone with me after another guy has implied that she doesn't make enough time for him. It was the busiest week of the year at work, and she just couldn't find the time to see him. "Yes, I get to travel the globe, wear gorgeous clothes, and I make a shitload of money. You know what? No apologies. I have a fucking fabulous career. But I never turned down a fucking proposal from an amazing guy because it interfered with New York fucking Fashion Week!"

I'm giggling again. Wynn never loses it like this. But I feel her frustration. I never delayed a marriage proposal from someone I loved because I had to wake up for an early-morning meeting. But I have been in several relationships where I learned the man had no desire to be committed to anyone long-term. I admit I may have stayed too long in one, hoping he would change his mind. But the more deeply I fell in love, the more deeply he dug in his heels, wanting to remain alone.

Wynn agrees. "And then on a first date, they have the nerve to ask you why you're still single!"

I've heard the refrain myself on first dates. "I don't get it," my dates will say. "You're attractive, smart, successful . . . Why are you still single? Are you just picky? I have a colleague like you at work— a 'career woman.'"

Then I say, "Why am I a 'career woman' but you're just a guy who hasn't been lucky in love?"

Then they say, "Hey. It's all good. You have other priorities."

Then me, generally to myself because I don't want to come off as defensive: *Having a job is not a choice. What would you prefer I say? That my father is still supporting me at my age?*

Women, certainly single women, need to work, just as men do. Having a job is not part of some feminist manifesto; it is not some radical way to demonstrate to the world that we are liberated. A so-called professional career, one that we work toward and work hard at once we're there, is the hardest to defend. Some men find them a turn-off. Jared, a divorced dad friend of mine, asked me to set him up. I acquiesced immediately; he's a nice-looking man, early forties, works in commercial real estate. I was sure he'd be a good match for one of my friends, so I asked him what he was looking for. He prefers tall brunettes, he told me, and someone, he added, who is "down-to-earth." This remark was curious to me. What did "down-to-earth" mean? Did he want someone who's charitable? Someone who wasn't materialistic? Someone who was sincere?

"I mean," he explained when I pressed, "I don't want someone with a fancy career like, you know, a doctor, a lawyer, or like a PR person. I want a teacher or social worker type." *Oh,* I thought

> " It begged the question: Are so-called career women really not interested in men, as is so often presumed, or are some men simply not interested in 'career women'? "

immediately. *He wants someone who won't threaten him.* "Fancy careers" were only for men, it seemed. It begged the question: Are so-called career women really not interested in men, as is so often presumed, or are some men simply not interested in "career women"?

Joanna is thirty-eight, never married. She tells me she's recently had a career change. "When I was thirty-two, I was on the partner path," she explains, "but I was working day and night and rarely dated. It's not that I didn't want to date, but the men I met weren't accommodating of my schedule. They'd get frustrated if I had to break a dinner date because I was still at work at 9:00 PM, implying I was trying to prove myself, or that I didn't care about the relationship. Worse, some men weren't interested in dating me, simply because I was a corporate attorney. How was I supposed to know when I went to law school that my biggest battle would be proving that I'm just a girl who wants to be a married mom? I knew that if I wanted to get married and be a mom, something had to give."

At thirty-two, Joanna gave up her career path and took a job in legal marketing at the same firm. The partners were disappointed in her, telling the want-to-be bride that she was being groomed to become a partner one day and that she was giving up too much. They would have understood if she were a new mother, but the male partners could not understand why she, as a single woman, would take a step down.

"It was more like ten steps down!" Joanna exclaimed. "I gave up more than 50 percent of my annual income and settled into my new role. But the men I met were *still* not satisfied. I couldn't find a man who challenged me the way my work used to. I missed being an attorney, and I was envious, watching my colleagues move up to bigger cases. But I held steadfast to my decision. I truly believed I was making the right choice. So here I am at thirty-eight, almost thirty-nine, still single, still not a mom."

Joanna made the decision last month to get back onto the partner track at the firm. "If I'm going to be alone, which I still hope I won't be, at least I'll have a big apartment and a walk-in closet to show for it! You know, Melanie, they talk about 'having it all,' but when it came to my career, I had it all, and I gave it up to have all the other stuff, too. So now I'm back to having it all right now."

Later that week, I'm splitting a cab with Dana, a woman I met at a charity event. Rumor has it that when she was just thirty-four, Dana did a deal so big at the hedge fund where she works that she won't have to worry about money for a long time. Now thirty-six, Dana is thinking about doing much more volunteer work. "My job is suffering, but I want to give back," she explains. "And besides, you know, I've been a 'career woman' all my life. That's why I'm not married and not a mom. It's my fault."

I have to ask. "Did you ever break up with a guy because he wanted to get married and you were too career-focused?"

"Ha!" Dana laughs as the cab hits a pothole, partly in shock. "That's funny. Look, I got lucky with this hedge fund stuff. I mean, I worked hard for my success, I admit that. But dating, marriage, and children were always a priority for me. However, it's been one broken heart after another, unfortunately."

"Then why did you say you're a 'career woman' just now?"

> 66 Single, childless, 'career women' are, on the one hand, expected to stay late at work or work over the weekend because they don't have responsibilities at home, it's assumed. On the other hand, they are vilified for not understanding that 'not making time for dating' is bad for their familial pursuits. Women of the Otherhood simply can't win. And they are fed up. 99

"Isn't that what I'm supposed to say?" We hit a pothole again, and we both laugh hysterically at the absurdity of it all.

Single, childless, "career women" are, on the one hand, expected to stay late at work or work over the weekend because they don't have responsibilities at home, it's assumed. On the other hand, they are vilified for not understanding that "not making time for dating" is bad for their familial pursuits. Women of the Otherhood simply can't win. And they are fed up.

I have invited Rae, a thirty-nine-year-old woman in TV production; Lana, thirty-eight, in management consulting; and Sasha, a forty-two-year-old entrepreneur, out for late drinks to talk about being single and childless in the workplace. It's 9:20 PM and Lana has just arrived. Her flight was delayed.

"What are we drinking?" Lana asks as she sits down. Lana is a stunning, tall, thin, African American woman who wears clothing so effortlessly it's like she's a mannequin. She shrugs her blazer off behind her to reveal a silk mustard-gold camisole that makes her skin glow.

Sasha and I are meeting Lana for the first time tonight, thanks to Rae's introduction: "Lana is an amazing godmother to her niece, and she's absolutely freaking fabulous. We went to college together, and she's been my girl crush for like the last twenty years. You have to meet her!"

Our newest arrival orders a Mint Julep and we continue the discussion. Rae tells a story. "A few months ago, the executive producer brought the production team into a meeting to tell us that, due to a more aggressive programming schedule, our production schedule would be changing, which meant our team would have to work later into the evening than before. There's this mom on the team who always feels entitled to leave earlier than the rest of us, which means that I am always working later in order to pick up the slack when she takes off. She stands up like this new assignment schedule is a personal affront to her and her son, and she basically shouts, 'I am sorry but there's a little boy with a name who's waiting for me when I get home! I'm leaving at 6:00 PM as always and that's that.' And my boss, a married dad, nods like he totally understands, and I know I'll be the one to make up for it. It was the straw that broke this single girl's back.

"So I get up and say, 'Well, I have a fucking Martini with *my* name on it waiting for me when I get home, so I'm leaving now and that's that.' And I grab my notebook, my pen, and my 5:00 PM latté and leave the room. I'm tired of people assuming I have nothing going on in my life because I'm unmarried and not a mother. And you know what? Who cares if I don't have anything vitally important going on at home? I am tired of making up the time and work for working moms!"

She's riled herself up. And she's riled up Lana. "At my firm, the only way to get any respect for your time is to get married. It's an invisible discrimination against single, childless women," Lana insists. "The best way to get staffed for a project that doesn't move you to some shitty town—where, P.S., there are never any direct flights and you're spending hours of time on red-eyes and layovers, hence my tardy arrival tonight—is to be married and have a kid.

Lana continues, "I had a younger female colleague who was always complaining to me about how they assigned her to these crappy projects in the middle-of-nowhere-America, and literally the day she returned from her honeymoon, she was placed on a new project closer to home. Then the minute she had a baby, she was told she could work 'in town.' That was the firm's code for working from home, so she could be near her family. Guess who got her (Lana is using air quotes) 'plum' assignment 350 miles from home?"

Rae shakes her head. "I mean, didn't you miss your goddaughter's birthday or something?"

"It was her ballet recital," Lana corrects her, "and I was in Albany. I really thought I could get there by train, but the client was a full-on headache, and I missed it. I think I was sadder about missing it than my goddaughter was. I was the one who paid for her ballet classes, by the way! All I wanted was to see her dance around in the tutu I bought her for Christmas.

"I literally said to my boss the next day, 'Is the only way to get some downtime around here to spread my legs and get knocked up?' Saying it out loud makes it sound a little harsh, but that is exactly what I said!"

"How did he respond?" I ask.

"He shrugged. He literally just shrugged at me. Look, I totally get that mothers have to be near their kids. I would want that, too. But what I can't understand is why my life outside the office isn't valued, too? I'd love to go on some dates or to a party where I might meet someone. I'm thirty-eight! I can't meet someone if I'm traveling all the time."

"That's one of the reasons why I started my own business," Sasha, a former national sales manager for a personal care company, says. "It's not that I expected to have more time to myself, but I thought that if I was going to work crazy hours and travel two or three weeks out of the month, they would be for me, not for some big firm or to subsidize a mother's schedule.

"I left my job at forty, when I realized that my life choices were never going to be valued," Sasha adds. "Look, I wanted to be married and have babies. And even though I'm forty-two, I still hope those things will happen. But I didn't just want time off to date or go to social events so I could get married. By forty, marriage was no longer my singular life goal."

Rae bites into an olive while in thought. "Maybe it's the Martini talking, but I just realized you're right. I remember it was Valentine's Day, a couple of years ago. I was working on another show at the time and the production team was a little older and mostly married. I was a little depressed because it was Valentine's Day and I had no date—not that I even give a shit about Valentine's Day—but the whole team was like 'Rae, do you have a Valentine?' So you know what I did? I lied. I said I had some hot date with some hot guy and had to leave at six o'clock to get ready. Funny enough, the EP, another married guy with kids, practically threw me out the door at 6:00 PM! I didn't know what to do with myself! I think I went to the gym for two hours.

"The next day, when they asked about my date, I said it was great. I think I pretended to have a boyfriend for a couple of months and by then, production on the show was over, and I was looking for my next gig."

Sasha is nodding. "This whole Sheryl Sandberg thing of telling moms to 'lean in' to their careers is fine, and I heard her use the term 'invisible' in reference to those of us who are single in the workplace, but I heard her on TV once, and she focused on the idea that single women should be able to have time to date and not be stuck in the office until all hours while some parents are able to leave at a more normal hour to be with their families. That is definitely a piece of it, but more important to me is learning to have an off switch and actually stop taking on everything that comes my way because I am petrified of not being able to support myself as a single woman business owner.

"I feel like I have to lean in on everything big or small. I'm leaning in so hard that I'm going to fall over! And I have no net! Single gals bear 100 percent of the consequences and the responsibility of our livelihoods. I'm trying to figure out how to allow myself to lean back!"

"Here, here," says Rae as she motions us to lift our glasses. "To all the single ladies!" Rae cheers. And all four women lean in for a toast.

BABY SHOWERED

W*e're having a baby!!!*
It's 8:32 on a Thursday morning and a text is breaking my heart a little.

It's not that I'm not happy for Caroline and her husband. I am. They married a couple of years ago; she was thirty-nine and he forty-two. They knew having a baby would mean a move out of the city to the suburbs and they felt they had waited so long for the right partner, they wanted to enjoy married life a bit before parenthood. They also realized that time wasn't on their side. Caroline and Bobby had debated the pros and cons of becoming parents. Their nephew was the light of Caroline's life, and she told me she didn't need more. I therefore assumed they had opted out of parenthood. So the text was a surprise. And it gave me a little ache in that place reserved for life opportunities I haven't achieved. No matter where I am that day on an emotional level, usually happy in my little corner of the world, the reminder that some couples move forward with parenthood while I remain as single and childless as ever is always a little heartbreaking for me. It's not their fault that I feel this way, of course, and I know Caroline and Bobby want me to have love, marriage, and motherhood. But the text is a momentary reminder that I am not a mother and may never be one.

Baby girl due on July 4! another text pings seconds later. *We're looking for a place in Long Island. Hope you'll visit us out there!*

An Independence Day baby! I text back. *So happy for you and Bobby!!! What a lucky little baby girl she will be to have you for her parents!* But in truth, I felt more like mourning my own aloneness than celebrating an Independence Day baby.

The little reminders of my childlessness, of never celebrating my pregnancy, are everywhere.

There are pregnancy and birth announcements on Facebook, images of women sharing their pregnant belly growth monthly, sonogram images of a fetus replacing profile images, and images of an exhaustedly exquisite new mom holding her newborn for his or her first photo minutes after coming into this world. They all hurt a little.

And pregnancy and motherhood have become such a fascination in the media. Images of pregnant celebrities cover magazines and website homepages, not to mention general TV news. And the assumption others seem to have that I never wanted children, or that I am immune to the pain of childlessness because I'm not actively trying to have a baby, is hurtful.

"So you never wanted kids?" a younger woman asked me in the greenroom minutes before a TV segment we were appearing in together.

"I always wanted kids," I replied. "I just haven't met the man I want to have children with." She didn't mean anything by it, but it cut like a knife.

I met a man at a premiere. He asked what I do for a living, and I tell him about Savvy Auntie, the lifestyle brand I founded for women who don't have children of their own, for whatever reason, but love the children in their lives. He responded with how wonderful his

> 66 There are pregnancy and birth announcements on Facebook, images of women sharing their pregnant belly growth monthly, sonogram images of a fetus replacing profile images, and images of an exhaustedly exquisite new mom holding her newborn for his or her first photo minutes after coming into this world. They all hurt a little. 99

children are and asked me why I didn't want to be a mother. "I'm single," I replied. "I never met the father of my children."

"Well, being a parent is just about the best thing in my life," he replied, not hearing me at all. I smiled politely and walked away. But sometimes, I can't just walk away.

A cousin I once held in my arms when she was an infant calls to tell me she is expecting her first child. Or another younger cousin calls to tell me how she and her husband are having difficulty conceiving and how hard it is for her. And I'm sure it is very hard for her. But I feel as if I'm invisible. It's like if I'm not married, I couldn't possibly feel the pain of infertility. Yes, it's brought on by circumstances, not biology, but it's painful. And it's invisible. And so I feel as if I have to reply with sympathy, not empathy, for any married woman suffering from infertility. Likewise, I feel as if I have to reply with excitement and confetti when anyone shares that they're expecting, instead of disclosing the grief their good news brings me.

And even those women who are doing things I do not have the courage to do, to become single moms—of them I also feel a twinge of envy. Their determination to become mothers by choice is something I admire and honor. And while I chose not to even investigate single motherhood myself, I am envious of those who did and are on their way.

Even an email from a friend who has been through so much, who was told by one fertility specialist that she would never be a mother, relays the news that she might have a chance to get pregnant. "They found a follicle! They retrieved my egg this morning. I selected my sperm donor. I can't believe it! This might actually be happening!"

I reply with love and honest happiness for her, but I am a little sad for myself. For a minute I wonder if I have made a mistake by not choosing single motherhood. I am in my early forties and at *Borderline Regret,* a short window of time in which to make a choice, with possible regret waiting for me on both sides of that choice. It's a very different border from the one I crossed twenty years ago when I moved from Montreal to New York City in a car filled with my most important belongings and expectations of love, marriage, and children ahead.

I am reminded of my dream later that night when I bump into Aashna at a reception celebrating International Women's Day at the private residence of Danièle Ayotte, the Canadian deputy consul general. Like me, Aashna was born in Montreal and moved to New York after college. Now forty-three, Aashna is the marketing director for an international jewelry designer.

She pulls me aside. "I want your opinion on something," she says softly. Aashna has a voice that could calm a screaming baby or disarm a male CEO. It's as if it's lined with velvet. "I'm invited to a baby shower next month in New Jersey for a friend I've worked really closely with for years but I just . . . I just can't go to a baby shower. But I know I will. I have to . . . " she says, still considering her words. "I have to, right?"

Aashna is single, no children. "Time just flew by," she told me the night we met at a birthday party for Wynn. "And here I am living a fabulous life without anyone to share it with." Aashna had been engaged to a man she dated through college and then lived with when they moved to New York. "I was at the stationery store deciding on fonts for the wedding invitations. And when the saleswoman showed me how the invitation would look in calligraphy, I felt sick. I was doing everything I was supposed to do, being the traditional woman who gets married after college. But it wasn't what I wanted to do. Yes, I loved my then-fiancé, but I wasn't in love with him. I didn't want to spend my life with him. I didn't want to have babies with him."

Aashna spent the rest of her twenties enjoying the single life in New York City. "I really enjoyed being single. I went out all the time and met a ton of guys. I wasn't serious about getting married, feeling liberated from my engagement. I was having the time of my life." But before she knew it, Aashna was thirty-six. "I started to get serious about meeting someone, but it was harder than I imagined. The men I met either didn't want to be married or weren't marriage material."

Back at the consulate general's home, she continues the story. "At thirty-nine, I was dating André," she says. "And he wanted to marry me. When we first met, I fell in love with him deeply. He put on a great show at first, telling everyone how successful and talented I am. But when I was promoted to senior vice president, he shut down and became aloof.

"André is a good man, but he wasn't ambitious at all. He blamed the recession for not going out to find a job that would challenge him, but I think it was just an excuse. He didn't want to push himself forward. And whenever I tried to motivate him, he'd tease me about my career, saying it was more important to me than he was.

"Ironically, he might have been right, but not because I was putting my career above André or marriage, but my career keeps me growing intellectually. And I'm appreciated at work. André would have been happier if I was ambivalent about my work like he was about his. He was bringing me down. So instead of accepting his ring, I broke up with him."

She continues, "Melanie, it was the hardest thing I have ever done. I knew that I wasn't just ending a relationship, I was potentially giving up my chance of becoming a mother."

Aashna is dating someone else but she's not falling in love with him. "I'm beginning to wonder if there is something wrong with me, but as much as I want to be a mother, I can't marry someone who I'm not in love with."

Aashna is choosing love over motherhood, a theme I have been living myself.

"And now, I have to go to this baby shower. This friend is the one I used to go out with to meet guys when we were both single. We've been working together for over ten years! I have to go. But she keeps sending me photos of her sonograms and telling me about how hard it is to find maternity clothing she likes, and I can't take it anymore.

"How can she be so un-empathetic to my situation? Just a year ago, she was in the same boat."

It's Aashna and I who are in the same boat tonight, wondering if our ship has sailed.

THE SAVVY AUNTIES

Wynn is at a loss. Her best friend, Kate, said something hurtful to her, and she is struggling to deal with it. She called me just a half hour earlier, asking if I would meet her for a drink. I knew something was up. She's nodding across the table in disbelief when I arrive, and uncharacteristically, she is near tears.

Wynn and I normally have to plan our nights out together way in advance because her career as a PR executive for a global fashion brand takes her around the world and back again, and she leaves her free nights open to dating and weekends open to seeing her three little nieces, her older sister's kids. Today, Wynn spent the day with Kate, Kate's husband of five years Gary, and their two boys. She had agreed to travel with them to Long Island for another friend's son's second birthday party.

If you met Wynn, you wouldn't believe how much time she devotes to the children in her life. She's the typical Savvy Auntie and one of the women I had in mind when I established my company. A total knockout, stylish, and very successful, Wynn is also a very generous and good-hearted soul when it comes to her family, her friends, and their children. It's not unusual for Wynn to find a one-of-a-kind gift for a niece's or nephew's birthday or to spend a day with her three little "FashioNiecetas" by taking them shopping for new outfits at the beginning of a new season.

But it was to Kate that Wynn was especially benevolent. When Kate was in labor a month earlier than expected with her second son, it was Wynn who stayed overnight to take care of Kate's older son, Jacob, at the very last minute. He's got asthma, but aside from his parents, he'll let only Wynn nebulize him, so it was important with his potential stress with mom and dad in the hospital that his Auntie Wynnie was there. And it was Wynn who went to the hospital the next day to deliver some of Kate's beloved things to help make her more comfortable, along with a grocery bag filled with Zabar's bagels, lox, and cream cheese—Kate's very favorite—to help her friend recover from the unexpected trauma of premature labor.

Soon after baby Isaac was born and needed his mom's full attention, Jacob's third birthday was approaching. Wynn offered to put together the party for Kate. She baked four dozen cupcakes and decorated Kate and Gary's apartment in an airplane theme, at Jacob's request. Wynn even hired her intern to DJ the party with kiddie songs. From serving the food to cleaning up, Wynn took care of everything, making sure each child left with a goodie bag of her own creation.

Today was another birthday party and another day of deep breaths for Wynn. At forty, she always assumed she'd be married with kids by now. But the men she dated were either too immature to want what she wanted or too competitive with her success. Sitting in the backseat on the way to another child's birthday party in Long Island without a man of her own, knowing she'd be the only single woman there, Wynn felt sad. Fortunately, as she sat between a sleeping Isaac and a happy Jacob, she felt better.

> ❝ There is a standard misconception about childless women, no matter their age, education, work ethic, health, or lifestyle. Many people, perhaps even subconsciously, assume that because they don't have families of their own, they are too irresponsible or carefree to understand the true meaning of motherhood. ❞

As they got out of the car, Jacob insisted Wynn carry him into the house he'd never seen before. As she stepped forward, a heavier-than-she-remembered Jacob in her arms, Kate turned to take him from her. "We wouldn't want anyone to think he's your son, so I'd better hold him as we walk inside," she said.

"Can you believe that?" Wynn asks me. "I felt like I wanted the ground to just swallow me up so I didn't have to walk into that party. The only redeeming thing was seeing Gary wince when he heard her say that."

As Wynn tells me the story, my mouth is agape. I don't know Kate well, but her actions surprise me. Did she really believe Wynn was trying to convince others that Jacob was her son? Was she that insecure, with a great husband and two beautiful kids at her side, to care whether some acquaintance thought her best friend was her son's mom?

There is a standard misconception about childless women, no matter their age, education, work ethic, health, or lifestyle. Many people, perhaps even subconsciously, assume that because they don't have families of their own, they are too irresponsible or carefree to understand the true meaning of motherhood. Put more simply, because they are not mothers, they are seen as less maternal than mothers and less capable of being maternal.

A common refrain goes something like this: "You'll never know love until you have a child of your own." Or should a childless woman contribute thoughtful advice to a mother who is dealing with some sort of issue with her child, she is immediately thrown down with a comment like "You are not a mother, so you really can't give me advice on what to do with my child."

That's not to say that every word of advice from a childless woman is good advice, but we all receive advice from friends and family who are trying to help.

In December 2012, I co-released a national joint study on childless aunts with Weber Shandwick, a global public relations firm, and KRC Research, a market research firm. The study was called "The Power of the PANK." We discovered that twenty-three million Americans are PANKs, or Professional Aunts No Kids, the term I coined for women age eighteen and up, single, married, gay or straight, who have at least one child in their lives, by relation or by acquaintance, whom they love and adore. That's one in every five women. That a demographic that large is so misunderstood or, perhaps worse, cast aside as less-than or completely unsavvy about children, is not only unproductive but also hurts women, the children they love, and the parents who can often use a helping hand. Take Kate, Wynn's friend, as a good example of a mother who relies on Wynn's love and devotion to her children.

Wynn spends her time and income not only on her three nieces by relation, but also her nephews, who are nephews "by choice"— what I call nieces and nephews we choose to love despite having no blood or marital relation. While Wynn has no children of her own by circumstance—because of her singlehood—her enormous gener-

> " I say, babies are born from the womb. Maternity is born from the soul. There are many ways to mother. "

osity to her nephews is taken for granted, as if in some way her not being a parent means she owes them her devotion. Of course, the opposite is true. An aunt, even one who is an aunt by blood, has no responsibility to love a child not her own. And yet, so many family members and friends take that gift for granted.

We've all also heard the proverb "It takes a village to raise a child." And yet, the women who help to raise the nation's children—the aunts, godmothers, cousins, nannies, teachers, coaches, neighbors, and so on are sometimes thought of as "less-than" women because they are not mothers. They are the "other mothers," and their selfless devotion to children not their own should be celebrated and honored, not overlooked.

As the founder of Savvy Auntie, and as one who writes on the subject of childless women on platforms like *The Huffington Post* and PsychologyToday.com, I have received comments and letters from those who believe that childless women, even the most devoted aunts, are not truly maternal unless they prove their maternity by having children of their own by birth or adoption—or worse, that they are not fully women until they become mothers. But what I know is that motherhood shows up in many ways, and the childless Savvy Auntie, whether childless by circumstance, choice, or biology, shows enormous maternal offerings without having birthed, adopted, or become the legal guardian of a child. I say, babies are born from the womb. Maternity is born from the soul. There are many ways to mother.

I've personally heard countless stories from aunts who go above and beyond what people's stereotype of aunt behavior is, that is offering kids grandiose gifts and leaving the minute a baby poops or a child cries. That's not to say aunts don't offer gifts and adventures children love, but the role they take on is much more involved than that.

Even small things like unstructured play, reading to small children, baking cookies with them, helping them build toy railroad tracks, or taking them to the beach to build sand castles can help develop the cognitive, social, and emotional skills they need as they grow. I've dubbed this "QualAuntie Time," as time children spend with their aunt is often uninterrupted, adult-led playtime, exactly the type of playtime the American Academy of Pediatrics recommends as essential for childhood development. So most aunts, even those who can visit only now and again, are contributing greatly to the welfare of the children they love.

But there are aunts who go even further. Some have shared that they will leave work early or take their lunch break to go to a sibling or friend's home to take care of nieces and nephews who are being neglected by their parents. I've heard stories from aunts who have taken in a teen niece or nephew who would otherwise be on the street because they no longer can or want to live with their parent(s). I know of aunts who have taken a leave of absence from work to take care of their nieces and nephews while the children's mother or father is ill or has died. And I know the guilt they are made to feel by others when they want to return to their lives in their own homes, cities, or countries, after some time.

And some aunts, whom I call "ParAunts," completely change their lives, often overnight, to become the guardians of nieces and nephews whose parents are no longer able to take care of them due to incarceration, abandonment, illness, or death. Unfortunately, sometimes the parents have not done the necessary legal work in advance, putting the children at risk of being taken away from their devoted aunt. Some aunts who were not made legal guardians have to go to court to fight to keep their nieces and nephews who otherwise would be turned over to the state.

And while these may be more extreme cases, our "The Power of the PANK" study shows that more than one-third of PANKs say they take pleasure in simply running errands with and for their nieces and nephews, like taking them to their sports events, walking them to school, taking them to the doctor, and so on. Many aunts have told me that they regularly tutor their niece or nephew struggling at school or teach them a skill like painting or playing an instrument. Roughly seven out of ten PANKs say that they are role models to the children in their lives. And it's not just time and positive influence that PANKs offer so generously. Our study shows that 34 percent of PANKs contribute financially to a child's education, and 45 percent of PANKs say that they have given gifts to parents so that they can provide for their children.

Jacqueline, a thirty-five-year-old, single, and childless successful real estate agent, is the perfect example. She explains: "When my goddaughter was born, I knew that my best friend Jeanine and her boyfriend, her daughter's father, would have a tremendously difficult time raising her in New York City while they both pursued their careers in entertainment. I had had a really good couple of years in real estate at the time, and it was important to me to know that my goddaughter's education and day care expenses were not adding more pressure on Jeanine. She is an incredibly talented woman, and I knew that she would be able to pursue the right opportunities only if she did not have financial stress.

"I opened a trust for my goddaughter, and I opened a 529 plan for her college education as a gift to Jeanine, which, even in the more difficult times in the real estate market, I contribute to annually. The trust is really an emergency fund. It's there for her school costs, day care costs, medical needs, whatever she may need that her parents come up short on. The trust has nearly tripled in value since my goddaughter was born, which makes me so happy. It's there to protect them from financial ruin if something truly devastating ever happened."

And while Jacqueline is financially able to help in this way, and not all aunts are able to, many aunts contribute to their family and friends in other invaluable ways. Here's Kristin's story: "My sister and brother-in-law were going through a nasty divorce, and I knew that my sister and niece needed my support. Since then, I've been flying to Baltimore every month to spend a weekend or longer with them. But I know even with that I'm missing out on many of my niece's milestones. Sometimes, I send my sister a little cash to pay for something like a birthday party I can't get to or babysitting money so my sister can have a night out with her friends. My niece is also the beneficiary of my retirement and life insurance policies. I know it sounds a little morose, but I don't have a family of my own, so there is nobody for me to leave it to but them, and of course my parents, but for now, it's just them."

And other Savvy Aunties contribute to their community, or the global village, in invaluable ways. Our study shows that 57 percent of PANKs say that they get personal enjoyment out of community service, charity work, or volunteering. And that's not just locally. Some Savvy Aunties offer love and devotion not only to the children in their lives but also to foreign exchange students they welcome into their homes, while others focus their careers on teaching, coaching, or supporting the talents and welfare of other children. And some travel to areas nationally and around the globe to help children and families in need.

Back with Wynn, she tells me that however difficult it might be, she plans to tell Kate just how fortunate she is to have a friend like Wynn in her life—a friend who loves her children like family. "I want her to know that her children will always have me in their lives, but I need to know that she respects me and what I give them—and her and Gary."

Wynn vows to never go to a child's birthday party again, apart from her own nieces by relation, as she can't take the hurt anymore. "I don't blame you," I say. "You have to protect yourself and your feelings."

I remind Wynn of the number one Savvy Auntie Principle: Aunthood is a gift. Just as a Savvy Auntie is fortunate for each and every niece and nephew who enters her life, the love she shares with these children and their families is an incredibly generous and precious commodity. Although an adoring auntie may feel as if she can't help granting her loved ones' every wish and desire, the truth is that everything a Savvy Auntie offers them is a gift. Savvy Aunties know they need to be valued and respected in kind.

"Cheers to that," Wynn says, with a smile.

The server comes by, and I order us two more Savvy Auntinis. "And cheers to you," I say.

IZZY WAS ROBBED

I walk into a high-rise apartment elevator not knowing I'm about to experience another broken heart. The little, old, white-haired woman and her little white-haired dog who are there with me pay no attention. We're all clueless. But the story is so unbelievable that I can't blame myself for not being prepared.

Izzy opens the door with a wide smile and an apology. "I'm so sorry for how I look. I'm just so tired," she says. Izzy in yoga pants and a hoodie is more attractive than most women on their best day. She looks fabulous.

"I'm jealous that you are so comfortable!" I say as we kiss hello. And I am. I'm tired, too. I've been running up and down the city for almost two decades now. I have yet to meet "him" at a stoplight, on a bus, sitting at the bar at a restaurant, or walking around Bed Bath & Beyond in search of nothing in particular that will help make my apartment feel more like a home.

"It's the entrepreneurial life," Izzy says, with a knowing glance.

But I can see in my friend's eyes that she's not just tired. She's sad.

Izzy is a gorgeous, savvy woman who started a digital ad agency over a year ago, a dream she's had for years. She found the investors she needed and was knee-deep in building her business. She and

Chris, her long-term boyfriend, had recently moved to Brooklyn. It was in their apartment that she shared the shocking news with me.

"Chris and I are over," Izzy says, eyes welling up as if she were realizing it for the very first time. "I found out a few weeks ago that he had been cheating on me for years, and he's now with her."

"What?" I say a little too loudly, wondering out loud what man would leave Izzy for another woman. I had last seen her just a couple of months before. She didn't know about his cheating then, but she had been beginning to suspect something was not right.

"Apparently, Chris was leading a double life. He'd been seeing her when I was in the city at the office. I suppose this woman gives him something I can't."

It's difficult to imagine what a man would need that Izzy didn't offer. Perhaps it was that she had too much too offer. "How did this happen?" I ask, again too loudly.

"A few weeks back, I spotted a text from a girl on his phone that said *Where are you, baby?* and when I confronted him about it, he made me believe it was a substitute teacher who taught at his school where he's the principal, and she just had the dates confused about some meeting. But a couple of weeks later on a weekend, Chris left his phone in the apartment by mistake and I saw another text from the same girl and it read *Where ARE you?*

"I figured if I confronted her, she'd leave my man alone, so I texted her back: 'Why are you texting my boyfriend?' And would you believe she called his phone immediately? She told me that I should know Chris was leaving me for her. The next few minutes were a blur as she went on about how long they had been in love. And then, Melanie, I hear Chris say, 'I'm pulling over.' And I'm like what? She's in Chris's car? With Chris? And she says: 'See, Chris is with me now.' And I swear to God, I might have fainted. It was otherworldly. Then I hear his voice on the phone and all he says is 'It's over, Izzy.' And, Melanie, as sure as this is Friday, that was that."

I'm in shock. I had never met Chris but had heard only good things. Chris may not be the wealthiest guy or the most ambitious guy, but we all knew, expected, that he was a "good guy."

"It just happened five weeks ago, Izzy says, grabbing a tissue. "It's still so raw."

I can't even imagine . . .

"So anyway," Izzy says, sitting up straight and drying her eyes, "This whole debacle just proved to me that I can't wait for a man to make my dreams come true. I want to be a mother. I'm going to have a baby on my own. I don't care what it takes. I'm determined."

Izzy is doing what so many women approaching forty are thinking but few are able to do, for many reasons.

"I'll be forty in a few weeks," Izzy says. "I'm going to have kids. I just really thought that I had met the kind of man who wanted to have a family. He wasn't by any means like the men I had previously dated. When we first met, he was a math teacher who loved his students. He'd always wanted to be a teacher. I fell in love with how he talked about his students, how much their perseverance impressed him, and how committed he was to them. But when it came time for us to talk about having kids of our own, my perseverance was less impressive to him. He would tell me I was putting all the pressure of my timeline on him, like my fertility was something I could put on hold until he was ready.

"Melanie, I honestly thought I was making the right choice by being with him. Before Chris, I dated these high-powered New York City guys with money beyond money. But they didn't want to settle down. I made a stupid mistake thinking that's what Chris wanted, or at least that he wanted it with me. And it's not like we didn't talk about it when we first dated. He said he wanted kids on our very first date!"

It turns out Izzy's math teacher boyfriend was more calculating than she had thought. "And even though we moved to Brooklyn when he landed the principal position, I still paid the rent because I wanted a two-bedroom, anticipating we'd finally try to have a baby. He thought we didn't need a two-bedroom apartment and was like, 'If you want a two-bedroom, then you pay for it.' I was totally fine with it, but I think he resented that I could afford a two-bedroom and he couldn't. And when I got funded, he grew more distant than ever. He'd make snide comments about me and my 'entrepreneur women friends taking over the world.'"

"Do you think this was a power-struggle issue for Chris?" I ask.

"I have no doubt," Izzy says. "The girl he's with now is in her midtwenties, and he's the principal of the school. She's a substitute teacher, so he's clearly making more money and has more power than she does. She probably looks up to him like he's a freaking god!

"Now I know he didn't want to have a baby because he was with someone else. But now . . . " Izzy's voice drops and her red eyes fill with tears again. "Now I can't have a baby. I went to see a gynecologist who specializes in infertility, and he told me that my FSH levels are too high. He wouldn't even try to do IVF on me."

FSH levels, or follicle-stimulating hormones, are one measure of a woman's fertility. A low FSH level means excellent fertility. A high FSH level can mean infertility. Izzy's FSH level is 17, which is painfully high.

"But I don't care," Izzy says, choking up on her words. "I want two kids. I will have two kids. I will get donors eggs, a surrogate, whatever it takes. The money I was saving to buy a house for Chris

66 I can't think of anything worse than a man who steals a woman's fertility, which is essentially what he did by asking her to wait until her fertility became compromised to tell her he did not want to be with her. 99

and me to live in is now going to rent a womb or two for my babies," she says with a tearful sense of humor.

I'm so angry with Chris. I can't think of anything worse than a man who steals a woman's fertility, which is essentially what he did by asking her to wait until her fertility became compromised to tell her he did not want to be with her. He had no intentions of having children with Izzy, and he led her on while she paid the rent and tried to be patient. I have found some men to be so cruel and unsympathetic about women's fertility.

I know another gorgeous, successful, philanthropic woman who had been talking to her husband about having a baby since she was thirty-nine years old. He has a daughter from a previous marriage who lived with them. My friend thought that being a stepmother would be enough for her. But a couple of years after they married, she realized that she also wanted to mother her own baby. He kept putting her off, saying yes but that the timing wasn't right. The week she turned forty-one, and a month after she closed another huge business deal, he left my friend for a woman in her twenties.

"And there went my chance to have a kid," she said to me over drinks at the Four Seasons the night she revealed she had separated from her husband. "I was trying to be patient, but he was deceiving me on every level. He just preferred a girl who was willing to play nice little 'wifey,' and while I did my best to always make sure dinner was on the table and he had clean drawers in his drawers, I wasn't always there the minute he got home from work. I think he resented that."

Men who leave a wife or girlfriend for a younger woman are nothing new. But when a man stays with a woman and pushes off a pregnancy he never intends to go through with, it's heartless.

And to think women are the ones often blamed for not having babies while they are young enough and accused of not knowing how precious our fertility is. We're called "naïve" about the delicacy of our fertility and, more often on the other end of it, desperate.

Things hadn't worked out as Izzy expected even with her vigilant forethought. "And I thought I did everything right," Izzy says. "I had had my FSH levels tested every year since I was thirty-six. I kept telling Chris with each result going higher and higher that we had to start trying, and he would balk and talk about pressure and not making enough money. When he got that new job as principal at a school in Brooklyn making more money, his new job was the excuse. 'Let me get my feet wet as principal,' he said when I came home with a level 14 a year ago.

"It was like *he* was doing all the compromising! I never put pressure on him to marry me or anything. But he always talked about the pressure I was putting on him."

I admire Izzy so deeply. And I'm not surprised at her resolve. Izzy was determined to get her business started, and she did. She's already seeing extraordinary success from her efforts. And I wonder whether Chris saw this in her, too, and how that might have affected their relationship.

"And the crazy thing is," she says. "He was so romantic. He would text me how much he loved me when I was at work, or I

> 66 And to think women are the ones often blamed for not having babies while they are young enough and accused of not knowing how precious our fertility is. We're called 'naïve' about the delicacy of our fertility and, more often on the other end of it, desperate. 99

would come home to a candle-lit dinner. I honestly thought we were madly in love. I really had no clue."

I left Brooklyn deflated. Later that evening, I was having dinner with Erica, a married friend, mom of three. She knows Izzy and her story. We're both angry on her behalf.

"I'm telling you, Melanie, men can be assholes. I think Izzy has the right idea. If you want to be a mother, forget waiting for some guy to sweep you off your feet. If you really want to be a mother, you have to have a baby on your own. That's it. Period."

"I have no backup, Erica," I say. "My mother died over twenty years ago, and my father lives hundreds of miles away. My brother has his own children to take care of. What if I have an emergency? Who will take care of my kid? What if the child has special needs? Who will help me manage that?"

"Oh, stop being so negative!" Erica says loudly. "Why are you thinking you're going to have a baby with special needs?!"

"Because it's a possibility, Erica," I say, calmly. We can all fantasize about the most beautiful moments of motherhood, but there are challenging ones, too. Some last a lifetime.

I wonder why people think I'm being too romantic when I choose to be with a man I love before having a child, but too practical when I consider the real, possible challenges of single motherhood.

My infertility wasn't caused by biology. It is a result of my circumstances.

"All I'm saying is that you talk and talk about how you're so maternal, but you are not willing to be a mother, so it's all bullshit to me. Sorry. Just being honest," she says.

I know she's angry at Chris and who knows what else, but I'm speechless. Apparently the only way I could prove to Erica how much I want to be a mother, when it's all I've ever wanted, is to become a single mother by choice in my early forties. I'm not going to become a single mother to prove I am maternal or that I've wanted a baby so much I have often felt like a failure as a woman because that hasn't happened for me.

Erica could tell she had overstepped her bounds. "Look, I'm sorry. I just don't want you to miss out."

Didn't she understand that I already missed out? Didn't she understand that I know what not finding love means for my ability to have a baby? A family? Didn't she understand how I not only don't have a child, but I also don't have a love? I'll never be a young mother, or a thirtysomething mother, or most likely, a mother in my forties. I will never cry into my husband's chest when later-stage infertility has caused another month to go by without conception. I will never hold my pregnant belly or feel my baby kick inside of me. I'll never complain about morning sickness or swollen ankles. I'll never hold my baby, seconds old.

Did I really need a mother to remind me I'll never be a mother unless I have a baby on my own? Did I need her to remind me of what I'm missing? If I had been married and was having trouble conceiving, would I get the same speech about missing out? Obviously, the answer is no. My infertility wasn't caused by biology. It is a result of my circumstances. I am single. I want a man I love to have a baby with me. Why does that mean I don't sincerely want to be a mother?

"Trust me," I said. "I know what I'm missing."

MY LONELY GRIEF

When I was about thirty-five, I had a night I can't forget. Actually, I had many nights I can't forget, all of which have now melted into one memory, one dark time. These nights looked and felt the same. Sometimes they were days apart, sometimes months apart, but altogether, they were years full.

Imagine it: I'm lying in my bed at night in the dark. The walls are closing in on me. The days are running into each other like minutes . . . like seconds. I'm excelling at work but frustrated there because I'm not able to do more, go deeper, better live my potential. *Is this it?* I would ask myself. *Is this my life?* And I'm probably depressed. But no one knows. Not even me. I'm making some new friends, but I'm not meeting many new men.

Summer rounds into fall . . . rounds into winter . . . rounds into spring . . . rounds into summer, and there it goes. And I'm lying in my bed, and I'm crying. I'm not just crying, I'm sobbing. I'm desperately, desperately sad and alone. And I'm wondering aloud, "What the hell happened? How did I get here?"

I take a day off from work—a "mental health" day, as they call it. It's a day to regroup or to walk or to think or to dream—to find my way again. I walk all day. I walk around downtown. I walk around Midtown. And then I come back uptown and walk around some more. I spot a young boy run up to his mother carrying a big green butterfly made from construction paper and finger paint. He runs into her arms and gives her the butterfly. I get the butterflies, and I run home. And I cry.

Where is my *baby?* I ask God or the universe or my mother up there in heaven. I ask the room; I ask the walls closing in on me. And I ask myself. *Where is your baby? Where is your love? Why is this so hard?*

At the time, I'm living in New York City, and I work for an outstanding global beauty brand and I have to look the part. And so every day I brush on the blush, put on something fabulous, and slip on my high heels. And every day, I wake up and go to work and I focus on doing well.

And I turn thirty-six. Summer rounds into fall . . . rounds into winter . . . rounds into spring . . . rounds into summer, and there it goes.

A guy I might be interested in isn't interested in me, or one who's pursuing me isn't moving me. There's another party, another disappointment. On Sunday, I shop for new jeans or new shoes or a new dress for dates I don't have. Dates with men I don't meet.

I go to Paris for just one day, leading a meeting in French. It's empowering. After the meeting, I hop on the back of a colleague's *moto* to tour his extraordinary City of Lights: the Eiffel Tower, the Seine, the Louvre. It's exhilarating. Soon after that, I take a week off work and travel with other singles. I float on the Dead Sea, looking up at the sky above the most spiritual place on earth, and I pray to see my life in a new way. I make new friends, and I feel like my life is fresh and new and has potential. And yet, *the more things change, the more they stay the same.*

> **Where is my baby?** I ask God or the universe or my mother up there in heaven. I ask the room; I ask the walls closing in on me. And I ask myself. *Where is your baby? Where is your love? Why is this so hard?*

I turn thirty-seven. Summer rounds into fall . . . rounds into winter . . . rounds into spring . . . rounds into summer, and there it goes.

This isn't me. It can't be me. I can't be grieving the loss of babies I never had. I have to find a new path. I have to breathe again. I have to begin smiling for real again. As far as anyone could see from the outside, I had a gorgeous life. I felt disappointed in myself for not appreciating everything I had, everything I had worked hard to create for myself. My life was magical, and yet, I was grieving.

Cut to today, now I'm on the other side of hope. And thankfully, I'm on the other side of grief. I'm sitting at an airport gate next to a woman in her late forties. We start to chat.

"It's my first time on a plane alone in I don't know how long!" she says, thoroughly excited. "My kids are grown, and I'm finally able to travel on my own."

She's maybe five years older than me and already an empty-nester. "You must have had your kids so young," I say to compliment her youthful appearance.

"Not really," she says. "I was twenty-six and twenty-nine when I had my kids."

I realize in that very moment that somehow I've lived an entire generation of time without having children of my own. I feel in that moment like my time has truly passed. I reply, saying something I've never said aloud before. "I couldn't have children," I say. "But, wow, I guess if I did, I might be an empty-nester already!" And I wonder to myself how many plane trips I would have taken with my family. How many vacations we would have had together. And how, now that I'm forty-three and I'm being honest with myself, I know I'll never have that. I've passed that life; I've missed my flight.

I know I've made this woman believe that I had a biological issue with my fertility. I don't want to admit I'm single and never met a man with whom to have a family. I don't know if she'll understand. Besides, for all intents and purposes, I couldn't have children because of my circumstances. And that grief, while different than the grief of women and men who suffer from biological infertility, is still grief.

I'm used to the sad feeling. In my twenties, I'd feel sad as, one by one, my friends got married, had a baby, a second baby, moved to the suburbs or other cities altogether. But I'd be scrappy, start again, and find new friends. I kept believing it was only a matter of time. How could it not be? How could it be possible that I wouldn't be a mother? I couldn't fathom it.

In my midthirties, I had a life-changing conversation. It looked something like this: We're three old friends catching up on each other's lives. One of us is a married mom of two. One is newly married, pregnant with her first. And one is a single woman in her midthirties about to lose yet another unfertilized egg. I was the last.

We used to chat about the men we were dating, wanted to date, or were sadly breaking up with. We shared news about a new job or promotion or the larger apartment we were moving into. We talked about the cute new outfit we found on sale or our latest adventures with our nieces and nephews. Over time, talk of engagements, marriages, and pregnancies crept into our conversations, but they were always balanced with other topics and the presumption of a common eventuality: We'd *all* get married and have kids. Until we didn't.

That night at the restaurant, the disparity is evident. Once we order, talk immediately turns to things maternal. The two who share the common experience of pregnancy swap stories about the burdens of burgeoning bumps. I quickly learn what gave one of the women third-trimester heartburn and how the other is managing her elder child's eating habits while trying to lose her postpregnancy weight. Topics like fashion come up, but in relation to new jeans that "totally don't look maternity!" They go through the list of mutual friends who are expecting. Then, they move on to one of our friend's younger sisters, recently married and having trouble conceiving. Understandably, the conversation turns somber as they share thoughts on the grief she and her husband must be experiencing.

I remain quiet. It's not that I don't feel sympathetic. It's not that I don't appreciate the challenges of my mom friends, even if they're not my own challenges. And it's not that I don't celebrate their children and their joys. But what's becoming clear to me is that the kinds of conversations we used to have, topics that were still most relevant to me, are no longer relevant to them. It feels as if I am suddenly an outsider in my own group. I have gone from being a compatible girlfriend to a silent audience member. So I just sit there, moving tomatoes around my salad plate with the tip of my fork, as they continue for what seems like an eternity. But when the dialogue about baby weight gain and toddler temper tantrums and new IVF trials and "Did you hear that Audrey is expecting twins?!" and fingers tapping a pregnant belly and heads nodding in total heartburn sympathy goes on past the appetizers and well into half a bowl of pasta, I lose it.

"Stop! Talking! About! Babies!" I shout, catching even myself by surprise. My friends awkwardly change the subject but not before looking at me as though I am completely out of line.

Perhaps I'm being inappropriate, but the subjects they'd rattled off, like items on a menu, were everything I was hungering for. What I wouldn't do to have a reason to buy maternity jeans! What I wouldn't do to hold my pregnant belly as I listened to my friends talk about their children, knowing my own was coming just a few months down the road. What I wouldn't do to be able to bury my head in the arms of my loving husband as another month passed without getting closer to parenthood. What I wouldn't do to have a husband at all . . .

But instead, there I was, in my midthirties, with no romantic partner in sight. Finally, on that night, not only did I have admit to myself that my life was not the way I had expected it to be, but also I had to face the fact that my dream of marriage and children may never come true. It was the beginning of a silent grief that would accompany me on lonely weekends with no dates or friends, as well as some nights when I went to bed realizing that more days, weeks, and months had passed since I had met anyone with whom I felt a connection.

During the day I found myself noticing pregnant women and young moms everywhere. The Upper West Side of Manhattan is brimming with babies, often twins rolling side by side down Broadway. Every baby I passed by and every pregnant woman I offered my place to on the subway stirred something within me. I was supposed to be preoccupied with finding a husband, moving one step at a time. *It's not your turn to grieve your infertility just yet.* The pain of childlessness is reserved for couples who are trying to conceive. I wasn't even trying.

"I hear Helena is trying to have a baby," reported a friend. "Isn't she turning forty? She has two kids. She really shouldn't try for a third now. It's just too late."

I was only thirty-seven. My period would come, and I'd acknowledge the death of one more egg. And I'd lie in bed, swelled

> 66 The type of grief I experienced and many women of the Otherhood experience is referred to in psychology as disenfranchised grief. Because there's no marked loss for others to visualize, it is not understood or accepted. There's no witness like a husband or lover to share your grief over your infertility. Many don't recognize it as something real. 99

by hormones and discomfort, and I'd cry into my pillow. I grieved alone. I was in mourning. But it was the kind of grief that isn't acknowledged. Unlike the grief a couple goes through due to biological infertility, the sadness over childlessness for a single woman in her thirties or forties is not generally accepted by our culture. And we grieve alone, without a shoulder to cry on.

The type of grief I experienced and many women of the Otherhood experience is referred to in psychology as disenfranchised grief. Because there's no marked loss for others to visualize, it is not understood or accepted. There's no witness like a husband or lover to share your grief over your infertility. Many don't recognize it as something real.

The double whammy of being alone and being childless is a silent grief for so many women. Society insists not only do we not have the right to grieve our childlessness, since there are alternative ways of becoming a mother (never mind the challenges that come with any of those paths), and many ways of finding love and marriage (no matter how hard we've tried), but also that the only "real" woman *is* a mother.

A comment on *The Huffington Post*: "If you *really* wanted to be a mom, you'd be a mom! Women today have children if they *want* children. Clearly that's not what you *want!*"

A letter from a stranger: "If you were *really* mother material, you'd adopt. Otherwise, get over yourself."

A woman I meet at a conference who learns about Savvy Auntie: "So you never wanted kids?"

I find myself wanting to prove to friends and strangers how much I have truly always wanted to be a mother. My childlessness is not something many have sympathy for; rather, many see it as proof that it was not meant to be for me, or worse, childlessness is a choice I made.

A fertility expert once referred to me as "child-free," the term used by those who have chosen never to have children, happily living their lives free of kids. She explained that since I had not chosen to become a single mother, I had in fact chosen to remain childless. "It was still a choice," she explained. Somehow, by not having a baby on my own, I have to be labeled as one who chose to live my life without children, and happily so? No.

Some believe that the term "child-free" is a more empowering label for the childless woman in her late thirties and older to wear, as if being "childless" is too passive, too unnatural a state, for a modern woman who is able to control most other aspects of her life to find herself in. I have wondered at what point it becomes unnatural for a woman to be childless.

If we have babies *before* an age that society deems acceptable, it's unnatural. Age sixteen seems to be the youngest at which we are mildly comfortable with a girl's pregnancy. Even then, we are not entirely comfortable with it. On the other hand, once a woman is in her late thirties, it's considered unnatural for her *not* to be a mother. And once she's reached her midforties, it's unnatural for

> 66 She explained that since I had not chosen to become a single mother, I had in fact chosen to remain childless. 'It was still a choice,' she explained. Somehow, by not having a baby on my own, I have to be labeled as one who chose to live my life without children, and happily so? No. 99

her to be pregnant; society is uncomfortable with that circumstance as well. So there is a relatively short window of time for a woman before which being a mother is unnatural and after which not being a mother is unnatural.

We are not only childless, but also made to feel as "less-than" women because we are not mothers. And whether or not we refuse to believe that we are—and I do refuse—we sometimes can't help but feel outside the norm. We grieve not only our childlessness but also the seeming dilution of our womanhood.

But then, as summer once again rounds into fall . . . rounds into winter . . . rounds into spring . . . rounds into summer, and we reach the end of our fertility, certainly not the end of our womanhood, we grieve less as we embrace life as it is, no longer focusing on what it isn't or what we aren't. And one day, if we're fortunate enough to realize how much more spectacular life is when we truly look at it for all its gifts, when we witness it and actively live in it, we begin to be able to grieve no more.

No matter how tightly we hold on to how we envisioned our lives to be, the natural cycle of seasons still goes around. And so choosing to live the lives we were given and the lives we are creating for ourselves, and loosening our grip on our own expectations of how, when, and what our lives should be or should have been, never mind society's expectations, is the most empowering choice we can make. Grief over what one has lost, or does not have, is natural. So is the cycle of life. And lucky for us, no matter what, life goes on.

OUR NEST EGGS

I'm early to meet Nicole at a café on the Upper West Side, so I order a coffee and prepare to catch up on emails. I'm quickly distracted. Two women sit down at a table next to mine. Within minutes, one shares the latest tale of her mischievous toddler. The other woman explains that she's not a mom, but she's an aunt. She quickly pulls out her phone to share a photo of her niece.

"I'm thirty-nine and, uh, you know, I don't really want kids," she explains. "But my niece Kaitlyn is like my mini-me! I can't even tell you how much I love her!"

I can't help but interrupt and hand the aunt my card. She laughs, happily. She follows my Savvy Auntie account on Twitter and says she recently purchased my book. In fact, she's a big fan of the Savvy Auntie movement. Just then, Nicole finds me and sits down. I introduce her to my new friends, and Nicole is proud of me for finding a Savvy Auntie on a random Wednesday afternoon.

"It's what I do," I say gleefully.

"I'm an auntie, too," Nicole tells the women. "I hope to be a mom, too, one day, but in the meantime, I just love being a devoted auntie."

Alyssa, the other proud aunt, now that she's among cohorts while her friend has gone to the ladies' room, wants to explain that earlier, when she said she didn't want kids . . . well, she said that only because she's learned that if people hear she wants kids, they go through a gamut of ways she can still become a mother. Alyssa adds, "If I have to say why I don't want to 'just have a baby on my own' one more time!"

"Oh, I know," Nicole confides. "I'm over it, too."

It's been a while since I've seen Nicole. She's been busy with her new job as a market researcher traveling all over Europe. And she has news for me.

"I've frozen my eggs," she says in a hushed way that makes it sound as if she's done something terribly daring and courageous, which she has. "When I turned thirty-eight this summer, and it had been a couple of years since I'd had a serious boyfriend, or even a date I could take seriously, I decided it was time."

I'm trying to hide my slight envy. It was at age thirty-eight that I first heard of egg freezing as a serious thing, and even then, it had a much lower rate of success than now. Plus, I had just invested everything I had in my business. I didn't have the funds for that kind of investment.

"I had to ask my parents for the money," Nicole reveals. "It costs $10,000, and I just got that new job after being hit by the recession for over a year. I just didn't have the money."

I nod, understanding all too well.

"I was afraid how my parents might take it. They're pretty conservative, but I don't know why I was so worried. Not only did my mother pull out her checkbook right then and there, my father drove me to the clinic when I went through the procedure. They thought they couldn't possibly spoil their future grandchild any more than by giving him the possibility of life."

I smile. It's heartwarming to hear.

"The whole process was much more involved than I imagined. I had to take hormones that made me all bloated and, well, hormonal. For a few weeks, I looked and felt pregnant."

I hadn't thought about it that way before.

"I told my girlfriends who are moms what I was going through, and they all opened up to me about their infertility issues. Just about every one of my girlfriends who got married in her midthirties has suffered in some way with fertility. I can't believe I never had any idea!"

I have my suspicions as to why. "Well, even though you weren't trying to get pregnant yet, freezing your eggs did bring you one step closer to motherhood—all of sudden, you were part of the mommy club," I say, hoping she's not offended.

"Yeah, maybe you're right. I mean, I was kind of hurt that my closest friends all knew about each other's fertility issues while I had been left out, until the egg-freezing thing. And I have to admit, it felt pretty good to have been included." Nicole looks wistful. "The day of the procedure was really worrisome. There were a few women sitting in the waiting room waiting to hear their verdict. A woman who looked to be in her late thirties was told they were not able to find any eggs. Another woman who was probably in her early forties had five. It's a low number. They say they really need to retrieve about ten to fifteen for the best success rate. So my heart was beating pretty fast. All of a sudden, I realized it was the most important number I could ever hear. Another woman had ten, and I felt a sense of relief for her. Finally, they told me I had twelve. It's a good number. Now my little guys are waiting for me to find their future dada."

Nicole is sullen once again. "You know, the weirdest part of this whole experience for me was that, after the procedure, once I was off the drugs and no longer feeling pregnant, I kind of missed it. I mean it, well, in a way, it felt like I gave birth, but I have no baby to show for it, you know?"

I understand.

The mom and aunt come over to say good-bye before they leave. "Aunties are the best!" Alyssa exclaims as she gives us both a hug.

"We are!" Nicole and I announce at once. I think the mom feels left out. I understand that, too.

Nicole and her decision to freeze her eggs are still on my mind when I meet Jill for coffee on the Upper East Side a few days later. Jill is pretty, smart, successful, forty, and single. And she's having a baby.

At least that's her plan. She's working on it. She has secured a very willing gay friend's sperm to create an embryo with her eggs. She'll begin the IVF process soon. She's smiling from ear to ear. She's finally going to be the mother she's always dreamed of being.

"Have you looked into it?" she asks me, referring to my having a baby on my own. "I am happy to give you the name of my fertility doc. He's the best in the city." She reaches for her BlackBerry. I recoil but try not to let it show. I can't imagine doing it on my own. The idea of having a baby on one's own is a hot topic among the single women of Manhattan. It's talked about over cocktails to help soothe a friend after her recent breakup from the man she thought was "the one." It's talked about on snowy Sundays over omelets at brunch. It's talked about during relaxing days at the beach while reading gossip magazines filled with the latest celebrity baby-bump sightings. It's talked about in the corridors of office buildings. It's talked about with close friends and new acquaintances. It's certainly talked about the days before or soon after a birthday. And it's almost impossible *not* to talk about in the doctor's office. It's even being talked about on the morning shows.

A few weeks after hearing Jill's news, I'm having another cup of coffee. This time, it's at home on a typical weekday morning while *The Today Show* sounds off in the living room.

Donny Deutsch, ad man turned cable TV host turned morning show "expert" on just about anything, is looking straight into the camera. Normally, he'd be looking at Savannah Guthrie, the moderator of this "Today's Professionals" segment, to share his opinions. But this morning, Donny seems to have something especially important to say.

"Today's Professionals" consists of a panel of three opinionated professionals: Star Jones, Esq.; Nancy Snyderman, MD; and Donny. It's filled with banter about the hot topics of the day, refereed by the moderator as the segment time counts down quickly. Today, as he takes on the subject of whether or not women are naïve about their fertility lifespan, Donny wants the viewing audience to hear him loud and clear. He directs his message to those single women of a certain age still hoping to find a mate and have a child.

It goes something like this: "Don't wait any longer," he warns as he stares into the camera. "Have a baby on your own." Then, to add a bonus to his Big Idea, he adds, "Trust me, men will find you even more attractive if you do."

I am flattered. It's an off-the-cuff remark that leaves me blindsided. The debonair Donny Deutsch, who fathered his last child at age forty-nine, is telling single women what to do—no, he's *warning* women about what to do.

Back at coffee with Jill, she's encouraging me to really consider having a baby on my own. "Here's my doctor's number," Jill says. She nods at the server for a refill. With her cup half full of optimism, she adds, "I don't know what I'll do without coffee when I'm pregnant."

I don't know what I'd do at all, I think to myself.

> " When a woman is reaching the end of her fertile years, and she makes the decision to conceive a child on her own and to raise that child on her own should no man ever appear, she's committed to doing it. She can't stop to second-guess herself. And she can become an evangelist to all women she meets. "

I notice my cup is half empty. "I just don't think I could do it. I don't have any support," I argue rhetorically. "My mother is no longer alive. My father lives in another country. My brother has children of his own to worry about. If I want to keep moving forward with my business, I wouldn't be able to take maternity leave for a day, let alone weeks. How could I earn a living and raise my baby—let alone be available for the baby? You can't easily be a stay-at-home mother and pay the rent without a partner."

But Jill, an independent woman with means, is nonplussed. "Where there's a will, there's a way!" she chirps. The server returns with a fresh pot and pours more coffee into her cup. It smells good.

When a woman is reaching the end of her fertile years, and she makes the decision to conceive a child on her own and to raise that child on her own should no man ever appear, she's committed to doing it. She can't stop to second-guess herself. And she can become an evangelist to all women she meets.

"It's the best decision I ever made!" exclaims Heather, a single mother to twins I met at a Manhattan event a couple of years ago. She often finds an opportunity to remind me what I'm missing by not having a child on my own. "I can't imagine my life without my babies. Do it! Get pregnant! Have *babieeeeeeees!*"

And after meeting up with Jill, I'm actually considering it. I jump on the 1 train back to work (no cabs for women saving up for a baby!) and think about how much money I have in savings. I think about who I could ask for financial help if I needed it. I think about who would be there for backup. By the time I'm home, I add Jill's fertility specialist's name to my contact list. I don't think about it seriously again after that.

My dream was to get married to a man I love, get pregnant, go into labor with him holding my hand, see his face when he first saw our child. The child we had made together, in love. The child we would raise together. She'd have my eyes and his chin. He'd have my restless creativity and his pragmatism. That's still the dream I want.

I used to throw dinner parties. I'd plan well ahead and obsess about the details. For a Passover Seder I once threw, I bought a whole new set of dishes and wineglasses. There were fresh spring-inspired cloth napkins and a new Haggadah at each place setting. An hour before the holiday, I ran to Pottery Barn to pick up a new vase so the orchid I purchased would sit perfectly in the center of the table. There was not a detail left undone. The night was spectacular. My single friends and I enjoyed the rituals, the conversation, and the food.

And then they left. Lovely as they were to help clear what was left of the Seder table, in the end, all I was left with were dirty dishes, some leftovers, and a single orchid sitting flawlessly in a vase for only me to enjoy. It felt lonely.

All this is to say that I want to be pregnant in theory. I would love to cup my belly in the way that makes an expectant mother look angelic. I want to feel my baby kick inside of me. I want to have conversations about everything pregnant women and their pregnant friends talk about. And I want to hold my newborn in my arms, minutes old, and make promises to love her or him unconditionally and wholeheartedly—but I am petrified of walking through my door a couple of days later to an empty apartment. Yes, my life would be more full with a child, that's obvious. My heart would swell with love, I don't doubt it. But I'd still be in grief for what I don't have—a husband to share it with.

After I turned thirty-seven, both my former internist and gynecologist asked me if I'd considered having a baby on my own. My male gynecologist at the time was not sympathetic to my situation of being single. The "she'll regret this" look I saw on his face was almost audible. There was this "tsk tsk" air to the discussion. Maybe he'd seen as many women my age in his stirrups as he'd seen sixteen-year-old girls asking for the pill and he'd lost his sensitivity, if he ever had any to begin with. My internist, a lovely woman more sympathetic to the plight of being single at thirty-eight, lowered her eyes when I said I'd wait until I was forty to make that decision. Her face said it would be too late. My heart said I'd have to wait.

If you'd told me when I was in my twenties that women in their late thirties and forties would be having babies on their own in a way that society accepted, while I'd be judged for not making the same choice, I'd have laughed. Somehow being, happy, kind, well-educated, and successful is no longer enough to be considered everything you can be. In order to be a full woman, one must be a mother. But I know better. I know that while I have moments of sadness over not having children, I am fully engaged in my life. Donny's words that women who make the choice to have babies on their own are more attractive to men was the straw that broke my womb in half. I wrote about it for *The Huffington Post*. The morning after, a *Today Show* producer invited me to talk on-air about what I wrote. Three hours later I was calling into "Today's

> " If you'd told me when I was in my twenties that women in their late thirties and forties would be having babies on their own in a way that society accepted, while I'd be judged for not making the same choice, I'd have laughed. Somehow being, happy, kind, well-educated, and successful is no longer enough to be considered everything you can be. In order to be a full woman, one must be a mother. But I know better. "

Professionals" to give Donny what for. Savannah and Star, then forty and fifty respectively, both childless after failed marriages, joined me, reiterating my points. They had been miffed by Donny's point, too.

Savannah Guthrie, now engaged, agreed with what I'd said in writing, that Donny had made us single women feel worse for not deciding to do it on our own. Star Jones said that she simply never wanted to be a single mother, but not because she didn't want children. All three women, including Nancy Snyderman, supported my points about the financial means and familial support a single woman needs to consider. And all three agreed that many women want to be in love and in a relationship with the baby's father.

When the segment that morning was done, I poured myself another cup of coffee, and lifted my mug to the women on the screen to thank them. I had backup.

Funnily enough, I met Donny in person a few months later at a dinner party for a mutual friend. He generously apologized for not understanding my point of view. I humbly apologized for telling him off on national television and told him I understood he hadn't meant to hurt anyone. He said he wants women to have the babies they want to have and not feel as though they shouldn't have those babies on their own because some men—and women—may judge them for it. Of course, it's not a choice everyone can make, or wants to make. But Donny and I both agreed that for those who can and do make that choice, it's a wonderful and extraordinary choice to make.

MIRABELLE IS
HAVING A MOMENT

Mirabelle is running late to meet me for dinner. She's easily forgiven. It's Mirabelle, after all, there are few women I adore more. She and her husband, Doug, have been struggling with infertility for a couple of years. She is about to celebrate her thirty-sixth birthday. IVF is the next logical step. She also knows how much I've wanted a child and a man I love to share that child with.

It began as the perfect happily-ever-after for Mirabelle and Doug. They met one night at a friend's going-away party and that was it. It truly was love at first sight. A couple of years later they were married, got his-and-her dogs, and moved to Brooklyn in a space big enough to hold the four of them, plus room for a couple more. Now Mirabelle works as a powerhouse marketing executive. No one at work knows what's going on with her. They just assume she and her husband have chosen to be child-free.

After ten or so minutes, Mirabelle appears, carrying two large bags, one for work, one for whatever reason women carry large bags. She's visibly ready for a cocktail. We order.

"You have no idea the hilarity of my morning," she says immediately. "Doug and I are at the fertility clinic which is in and of itself surreal. *The Today Show* is on in the room where I'm about to have the procedure done. We hear your name. You're giving Donny Deutsch hell! We're pointing at the TV saying, 'That's our friend Melanie!' And the nurse is cheering you on, too! Way to go! I'm telling you, Mel. This morning was *surreal!*"

It feels surreal to me, too. It's not every day I get into an argument on national television.

"How does Donny Deutsch expect women to just go have a baby on their own?" Mirabelle says, echoing my feelings. "I can't imagine going through all this without Doug. I told him and the nurse—who is now your biggest fan, by the way—that I was seeing you tonight. She wanted me to say hello!"

I smile and ask Mirabelle to explain to me the procedure she had done this morning. She does, without that I-know-more-than-you-know tone some people have when explaining things. Unsurprisingly, she is taking today's procedure in stride.

"Whatever happens, happens, right? I mean, we want a baby, and we're focused on making that happen. In the end, it's in God's hands."

I say a quick little prayer in my head for this first round of IVF to work.

"What's going on with you?" she asks with sincere interest. What I love about my time with Mir is that there will be no judgment if I still haven't made any progress on meeting someone since our last dinner. We talk about a couple of projects I'm pursuing and some other work-related ventures I'm excited about. I allow myself to tell her the no-news news. "But, nothing is going on romantically. I've had some dates here and there. No one I am interested in."

> " There is a potent connection between women who appear to have it all on the outside but on the inside feel like failures of fertility. Heads up, shoulders back, we're strong. And then we look into each other's eyes, and we let it go. It's a secret we share with each other. The courage of vulnerability is something powerful women allow in one another. "

Even though I am careful to sound carefree about it all, Mirabelle can tell I'm worn out from disappointment. I allow myself to be honest with her. "I can't believe I have so many exciting things going on with my company but in love, I have so little to speak of."

She holds out her hands across the table and takes mine in hers. She looks at me the way only people who love you look at you. "Melanie, you're special. He's out there. I believe he is. There's a reason why you haven't met him yet and it's not because you're undeserving. Life is no flawless romance. We both know that you have to believe in something bigger than yourself to be bigger than you thought you could be. And you are a perfect example of that. You are doing incredible, incredible things for women. You're touching women in very powerful ways, giving so many a voice."

I'm now crying tears I can't wipe; my hands are in Mir's. My vulnerability is released with a sense of relief; it's given permission by the compassion of a good friend.

"You're making women who can't have children feel a connection to their own maternity, and you're helping them be acknowledged for that powerful gift."

I am thinking of my mother.

"Believe me, Mel. You will find him. You will."

I'm nodding, choked up. Mirabelle knows what I need to hear.

There is a potent connection between women who appear to have it all on the outside but on the inside feel like failures of fertility. Heads up, shoulders back, we're strong. And then we look into each other's eyes, and we let it go. It's a secret we share with each other. The courage of vulnerability is something powerful women allow in one another.

The last time Mirabelle and I were in the same room together, we were seated at separate tables in an event space packed with an audience of reporters and producers. I was conspicuously seated at a round banquet table with several moms who blog about motherhood. Mirabelle was out of sight at another table with her marketing colleagues.

The reason for the breakfast was a "marketing to women"–type panel discussion about a new study released by the major media-marketing company sponsoring the event. I wasn't certain why I had received an invitation, but when I learned that the ever-lovely Sarah Jessica Parker would be there, to discuss her role in her then-latest movie, *I Don't Know How She Does It,* I knew I was not going to turn down the opportunity.

As much as I love SJP (and I really do) I have a beef with the film, which typifies the work/life balance mothers strive to achieve. While that is undoubtedly an important and valuable topic, the movie also takes good care to further mythologize childless women as heartless and completely unsavvy about children, as if only once a woman becomes a mother does she become maternal.

At the breakfast event, SJP's seated up on stage, and behind her there's a huge screen. The image projected on that screen makes me cringe. It's from some TV show about parenting, and it depicts a childless female character stereotypically holding her best friend's

> 66 The words 'women' and 'moms' are often used interchangeably, as if they're the same thing. It begins to seem like only mothers, not women in general, contribute to the economy. 99

baby at arm's length, with a cliché look of misery on her face, making her look maternally inept. As if on cue, my iPhone vibrates. Mirabelle's noticed the image, too.

So all childless women are morons? Is that what the research shows? Mir texts me. The image is clearly not the way to ingratiate the childless women in the room. But, sadly, I'm not surprised. Childless women are rarely shown much compassion. The event moves on to a panel of marketing executives discussing why moms are so valuable to their businesses and to the economy in general. The words "women" and "moms" are often used interchangeably, as if they're the same thing. It begins to seem like only mothers, not women in general, contribute to the economy.

You better say something at the Q&A part!! Mirabelle texts, exasperated. There's nothing like encouragement from Mirabelle to embolden me. The second the Q&A part of the event begins, I shoot up my hand like an overeager fifth grader. I'm handed the mic, and I step onto my virtual soapbox.

"If we're focused only on moms, we're missing nearly 50 percent of American women," I say, referring to the 2010 U.S. Census Bureau fertility data I know like the back of my hand, which reported that 47 percent of American women are childless. "As women marry later and have children later than ever before, we have a much longer lifespan between college graduation and our first birth. But that doesn't mean we're not spending money on children. We're what I call Savvy Aunties, spending our discretionary income and time on our nieces and nephews by relation, and our friends' children—our nieces and nephews by choice. We're like Carrie Bradshaw!" I look over toward SJP, who lights up as she looks back at me, smiling.

I continue, "We may be married. We may be single. We may be in love or looking for love, ever romantic. What we all have in common is a love for the children in our lives, like Carrie loves Miranda's and Charlotte's kids. Tell me something Carrie wouldn't do for them. And we're not just spending money on kids. Carrie knew how to spend money on herself and her girlfriends, too.

"So, panel, if you ignore these nurturing, child-loving women and assume all women are moms, then you're leaving millions of very powerful, modern female consumers off the table."

I step off my soapbox as the panel moderator, offering resounding support, exclaims, "I'm a godmother! So, yes! What about women like me?"

To give the marketers on the panel credit, they do seem to understand that Mom is not the only adult female consumer, but they fall short of acknowledging the consumer power of the childless woman. The panel discussion ends and a reporter immediately comes by to talk with me. "My aunt is a Savvy Auntie," she says. "She is always complaining that ads never speak to her." Even the top executives from the media company hosting the event approach me supportively, acknowledging the importance of this female consumer, too. Then some moms who agreed with me pat me on the back. Then a text comes from Mir: *Fabulous job!*

Even out of sight, Mir's always supporting my efforts to get us nonmoms noticed. That morning, it looked as if we were. And, as life imitates art, Carrie Bradshaw was there to notice it, too.

66 To give the marketers on the panel credit, they do seem to understand that Mom is not the only adult female consumer, but they fall short of acknowledging the consumer power of the childless woman. 99

Back at dinner, I am once again feeling empowered by Mirabelle's encouragement. She and I share a belief in something bigger than us. She convinces me that my love is out there.

"I love this time of year," Mirabelle says as we walk around Soho after dinner. Our beautiful city is filled with people enjoying a beautiful spring evening. I take a deep breath in.

"Love is in the air," I say reassuringly, to no one in particular. And I decide to believe it.

A couple of months later, Mir has an update. *It didn't take,* she texts about her latest fertility treatment, adding a sad face. I take a breath, crestfallen. I don't bother texting back. I call.

"It just didn't work," she says. "You know, I'll be OK." But I hear my friend choke up on the other side of the phone.

"It sucks," I say. These are the only words I can muster. I don't want to offer options or optimism. Right now it's about grief. And she's duly allowed it.

"You know, I waited for the right guy," Mir says in her own defense, "and yeah, maybe when things didn't just happen, maybe I waited a bit before opting for IVF. I just had so much going on at work, and I just couldn't bear adding this to the stack of stress. And now (Mir is starting to cry) I think maybe I waited too long. I feel such guilt for not being able to get pregnant. Did I put my career ahead of having kids? Did I think I was impervious to infertility?"

"Mir, thirty-six is not old," I plead. "It's possible there was an issue there long before you even started trying a few years ago. Please don't blame yourself or your career."

"This is the time of night I usually take my shot. I can't believe I'm grieving the shot!" Mir says with a little of her natural sense of humor. "I just want to take some time off from this for a while now. I don't even want to think about starting this all over again. I don't think I can take the rejection one more time. At least not yet."

I don't blame her. I don't blame her for anything, in fact. "Well, if there is anything good that comes out of this, it's that we can go out for a drink again soon," I say. I can hear a smile on Mir's face.

"Margaritas on me, my friend," she adds in her ever-generous way. "Thank you for listening to this. I know how much you want children, too."

We hang up but continue texting throughout the night and the next day. I want Mirabelle to know she's not alone. We end up trading stories about our nieces and nephews. No matter what, we'll always have that.

BASKET FULL OF
MIXED EMOTIONS

I t's spring, and there is hope in the air. Jennifer, Nadia, and I are
at the Carlyle with Kiki (née Katherine) to kick off her forty-first
birthday with a carb-filled breakfast.

As coffee is poured, Jennifer, who heads up development for a
large charitable foundation, is reporting on her early-morning appointment at the fertility clinic. "If my endocrinologist starts one
more sentence with 'At your age . . . ' I get it. I'm forty-two. I know
how old I am and that this situation isn't ideal, but what was I supposed to do about it? I met Rob when I was forty, and we married
ten months later. Two months after we said 'I do,' I made an appointment at the clinic. I'm moving as fast as I can!"

"Can I tell you something?" Kiki, the founder of a corporate
events business, asks. She and her husband Paul recently returned
from a trip to Australia, and she is beginning to see her life from
a new perspective. "I know you guys are going to think I'm like a
traitor or something, but I'm honestly not sure about this baby thing
anymore. Now that I'm officially 'in my forties,' I'm wondering if it's
what I really want."

I smile shyly at the server who places a basket full of baked goods on the table. I know I'm not going to have any even though they all look delicious and I wish I could. I'm feeling I need to hold back on the carbs. Nadia, a single attorney who recently turned forty-four, immediately grabs a mini bagel.

"I was in Australia," continues Kiki, "which is on the other side of the world, and the seasons are reversed, and maybe that was why I had this 'aha' moment. But I think the trip gave me a whole new perspective on whether or not I want children. I admit that, unlike most of my friends, I was never obsessed with having kids. But I always expected I *would* have kids. I never imagined I *wouldn't* be a mother. Anyway, Paul and I were looking out onto the sunset and he held out his hand to take mine and I realized: This *is* my life. It's an incredible life. I am so happy.

"I have an appointment next week at the clinic and part of me wants to cancel it. I want to move on, you know? But I know I'll go. I'll keep going through this process. Because what if? What if I don't think this way in a year from now? Or some day in the future?" Kiki takes a breath. "I honestly don't know what to do."

Borderline Regret, I think to myself, *is not where she expected her travels to take her.*

"I'm with you, Kiki," Jennifer says. Jen has been going through IVF treatments for months, trying to collect enough embryos for a first baby now, and perhaps a baby sibling in a couple of years. I know this because Jen is very open with everyone about the fact that she's going through IVF.

"I just don't see the point in hiding it," she told me a few months ago. "My friends see I'm not drinking wine because I'm not supposed to be drinking wine, and I don't want them to spend time wondering if I'm pregnant or trying to get pregnant. Plus, to be honest, there's no way I could keep coming in late to work or leaving early without telling my boss what's going on with me. It's no shock to anyone that I'm going through IVF, so why not just tell it like it is?"

I never have to worry about Jen telling it like it is.

"I mean, I get it," Jen says a little distractedly while looking through the basket and finally selecting a blueberry muffin. "Look, I'll be honest here, OK? I'm not allowed to go to the gym, so I'm gaining weight and feeling lethargic, and since I can't have a glass of wine when I go out with our friends, Rob and I are spending most nights at home. My work is suffering because I'm planning my treatments around my cycle, not around what's going on at the office. I love my life and I've worked hard to get here. And now I wonder if I care enough about having this baby. But like you said, Kiki, in five years when it's too late, will I regret that I didn't do everything I possibly could to become a mother?"

"Really?" Kiki says, partly shocked at Jen's confession. Kiki always imagined that Jen was one of her friends who really wanted a baby. Kiki's also relieved to learn that she's not the only one thinking twice.

"Yes," Jennifer says. "Now will you eat something? Have the most fattening thing here. It's your birthday!"

Kiki obliges and puts a mini croissant on her plate.

Nadia, who has been uncharacteristically silent, is finally ready to talk. "Funny enough, I've actually started the process of IVF myself," she says, nervously curling her long brown hair with her left hand. The girls are visibly surprised, including me. We hadn't realized Nadia was considering single motherhood.

"I didn't know you were thinking about having a baby on your own," Jennifer says. "I thought you didn't want to do it on your own. I'm so happy for you! That's amazing! I'll tell you everything I've learned with my process!"

"Thanks!" Nadia says, buoyed by Jen's positive reaction. "It's late to start the process now. I know. But when I turned forty-four I decided I had to try. I didn't want to regret not at least *trying*.

"I didn't get the man, but I am not giving up on my own biological baby. I realize it sounds crazy. It's a ton of money, but I have to try. I feel stupid that I waited this long to have a baby on my own, but now I'm determined."

Nadia and her last boyfriend broke up after dating for about eight months. She made it clear that she wanted to have a child soon (she was forty-two at the time), and he told her she was being irrational. He said that at her age, she should just be happy with her life the way it was. He offered that if she was willing to wait a few years, he would consider adoption. "There really is no difference," he had said. "A child is a child." That's when Nadia knew the relationship was over. It wasn't so much that he didn't want to have biological children. It was that he believed her desire to have a biological baby was completely irrational.

"Single women in their late thirties and early forties come into our clinic often racked with guilt, like their circumstances are their fault," says Dr. Marc Kalan, board certified in obstetrics and gynecology and reproductive endocrinology at the Center for Fertility and Gynecology in L.A. I spoke with Dr. Kalan over the phone a few hours after breakfast with the girls to get his thoughts. "But more likely, a combination of events got her there," he says. "These days, some men look at women who want children as somehow desperate and unreasonable."

I find Dr. Kalan particularly sensitive to older women who have either waited for the right partner, or the last possible minute, to conceive. He had agreed to speak with me about what he sees at his clinic.

> 'We see it here all the time,' says Dr. Kalan. 'Single women take on the responsibility for their childlessness, with society pointing a finger at them like they are naïve about their ability to have children after a certain time, or that their childlessness is completely their fault.'

"It's as if some men think it's unnatural to have the natural instinct to have children," I say with a tone of familiar incredulousness.

"Exactly," Dr. Kalan says. "It's inherently unfair that men judge women on any issue dealing with their fertility and their choices. As a man myself, I don't believe a man can have an informed comment on it. It's her biology. It's her natural urge and desire. It is not irrational for a woman who has been getting her period every month for around twenty-five or thirty years to want to give having a baby a chance."

"I still get my period," said Nadia when we met. "I have this monthly reminder that maybe I still have a chance." We all nodded supportively.

"We see it here all the time," says Dr. Kalan. "Single women take on the responsibility for their childlessness, with society pointing a finger at them like they are naïve about their ability to have children after a certain time, or that their childlessness is completely their fault. Some of our single patients blame themselves when our treatments don't result in a live birth. The say they feel like they are being punished for having waited for the right relationship. But, amazingly, these valiant women won't give up. It means too much to them."

"It would mean everything to me for this to work," Nadia said to us earlier. "Honestly, my fertility specialist says my chances of conceiving with my own eggs are pretty low. Like maybe 5 percent if I'm lucky. But I always dreamed I'd have a baby of my own." Nadia is not alone.

"The women who come to our clinic are among L.A.'s most sophisticated, successful women," Dr. Kalan says. "They are not unaware of their fertility lifespan or their limited chances of giving birth. But hope is stronger than analytical logic for them. For these women, who have made it very far in their careers and other areas of their lives, statistics no longer inform their actions.

"I see women who are forty-five and their chances of conceiving with their own eggs are about 1 percent. And even though we are very clear about the very low chances of it working for them with their own eggs, they insist on trying. And while they know the outcome will probably not be what they wanted, they are just as devastated when it doesn't work as a woman in her late thirties who has a 60 percent chance of conception is. Hope," Dr Kalan explains, "is a pretty significant feeling. And nothing will deter a woman with hope."

"Well, my friend Nadia sure is determined," I say. "And she told us that there's a partner in her firm who had twins at forty-five, so she's optimistic."

"Look, Melanie, it happens," Dr. Kalan says. "We had a forty-eight-year-old patient who conceived and had a live birth with her own egg. But it doesn't happen often. Most of the women who give birth at your friend's age became pregnant from donor eggs."

"I feel guilty," Jennifer said, referring to her contemplating giving up on IVF and motherhood while Nadia is so determined to do it, on her own, no less.

"No, please don't," Nadia said. "I am on a mission. Maybe things would be different if I was married and it was a decision I was making with my partner. Maybe I'm more empowered because I *am* doing it on my own."

"That makes sense," Kiki replied. "One of my friends who's forty is going through IVF now. She and her husband had to borrow money from their parents for their second round of IVF because the first didn't take. And she's so sad and obsessed over it. He is less so. He would prefer they put it all to rest. But she told me that if the IVF doesn't work with her eggs this round, she'll try with donor eggs. I don't know. I don't think I want it bad enough to go bankrupt over it or get a donor egg. But I know so many women who are doing that or have done it."

"That's the big secret in New York City," Jennifer said in a low voice. "So many of the older women get donor eggs; they are not always getting pregnant with their own eggs in their midforties. And you see younger women reading about these Hollywood stars who get pregnant in their late forties, and I know most are probably getting donor eggs."

"It's an insidious problem," Dr. Kalan tells me. "Women see other women their age or older having babies, and understandably the mothers don't want to make it public that the baby came from a donor egg, so there are misconceptions out there. And so the cycle continues."

"I want to try on my own before considering the donor egg route," said Nadia. "And believe me, I've done my homework. Once I decided to have this baby, I studied it like I'm taking the bar or something. I drive my poor fertility specialist crazy, I'm sure. I keep emailing him questions about supplements I read about or alternative Chinese methods and things that might help. But I'm determined. This is my absolute focus now."

Dr. Kalan isn't surprised. "It's actually pretty cool to watch," he says. "The independent women who didn't find a partner are

> 'The single, independent women around age forty are the most committed patients we have. They are on double duty, doing all the research, management, financials, giving themselves shots. Everything falls on them. But from their diligence about their choices of sperm donors to becoming experts on cervical mucus, they are wonderfully maniacal about it.'

taking control of their lives. They've always been successful at the things they can control, like their careers and their well-being. But they cannot control their fertility, so they are taking control of doing everything they can to conceive. And once they decide to have a baby on their own, they go for it with gusto. They are doing it on their own terms. It's truly extraordinary."

I think of Jill, my single friend who is having a baby on her own and encouraged me to do the same, and how proud I am of her.

"In a way, I'm happy I don't have a man holding me back on this," Nadia shared with us. "I doubt any guy would be willing to go through what I'm willing to go through to have this baby."

I admired Nadia's optimism. She spoke as if the baby was definitely on its way.

Dr. Kalan concurs. "It's the single women who are most energetic about the process. Maybe it's because they don't have a male partner holding them back. The men are much more, well, 'chill' about this stuff. The single, independent women around age forty are the most committed patients we have. They are on double duty, doing all the research, management, financials, giving themselves shots. Everything falls on them. But from their diligence about their choices of sperm donors to becoming experts on cervical mucus, they are wonderfully maniacal about it."

"I've been thinking about that lately," Kiki said, referring to whether being married is a help or a hindrance to her. "Paul surprised me the last few years. He really wants this baby now. He says he's almost forty-seven and wants to start a family. However, here's the thing. He's miserable at work and whines all the time about how he's not making enough money for the amount of hours he puts into it. (Paul works for a start-up and earns far less than Kiki.) And I totally agree with him. But when I suggest he try to find a new job, he hints that he should come work at my company. But I am petrified of that. I mean, I love him, but he is always asking me about what he should wear or to help him make a sandwich or something ridiculous. I'll end up having to take care of him at the office, too! I'm already managing most of the stuff that needs to be done with the IVF treatments."

I was beginning to understand why Kiki isn't sure about having a baby anymore. She might already have one at home. "I love my husband and we have a wonderful life," Kiki insisted. "But frankly, I'm the responsible adult in the relationship. I don't know how much more I can take on. And I don't just mean a baby. Everything I have to do to get pregnant is taking over my life. No one understands the amount of time it takes to go through infertility treatments. People talk about the money, and believe me, it's a ton of money, but it's the time I really can't afford right now. And Paul doesn't seem to get it. He actually missed one of our IVF appointments when I basically turned my week around at work to make it happen. He had to get his sperm checked and he kept delaying making the appointment. I finally had to make it for him. So I wonder how much he really wants this, which is why I think I'm second-guessing myself." Kiki finally gave in and took a bite out of her croissant.

66 Women of the Otherhood are often earning at least as much or more than their boyfriends or husbands. In some cases, they are the main breadwinner by far. It's a lifestyle and responsibility we never expected to have. 99

Jennifer agreed. "I don't think Rob understands it either. I always make sure to get the first appointment of the day at my clinic, but even then, it can take well over an hour and then I have to run back to the office. I don't even have time to take in what I've just gone through. And then Rob will forget to pick up the dry cleaning or something."

"I hear that friends of mine who don't work start lining up in front of Weill Cornell at 6:00 AM to get in for that vital morning appointment," Kiki said, uncharacteristically loudly. "It's like a cattle call. I can't imagine doing that. I *can't* do that.

"Look, Paul and I married when I was thirty-four, so it's not like I didn't have time to consider becoming a mother, but I was building my business, and frankly, I was doing better financially than Paul was at the time, and I felt like I needed to focus on that. I needed to get my finances in order, *our* finances in order, in order to even think about supporting a family."

Women of the Otherhood are often earning at least as much or more than their boyfriends or husbands. In some cases, they are the main breadwinner by far. It's a lifestyle and responsibility we never expected to have.

"I really would love to have a baby," Jen said. "But I realized something recently. I was spending so much of my energy wishing for something, instead of living my life in the moment and taking what comes. I realized that I missed out on forty. The whole year was so focused on getting pregnant that I can't tell you anything else that happened besides getting married that year. What a waste."

And then Kiki added the kicker. "In a way, I feel like I'm going through this alone, like you are, Nadia. I mean I know that's not fair to you, for me to say that. I realize that. But no matter how much Paul says he wants this baby, if I don't take care of just about everything, including managing the process, it wouldn't happen."

"I know. I understand," Nadia replied. "I don't think anyone at this table expected life to turn out this way. Don't laugh at me, but I always had that perfect white-picket-fence ideal for myself. I'd get married in my twenties, have my first baby before thirty, and my third by thirty-five. So trust me, the time I have spent making this decision has been the hardest, most painful time of my life. But once I decided to do it, I was relieved. It was like the sun was shining again and I was on it!"

When I share the morning's conversation with Dr. Kalan, he isn't surprised. "It's a very hard choice, deciding to become a single mother. It's very emotional for so many women whose dreams of falling in love, getting married, and having a baby with that man are coming to a close. But once they make the decision, there is so much to do that they don't have time to focus on the emotion. The grief is over and the focus on creating life is on. These women are proactive and dedicated to their goal."

"I love that Paul and I can take a couple of weeks and travel to Australia or wherever we want," Kiki said. "And I don't even mind that I'm the one footing most of the bill. But everything is scheduled around my fertility treatments. I had to plan the entire trip around my period. I'm telling you, my period is like my child. My whole life is centered around my period!"

"Well, I have something to admit to you," I said, "and I feel a little guilty about it, too. Now that I'm forty-three, I have to admit that I'm almost getting over it. Trust me, if it happens . . . if I meet someone tomorrow and he wants to have a child with me and somehow I become pregnant and have a baby, I would be so happy. It would be a dream come true. But I am realistic and know that that probably won't happen, and so I have been letting go of motherhood." It felt bittersweet to say it out loud for the first time.

Let me explain that this feeling comes and goes. I change my mind sometimes, wondering if it could possibly still happen for me. I try to manifest a story of a man coming into my life and changing my life . . . but then I don't allow myself to keep going with it. I'm afraid of feeling like a fool, I think, or that I'll be really disappointed if it doesn't happen, or disappointed in myself for believing that it could.

I wonder how it is that I have no limits to my professional aspirations, but personally, it's like I am blocked from believing it could still happen. I take solace from my friend and Manhattan psychotherapist Natalie Robinson Garfield, who once told me that while artificial reproductive technologies enable so many to have the children they always desired, it makes it difficult for the rest of us to move on past the grief. People want to tell you it's not too late. They share that so-and-so had her first baby at forty-three—by mistake! Or so-and-so had twins with IVF at forty-five. Or so-and-so celebrity is pregnant at forty-six! And you are not given permission to move on, Natalie said. And I agree.

"Oh, I get it," Nadia said that morning. "I've got a mom who can't wait to help me take care of this baby, and I know my firm will be flexible with my hours. And financially, I can do it. But it's not easy if you don't have all of those things. But yeah, starting this process at forty-four is not easy. Part of me thinks, I wish I had known what

> ❝ 'When women know that they will not be able to conceive due to a genetic condition and knew at a young age they would never have children, or if they have a medical condition that required them to either have to get pregnant now or never,' Dr. Kalan says, 'the blow can be a little easier on them.' ❞

my timeline was. Like if I knew at like thirty-eight that I had only six months to decide if I wanted to have a baby or not, I would have made a decision because there was a deadline. But every time there was a birthday, a friend would remind me of a friend of a friend who gave birth at that age, and I would hope that love would come around."

"When women know that they will not be able to conceive due to a genetic condition and knew at a young age they would never have children, or if they have a medical condition that required them to either have to get pregnant now or never," Dr. Kalan says, "the blow can be a little easier on them. They know it is the medical condition that hurt their fertility, not something like when they would meet a man, something they think somehow they could have controlled. Their social circumstance weighs heavier on them."

I am nodding on the other side of the phone. I wonder: *Had I known that I couldn't have children because of a medical condition, would not becoming a mother be easier?* I am not sure, but knowing I *could* have had a biological baby if only I met the right man at the right time does sometimes make me feel as if I failed.

After I divulged my new feelings, Jennifer rubbed my back and I attempted to catch my breath. I've said it. And I believed it. I will be OK if I never become a mother. I am OK not being a mother at

> ❝ I will be OK if I never become a mother. I am OK not being a mother at forty-three, which in a way, feels like the future me telling the younger version of me, who spent nights in tears, that she'll be OK. She'll be more than OK. She won't have the life she expected, but she will be fine. She will find a new kind of happiness. ❞

forty-three, which in a way, feels like the future me telling the younger version of me, who spent nights in tears, that she'll be OK. She'll be more than OK. She won't have the life she expected, but she will be fine. She will find a new kind of happiness.

I realize now that notwithstanding not having children, I have a fabulous life. I've founded a great business that celebrates women who love the children in their lives, and I am writing my second book (the one you are reading right now). I didn't predict I would author even one. I have wonderful friends, and I am experiencing incredible things. Meanwhile, some of my friends with kids are envious that I can do what I do. For the first time, I'm beginning to see my grass a little greener.

"We know how our lives turned out at forty," Jen said, as though she were reading my mind that morning. "And we know we're OK. But we don't know what our future selves will think when we're fifty or sixty or when our mom friends become grandmothers. Will we be sadder for not having had children? Will we be happier because we didn't have children? I think we romanticize what our lives would be like if we had kids. Maybe we'll be just as happy in the future without kids as we are now. I think I have to live for the

Jennifer I am today, not the Jennifer of the future. And the Jennifer I am today is stressed and pulled and prodded and pricked with needles. I'm exhausted. I need to take care of me."

"I know," I said, confirming my decision not to try to have a baby on my own for myself, too. "I meet a number of women who by the time they get to be around forty wonder if they'll just be too tired to deal with kids in middle age. But again, they also can't imagine a life without children."

I didn't think I could imagine it either, until recently. My realization even caught me off guard. It first happened a few months ago at the Fertility Planit conference in Los Angeles, where I had met Dr. Kalan. I was moderating a panel discussion titled "Letting Go of Having Genetic Offspring." I was surprised to see the room full of brave souls; it takes courage to concede that parenthood may never happen.

When the panel was over, a woman approached me with tears in her eyes, clutching a tissue and her last hope. "I'm your story," she said. "I'm forty-four, single, and trying so hard to have a baby."

But I could see from the desperation in her eyes that our stories weren't alike. And I felt pain, panic, and guilt all in one fell swoop. I wondered why I was not as grief-stricken as this woman was. Did I not want it enough? Or had I simply resolved to let go?

"I feel like my life is over, and I don't know what else to do," she explained. "All I've ever wanted was to be a mother, but I haven't met a guy. At forty, I took it into my own hands and found a sperm donor and after several tries with IVF, I got pregnant."

I knew her story wouldn't end well. "There was something wrong with the baby. I had a miscarriage. But I'm not giving up. I'm still trying. Because of the miscarriage, I now have a 'preexisting condition' and I cannot get health insurance, because I'm a business owner and not an employee. So now, on top of it all, I'm broke. I'm at my wits' end. I'm forty-four, single, and childless, and I feel like a complete failure."

My heart was breaking for her. On the one hand, her story confirmed for me that my decision not to try to have a baby on my own had potentially saved me from a lot of pain. It also made me realize how relieved I was not to be in despair. For so long I had been. My grief was ebbing. And I felt a little guilty about that.

Back at breakfast that morning, Jennifer was mulling over another treat from the basket while Kiki mulled over her circumstances. "Maybe if I knew Paul would be helping me as a caregiver and financially, I'd be thinking differently. It's not that we don't earn a decent living, don't get me wrong. But living in New York City is expensive, and add a kid to the mix and it's really hard. My business is in New York City and my network is here; I can't move out to the suburbs. Plus the commute would make it tiring, and I would miss that time with my child. I totally understand that these are Upper East Side couple problems, but even a two-bedroom apartment in Manhattan can cost millions of dollars. I can't give up my business or Paul's income, so we'll need a nanny, too.

"I just look at this whole endeavor much more realistically these days. And I am realizing that everything I've worked so hard for the last twenty years is at risk. Maybe that sounds selfish, but that's the honest truth," Kiki said.

"I can't pretend I don't have it easier," Jennifer admitted. "I feel very fortunate that Rob and I live very comfortably. And we can afford as many IVF treatments as we need, a bigger apartment, high-tech strollers, and a nanny—even a nanny to travel with us when we take a vacation as a family. So it's not about that for me. It's about how it's taking over my life. And I want my life back. Rob and I are madly in love. I finally found my soul mate and I want to focus on our life together."

"What would Rob say if you told him you wanted to stop the treatments?" Nadia asked.

"I think he'd be half disappointed and half relieved. He's an only child, so his parents are counting on us for a grandchild. And you know, we both agreed we wanted to be parents when we were dating. If he really wants this baby, then we'll keep trying. And I usually want a baby, too. Don't get me wrong. It's just that the doctor told me this morning that my FSH levels are really bad and maybe I'm feeling sour grapes. Who knows, ladies?! It's just good to confide in my friends about my mixed emotions," Jennifer added with a smile as she polished off another mini muffin.

"Now I must get to work. This was my treat," Jennifer said as the server laid down the check.

"Happy birthday, Kiki!" Jennifer added as the two women hugged warmly, perhaps for a few moments longer than usual.

"Happy birthday, Kiki!" Nadia said, and they hugged for a while, too.

I left the Carlyle and walked up Madison Avenue, breathing in the sweet, spring air. A woman in her early forties walked by me heading south, her newborn sleeping softly in her stroller. And in that fleeting moment, I daydreamed about the possibility of becoming a mother.

THE NEXT GIRLS

I'm in the bright blue sundress I wear when I want to feel like a girl, running in five-inch tan wedges to meet some girls for drinks. I'm always in a hurry, trying to catch up with time. The rush doesn't stop me from catching an attractive man looking at me in the reflection of a window as he passes by. I'm relieved he's not looking at me close up. If he knew I was forty-three, I wonder if he'd keep looking. Either way, it is exactly what I needed before I arrive at drinks—an ego boost to remind me that I'm still young enough to get a look from a handsome man, at least from afar. I'm old enough to appreciate each glance I used to take for granted.

I'm trying my best to look young and feel young because I'm getting together with Jessica, a twenty-seven-year-old entrepreneur, and Ava, twenty-eight, a marketing executive, both in the beauty industry. This latter fact is unsurprising; both women are natural-born beauties, Jessica with long, thick wavy brown hair and Ava with cream-colored skin and fair eyes.

We sit outside at Tolani Wine Restaurant on the Upper West Side and order a bottle of Sancerre. We give each other a quick update on work and dating. And before the wine is served, the conversation gets to fertility. "I was up late last night finishing a project with the designer I work with," says Jessica while slumping back in her chair with end-of-week fatigue. "We spent half the time talking about freezing our eggs." I'm caught off-guard. I didn't know about egg freezing when I was twenty-seven, let alone discuss it with colleagues . . . or friends.

"Egg freezing?" I ask softly, trying not sound like a forty-something-year-old woman. "Do you guys often talk about stuff like that, even with colleagues?" It wasn't a judgment of appropriate professional conversation, but rather a point of amazement on how ubiquitous the conversation has become.

"Are you kidding me?" Jessica says. "It's *all* we talk about. If you're having a conversation about dating, it quickly turns to figuring out what to do if we don't find the guy."

Ava nods in agreement. "Yep. I have a friend at work who just turned thirty and told me she's saving up to freeze her eggs by thirty-five."

"I've already started looking into it," Jessica says. "It's not just the procedure you have to save up for. You have to pay rent on those eggs each month! I have enough trouble paying rent in New York City for myself, let alone a place for my eggs," she adds with a sense of humor about it all. She takes a breath, leans forward, and gets serious: "I have to really consider it. I look around at the guys out there and I think, *what if I don't meet him?* I definitely want to be a mother." Then, as if making a resolution, she declares: "If I'm not married by thirty-two, I'll probably have a baby on my own."

Ava is less progressive in her thinking. She moved to the United States from Russia with her parents when she was a little girl. At first, her mother encouraged her freedom, something she herself was not able to have in her homeland, but now that Ava is in her late twenties, her mother is becoming impatient. "She's always asking me what I'm

'Are you kidding me?' Jessica says. 'It's *all* we talk about. If you're having a conversation about dating, it quickly turns to figuring out what to do if we don't find the guy.'

doing on the weekends, judging if I'm doing enough to meet my future husband. When I graduated college, I went on a ton of dates but never met anyone I wanted to spend the rest of my life with. Now I'm enjoying my freedom. There's nothing I enjoy more than a Saturday reading in Central Park, time for myself after a long week at work."

I nod, understanding. I relish my time alone. I've learned how to really relish it, not dread it. Ava adds: "I want to get married and have kids. I just don't know if and when that will happen. So in the meantime, I'm enjoying my life. I can't stand all the pressure my parents are putting on me. I feel so young."

I feel young, too, but I'm not. I'm trying to hide my envy of these women who are armed not only with youth, but also the knowledge of how life may not turn out as we planned, or how our parents planned for us. They're already preparing for how to preserve their fertility no matter what happens.

"I look at my mom, who got married when she was twenty and had my brother at twenty-one and me at twenty-three, and I can't imagine it," Ava says. "I think that at first my mom was happy for my opportunity to graduate from a good school and get a great job. But as time passes, she's getting worried about me. It's like there's this random moment between twenty-six and twenty-eight when being single goes from being exactly the right thing and to becoming a major concern."

> 'They want it both ways, I think,' Ava says. 'On the one hand they don't want to put much effort into courting us, making us understand that they want something meaningful, too, but then they judge us for being single.'

"I hear you," Jessica says. "And dating is not what I expected it to be once I hit my late twenties. And I use the term 'dating' lightly. I have guy friends in their twenties who use apps to find girls to basically have sex with. It scares the crap out of me. Not only is it demeaning because they are basically just looking for women for sex, not relationships—and by the way, I honestly don't care that the girls want it, too, because it makes women who don't want to do that seem like we're high-maintenance just because we want a guy to court us a little before assuming we are just going to have sex with them—but this whole hookup thing also makes the guys lazy. Dating is becoming a technicality. There's no art to it anymore. There's no effort. Never before has the idiom 'Why buy the cow if you can get the milk for free?' been truer.

"I started to exclusively look to meet and date guys in their midthirties, thinking it would work better for me. I thought older guys would be more inclined to know how to date. But most of them don't know how to treat me, either. Everything has to be so casual. Like, they don't plan a nice date, and on top of that, they arrive looking all disheveled, like the date is an afterthought."

"Agreed," says Ava. "I think they are confused. They think that equality means they should treat us like one of their buddies."

"Yes," Jessica says. "I honestly think they don't know what

women want, and we don't know how to explain it to them. But the fact that 'dating' has become uncool is really bothersome. I don't want to hang out with a guy I might be interested in with a group of his friends, including another girl he's been hooking up with. I want a meaningful relationship."

"They want it both ways, I think," Ava says. "On the one hand they don't want to put much effort into courting us, making us understand that they want something meaningful, too, but then they judge us for being single."

"Totally," Jessica adds. "I was actually on a date a couple of weeks ago with a thirty-five-year-old guy I met at a work-related event. He said to me, 'I don't get it. You're a successful, attractive girl. So what's wrong? What's your baggage? There must be something going on behind the scenes if you're not in a serious relationship by now.'"

The 'Why are you still single?' refrain is beginning for these young, fabulous women, I think to myself.

"I wanted to tell him that I'm single because of men like you!" Jessica says. "Men like him who assume that women who are well-educated, successful, and attractive must be deficient in some way if they are single. I am a provider. I provide for myself, I provide for my teenage nephews and nieces and my friends' babies, I provide for my dog. I will keep providing if and when I become a mother. If that's my 'baggage,' then so be it."

"Right?" Ava says. "They are confused that professionally, we exhibit traditionally masculine traits because we assert ourselves at work and hold our own. But on a personal level, we're traditionally feminine. I like being a girl, *and* I like that I can have a career that provides me with the income I need to live in New York City and enjoy a nice bottle of wine with my girlfriends after an exhausting work week."

> 'Being an independent woman doesn't mean that I don't want to have a partner in life and that I don't want to be a mother. I just don't want to be in an ordinary relationship.'

"I think they assume that if we are so-called career women, we aren't feminine, and if we are feminine, we aren't successful professionals," Jessica says. "Being an independent woman doesn't mean that I don't want to have a partner in life and that I don't want to be a mother. I just don't want to be in an ordinary relationship. I don't want to date a man, like my married friends say, that I'll warm up to if I give him enough of a chance. But these married mom friends of mine were always just looking for a good provider and a man who would be a good dad. They found that. But I'm not on the married-mommy track. My priority is to find a man who gives my life and our relationship balance. We will help each other in some ways, challenge each other in other ways. We'll be passionate about our careers, and each other's careers. I want a man who excites me, and someone I excite. I want to be in love with him. And then I want to have children with him. Why is that too much to ask for?"

"I know I need to start thinking about the possibility that I may not meet the man of my dreams," adds Ava, thoughtfully. "But I just want to live a little without the worry. Maybe things will change when those boys I am meeting now grow up a little. None of them want to get serious, even if I do. So in the meantime, I'm learning how to be alone. Maybe it's my way to prepare for my future."

I try to hide a sad expression behind my wineglass as I take another sip. Not only are these fabulous young women dealing with similar dating challenges my friends and I dealt with fifteen years ago, they are seeing that their older friends, like me, in our early forties are still unmarried and not mothers, and they realize it might happen to them. On the one hand, they have the good fortune my peers did not have to know that they may not be mothers until late fertile age, if ever, and can prepare accordingly. But they also miss out on the naïveté my peers and I had about our unexpected fates. Generation Y gets to have the conversations about preserving their fertility and the awareness to save money for egg freezing, IVF, and/ or single motherhood by choice. But I'm not sure their enlightenment is better than the ignorance of their older "sisters."

"It's like we are living double lives," Jessica says. "We are living for the lives we have right now, making room to date and be social. And we're working and planning for the lives we may have if we don't find a partner. We're working at careers that provide for us, we're saving and planning for babies late in life, and we're learning how to be alone."

"And all that while also doing everything to look great and keep in shape to boot!" Ava adds with a laugh to lighten the mood.

These women are presuming there is a chance they will be alone for at least a good part of their adult lives. They are each one coping, in their own ways. I want to tell them they'll be OK. They may have moments of grief. They may have big choices to make. But they are prepared for it all. I want them most of all to have faith that the right man is out there, or at the very least, that however their lives turn out, they will be happier for making the right choices and having faith along the way.

"I'm not giving up," Jessica says as the server pours the last of the Sancerre equally among our glasses. "But I'm also not giving into what others expect of me, not my friends, and not the men I date.

And I'm not going to lower my expectations in the men I date or what will make happy."

"Cheers to that!" Ava chimes, as she puts her arm around her friend. "I love you, Jess! You remind me that I need to be strong about what I know is best for me."

"Love you too, Ava," Jessica replies. "And hey, if we don't meet our guys by the time we're in our late thirties, maybe we'll have babies on our own and move in together and raise them together. Like a 2020s version of *Kate & Allie!*" Jessica is referring to a 1980s sitcom that was ahead of its time, featuring two divorced moms who move in together to raise their kids as a family.

I'm impressed with their maturity, and I admire their friendship. And I wonder if their *Kate & Allie* idea is not too far off from what may occur for this generation. Women of the Otherhood are independent but they are also adept at nurturing friendships. And since single motherhood is not easy, perhaps friends who become family is a good solution. In the meantime, I hope they find their path to what they want most: love, marriage, and motherhood.

"And here's to you two," I say, finally ready to show my age. "Because if there is one thing I've learned, being you is the very best thing you can be. The right man will be attracted to that. Keep the faith. Look at each day with possibility. You are two smart, beautiful, fabulous women with, dare I say, years of youth ahead of you."

Later that night, before I go to bed, I look at my reflection in the mirror. I am looking for a sign of my twenty-eight-year-old self. I want to hug her and tell her it will be OK. Her worst fears will manifest, but she'll be fine, more than fine. She'll be magnificently happy for all the unexpected joys she'll experience.

It's not the life I expected, but it's the life I directed. And I am ready for my close-up.

WE HAVE A LOT
TO CELEBRATE

Gigi, Wynn, Rachel, Jacqueline, Mirabelle, and I are meeting for drinks. We all have big news to share, and we decide to share it together.

"OK, who is going first?" I ask, as the server pours each of us a glass of Prosecco from the bottle we're sharing.

"I will!" Jacqueline says, unable to hold her news in any longer. "I bought my own place!"

"I love it!" Gigi says. "What made you decide to do that now?"

"Thanks!" Jacqueline says. "Well, I kept showing these fabulous apartments to other people, and I finally decided it was time for me to invest in one, too. It's in Chelsea, not too far from my office. It may not be the best area to meet a straight, single man, but the apartment is just stunning! The kitchen was completely renovated by the previous owners, and it's gorgeous!"

"That's amazing," Mirabelle says. "I'm so glad you bit the bullet and bought a place."

"Well, you know, it was always my dream to own my own home. I think I went into real estate in the first place because I just love being around homey spaces. I was tired of waiting around for some guy to purchase it with me. And Bernie, one of my gay friends, was like, 'Honey, you don't need to wait for a man! Go buy that apartment yourself.' And I thought to myself, you know, he's right!"

"Congratulations!" Wynn says. "I can't wait to come over and see it!"

"You'll all come over as soon as I fluff it up a bit more," Jacqueline says. "It's a little stark. It needs a little sex appeal. I'm thinking about a big shag rug for the living room and a big four-poster bed."

"I can't wait to help you decorate it," Gigi says. "I'll work with you on it so you can get my decorator discounts. Let's go shopping this weekend!"

"Thank you, Gigi! That's so nice of you!" Jacqueline says. "That really helps." We all notice that Jacqueline is welling up. "I'm being serious. You have no idea what that means to me."

"What's wrong, honey?" Rachel says as she wraps her arm around Jacqueline's shoulders.

"It's just that, well, I have to admit that as excited as I am to finally own my own home, I walked into the empty apartment for the first time as the owner, and I felt a little sad," Jacqueline confesses. "I realized that no matter what Bernie said, I wanted not only to own a home, but also to have a home, with a husband and kids, you know?"

"I get it," Rachel says. "But you know, your friends are the family you choose. And we choose to be your family. I say we all come over when you're ready and cook dinner together in your new kitchen. We'll warm up the place with a good home-cooked meal to help make your apartment really feel like a home."

"I know you're not Jewish, but how about a Shabbat dinner?" I offer. "We'll light Sabbath candles together and add a little prayer for you to fill your home really soon with a loving husband and kids." As I say that, I'm thinking of my Baba. Teresa had told me he was there with us in spirit at the bar that night we met for drinks, and that he wanted me to light Shabbat candles every Friday night, and when I do, to ask him and my late mother for what I want. I still do so, every Friday night, asking them both to help me find my love.

"I love it," Jacqueline says. "Let's do it! OK, Rachel, it's your turn. What's your big news?"

"I'm starting my own business!" she says.

"Wow!" Jacqueline says. "What kind?"

"Well, you know I've been in the beauty industry forever, and I needed a change. I was out with Harrison Black a few weeks ago at this great casual, open, and airy restaurant on the Upper East Side. We both love that place because it attracts an older, sophisticated crowd. And I was sort of fake-complaining that, because we love this place so much, I always have to come meet him near his apartment. And then I mentioned that I wished there was a venue just like it on the Upper West Side.

"Anyway, turns out that he's been thinking about opening a restaurant like that for a couple of years. He's got the finances and the network to make it happen. And he said that he knows I've got the aesthetic and that I know what women want and . . . "

"Oh my God, Rachel!" Wynn exclaims. "Are you opening a restaurant with Harrison Black?"

"Yep! We're already scouting locations. And Gigi, speaking of decorating, I wanted to ask you if you would consider helping us decorate the interior of the space?"

"Are you kidding me?" Gigi says with a big smile. "I would be honored to work with you on that! How exciting!"

"Oh, Rachel! This is thrilling," I add. "If there's any way I can help as a fellow entrepreneur, I am happy to do so. Just let me know."

"Melanie, I was counting on that!" Rachel says. And we clink flutes.

"OK, OK, my turn," Gigi says. "I have big news, too."

"What is it?" Mirabelle asks. "This gets better and better!"

"I am moving back into Manhattan! I love my place in Brooklyn, but honestly, it's time to make a change," Gigi says. "When I moved into my neighborhood, there were a few young families here and there. But now there are hardly any singles left, and I decided that while I may no longer be looking for marriage and babies, I do want at least the possibility of flirting with some cute guy I meet in line at Whole Foods. And I think moving out of a family-centric neighborhood into the hustle and bustle of the city is the change I need.

"Jacqueline, do you think you can help me find a place?" she asks. "I'm still a downtown girl, so maybe something in TriBeCa or Battery Park City?"

"I have a listing you'll love!" Jacqueline says.

"Does it have a—" Gigi starts to say.

"—a terrace?" Jacqueline answers, knowing Gigi well. "Yes! It wraps around the living room and bedroom. The interior is smaller than your Brooklyn apartment but—"

"—but you know I need my light for inspiration!" Gigi says.

"Exactly!" Jacqueline says.

"We can't wait to have you back in the city," Rachel offers. "Mir, are you staying put in Brooklyn for now?"

"For always," Mirabelle says. "Well, we never say 'never,' but between Doug and the two dogs, finding a place we can afford, never mind with outdoor space the dogs can play around in, forget about Manhattan. But I do have other news."

I'm hoping it's the news Mirabelle and Doug have been waiting for.

"I'm taking some time off from work. In fact, I resigned last Friday. I'm going to visit a friend of mine in Greece for a month. Doug is coming for the first week but then has to get back to work, now that he's the sole breadwinner and all. I've been poked and prodded and felt punched in the gut with the IVF thing too much lately, and I just need a break from it all. Work has been really stressful, too, and I think that's been affecting my ability to focus on my health and this baby thing. I'm leaving for Greece next week. And when I return, I'll figure out what to do next."

I am disappointed for Mirabelle and Doug but proud of her for taking care of herself.

"I think that's a wonderful idea," I say. "I've never been to Greece. But I love the food!" I add to lighten the mood.

"The food is fantastic!" Mirabelle says. "I plan to sit by the water and eat salads all day and fresh fish all night!" she adds.

"Sounds amazing, Mir!" Jacqueline says. "OK, Wynn, now it's your turn. What's your big news?"

"Well," Wynn says. "I know I said I wouldn't do it but . . . well . . . I froze my eggs."

"Wow," I say, cheerfully. "That's great news. What made you reconsider?"

"Remember that story you were telling me about that woman Nicole who borrowed money from her parents to freeze her eggs?" Wynn says.

"Yes," I say. "Of course."

"Well, soon after you told me that story, I was talking to my cousin who got married at thirty-eight and even though she tried to get pregnant right away, she found out that she had a really low ovarian reserve and that she had basically run out of eggs. She is really devastated. And it made me think that if I had the eggs to freeze, even at 40, I should consider it. And while it's not the way I want motherhood to happen for me, I spoke to my parents about it and they were surprisingly really supportive and even offered to lend me the money if I needed more than one round of egg retrieval. Anyway, it turns out I needed only one round. So now I'm cash-poor but egg-rich," Wynn says with a smile.

"Do you think, knowing you have your eggs frozen, you'll feel differently on dates?" Rachel asks.

"Yes, I think it takes some pressure off for me psychologically. But honestly, unless I wear a sign that says 'I froze my eggs,' it's not like the men I date will really know."

"Do you feel liberated?" Gigi asks.

"Well, I feel I like I made the right choice for me," Wynn says. "As you all know, I've always wanted children, and I didn't expect to ever find myself single and without children at forty. But yes, it does feel empowering to have done it."

"What if you meet the guy tomorrow?" Jacqueline asks. "Will you use those eggs? Or try naturally?"

"It happens that I am really fortunate to have some eggs left in me," Wynn says. "If it all works out and I meet him tomorrow, like you said, maybe I will have done it all for nothing. But for now I feel like I've planned well, just in case."

I look at Mirabelle, who doesn't seem surprised by Wynn's news.

"I wish I had known to freeze my eggs in my twenties," Mirabelle says. "But as you know, I don't even think that was an option then."

Wynn reaches across the table to hold Mirabelle's hand. "Mir has been so generous with me these last few weeks," Wynn says.

"Wynn asked me for the name of my fertility specialist because, as you all know, I love him. So I knew Wynn was doing this," Mirabelle admits.

> ❝'Well, what if you fall in love with someone who doesn't want kids or can't have kids?' Jacqueline asks. 'Like for me, I'd be thinking, what if I don't meet the man I love until I'm fifty? I don't think I'll want to become a mother at fifty. Do you think you'd feel guilty or something if you don't end up using the eggs?' ❞

"Mirabelle's encouragement has been amazing," Wynn tells us. "She is going through so much and was so nice to lend me her support with all of her own emotional roller-coaster fertility stuff going on."

"It was honestly my pleasure. I really admire you, Wynn." Mirabelle says. "You're like Joan of Arc, riding this new modern science! And it's not easy to do all of this alone."

"But I wasn't alone," Wynn says. "I had you."

Mirabelle smiles and says to Wynn, "Well, I have you, too," then turns to the rest of us and says, "It was actually Wynn who suggested I take some time for myself because she saw how the stress was getting to me."

"It looks like you two really bonded over this," I say. Their strength is palpable.

"We did," Mirabelle says and smiles at Wynn.

"I have a question," Jacqueline says to Wynn. "I hope you don't mind me asking, but it's something I've been wondering about."

"You can ask me anything, Jacqueline," Wynn replies.

"Well, what if you fall in love with someone who doesn't want kids or can't have kids?" Jacqueline asks. "Like for me, I'd be think-ing, what if I don't meet the man I love until I'm fifty? I don't think

I'll want to become a mother at fifty. Do you think you'd feel guilty or something if you don't end up using the eggs?"

"Well, I do think about these little eggs as having my DNA and potentially becoming little people one day," Wynn muses. "When I find the man with the sperm to fertilize them, that is. And yes, I think it might be hard to not use them, meaning to not have at least one child of my own. But like we all say, who knows what life will bring our way. I may feel totally differently when I am in the right relationship."

"Well, good for you," Jacqueline says. "I'm really happy for you." And we all clink our glasses in unison.

"So, Melanie," Wynn says turning toward me. "That leaves you. What is the good news you wanted to share with us?"

"My book is finished!" I say. "And I wanted to thank you all for your love and support throughout the process. I really appreciate it."

"Of course!" Rachel says. "We're always here for you!"

"Tell us what you learned!" Gigi says, enthusiastically.

Here is what I learned.

I got to meet and to know better so many extraordinary women of the Otherhood while writing this book, and I have to say, each is fabulous in her own way. That actually didn't surprise me at all, just as it didn't surprise me that these women are all a little frustrated about trying to find love or wondering if they'll ever become mothers. And they are aware of what others think of them, their circumstances, and their choices. But there is one other thing that all these women have in common that I hadn't really expected. At the start of this process, I thought a lot about whether we ended up where we are today because of choices we made, no matter the good intentions, or because of chance, fate, destiny—whatever you want to call it. What I've learned is that either way, no matter what the women of the Otherhood expected their lives to be, they are not

> 66 What I've learned is that either way, no matter what the women of the Otherhood expected their lives to be, they are not standing still waiting for someone else to make life happen for them, nor are they throwing in the towel on love and motherhood. 99

standing still waiting for someone else to make life happen for them, nor are they throwing in the towel on love and motherhood.

They all have faith. They believe in chance. But they also know that they have choices.

They can choose to have their lives mean what others believe it should mean. Meaning, they can choose to look at themselves as less-than because they are single and/or not mothers. Or they can choose to look inside themselves, to look at their lives, and find meaning in who they are and where they are, no matter their fate at this moment in time.

Each one of them is grabbing life by the horns. We may not ultimately have complete choice in what happens in our lives, despite our deep desires and long-held expectations. Nevertheless, we choose to find meaning in our lives today, and we choose to have faith in what happens next.

While some uncertainty might remain—will we find love? Will we have children? Will we have both? We certainly understand that uncertainty is part of the journey.

The women of the Otherhood know that they are neither a label nor a stereotype. They are not how many others perceive them to be. And they are certainly not inferior in any way to those who are coupled or have become mothers.

Those oppressed feelings that women of the Otherhood know all too well—that we are not enough, not full, or not complete because we are not mothers—are feelings that we have to understand, and we have to understand that sometimes those feelings are self-inflicted as well. They are shaped in relation to what others believe is enough, full, or complete. If we fall into the trap of allowing others to define our expectations of ourselves, then we merely become a reflection of the stigmas others project on us.

The women of the Otherhood are themselves, their true essence, and that speaks volumes about what they value most: searching for meaning and finding love with someone who sees them for who they are, someone who will walk with them on a shared journey. The women of the Otherhood do not allow others to tell them what or who they should settle for. They will never settle to satisfy others' expectations of them.

These women know that society looks at them askew, as odd, as outliers. But the confident women of the Otherhood are too busy looking within to notice or to let it affect their destiny. Among us women of the Otherhood, there remains one common conundrum: If I don't become a mother, will I remain or become unhappy in the future? Or will I be happier just living my life one day at a time and seeing what life has in store for me? Here's what I know.

As I find myself entering the other side of my fertility without becoming a mother, I can tell you that my life is extraordinary. I no longer feel an unbearable pain about my childlessness. There are brief moments of grief, certainly. And there is still a chance that motherhood will come, and I believe that. But I am no longer seeking out men. On dates, the roles have reversed. The men, who still call women between thirty-five and forty "too desperate" or "too anxious" to date seriously, are now wondering why I am not desperate

> 66 Those oppressed feelings that women of the Other-
> hood know all too well—that we are not enough, not
> full, or not complete because we are not mothers—
> are feelings that we have to understand, and we have
> to understand that sometimes those feelings are self-
> inflicted as well. 99

for them. My aura of confidence has attracted men who are instead seeking me out.

I have a fabulous business. I am completely and utterly besotted with my nephew and nieces. And I am enjoying friendships, new and old, as never before.

The experts I've spoken with agree. Sociologist Eric Klinenberg says that women forge such strong relationships and friendships that, even if they remain single past fertility, they are living the best of their lives, enjoying their careers, travel, aunthood—whatever they are most passionate about. Dr. Marc Kalan, the fertility special-ist who often treats women of the Otherhood, says that it's the single women who decide to have a baby on their own who have the most gusto of all his patients. The women of the Otherhood are focused and determined. There is nothing they won't accomplish once they set their minds to it, he says.

I realize now, as I complete this book, that we women of the Otherhood were never, in fact, the Other. We have always been our true, authentic selves. We are not the voice inside our heads telling us we are not enough. That voice comes from others, and it's only during those down times, when we believe that voice, that we are no longer true to ourselves.

Once we no longer define ourselves as the Other, as outside of the social norm, we are no longer concerned with how others define us. We are liberated to be our true selves. We are determined to be our true selves.

"Oh, Melanie," Rachel says after I've shared all this with the girls, "that's so true."

"Did your discoveries change your outlook at all?" Wynn asks.

"Well, as you know," I say, "I still don't have the man or the baby. But you also know that I am a happy woman. It's not that I am happier now, not having had those things in my life. I was happy before I typed the first word of my book, and I was happy when I typed the last. But I now realize that I'm liberated from what I thought my life needed to be in order to ensure that I would always be happy. I am finally, finally, me. I am not the woman who wonders what might have been. I am not measuring my life against what others define as life's true meaning. I have found meaning in being true to myself. And I have no regrets."

"Here's to no regrets!" chants Jacqueline as she raises her flute.

"And here's to the Otherhood," I add as we toast again. In unison.

And so, dear reader, here's a toast to your next chapter. How you find its meaning, how you choose to look at it, and how soon you choose to turn the page is entirely up to you.

ACKNOWLEDGMENTS

First and foremost, my genuine gratitude goes to all the many women and several men, friends and new acquaintances, who lent me their confidence so that I could shape their many personal stories into the composites of a few characters and events in this book. I thank you from the bottom of my heart for your generosity and honesty, and for your trust. I also acknowledge and thank those who inadvertently became part of some of the chapters. As the late Nora Ephron explained with sage words from her mother: "Everything is copy." When an author shares her life, and her life is filled with an abundance of people and stories, collective experiences can make their way onto the page. You are all generous and kind people who came into my life in colorful ways and then, in some fashion, found your way onto these pages. In return, I did my best to guard your anonymity. I appreciate you all.

Thank you to the experts I spoke with at length, all named in the book. You have added texture and context to a misunderstood generation and helped us all better appreciate these women and men, their experiences, and the time in which we live.

To my literary agent at ICM, Jennifer Joel, who patiently and persistently guided the proposal that became this book. And to my agents Josie Freedman of ICM, and Todd Hoffman formally so, who fervently believed in the story of the Otherhood before the book was even completed.

To the smart and passionate team at Seal Press, and their abiding love for this book and this story, thank you. Specifically, I warmly thank Krista Lyons, publisher, for deeply believing in me and our book, and to Donna Galassi, Eva Zimmerman, and Natalie Nicolson and the entire group of extraordinary people who collectively worked on this book and its publication. And before I submitted the manuscript, I was fortunate to have Rose Maura Lorre working with me, helping me organize my thoughts and research, and gently editing my reporting without altering my voice. And thank you to Daniel Weinstein for being a generous sounding board. I also thank Audrey Vavia for her invaluable help assisting my work in getting this book to market, as well as Ilya Welfeld and Susan Towers for their great expertise and support.

I also acknowledge the editorial team at *Huffington Post Women* for giving my posts such constant support. The response from readers there inspired me in part to write this book. Thanks to Sharyn Rosenblum for enabling my very first post there during the publication of *Savvy Auntie*, my first book. And I must say thank you to a few of my author friends for their invaluable "been there" advice: Jonathan Tropper, Karen Lehrman Bloch, Bruce Feiler, and Gretchen Rubin. It was Gretchen who introduced me to the editors at PsychologyToday.com where my writing also appears, and it was she and Samantha Ettus who introduced me to my agent, Jennifer Joel.

To the women and men who have come across my writing and/or the Savvy Auntie brand and have connected with me via email, Twitter, or Facebook to share your very personal stories and your support for me, and what I write and do, thank you for the frequent reminders as to why I wrote this book.

To my close friends whose patience, love, support, and enthusiasm have buoyed my efforts: You are the family I choose.

And to the family I did not choose, but would have if I could have: I am so grateful for your love. To my father and stepmother, who are unconditional in their support of my work, thank you for never asking me why I'm still single. And thank you to my brother and sister-in-law, who not only support my work, but also provide me with the best respite from writing with a warm home filled with the most amazing nephew and nieces an aunt could ever ask for.

And finally, to my late mother, who did not see me grow into an adult. I light my Shabbat candles every Friday night thinking of you, speaking to you, and knowing how happy you are to see how happy I am, despite how we both had expected my life to turn out. Thank you for the strength, wisdom, good humor, compassion, and empathy you embodied, enabling me to learn from yours and to put mine into words.

ABOUT THE AUTHOR

Melanie Notkin is the national best-selling author of *Savvy Auntie: The Ultimate Guide for Cool Aunts, Great-Aunts, Godmothers, and All Women Who Love Kids* and the founder and personality behind Savvy Auntie, the beloved lifestyle brand celebrating modern aunthood. In 2009, she established Auntie's Day®, the first annual day to honor aunts and godmothers. Notkin is the foremost expert on the emerging demographic of childless, often single, women in North America. She has shared her research, writing, and popular voice as a contributor to *The New York Times, The Huffington Post,* and PsychologyToday.com, among others, and she appears regularly on national television, radio, and the web. *Otherhood,* inspired by her life in New York City, was optioned by True Jack Productions and NBCUniversal for television.

Connect with Melanie Notkin:
On Twitter: @SavvyAuntie #Otherhood
On Facebook: Melanie Notkin and SavvyAuntie #Otherhood
On Instagram: SavvyAuntie #Otherhood
On the web: MelanieNotkin.com
Email: Melanie@MelanieNotkin.com

SELECTED TITLES FROM SEAL PRESS

How to Woo a Jew: The Modern Jewish Guide to Dating and Mating, by Tamar Caspi. $17.00, 978-1-58005-500-0. Advice for Jewish men and women on finding a soul mate from JDate's dating expert.

Airbrushed Nation: The Lure and Loathing of Women's Magazines, by Jennifer Nelson. $17.00, 978-1-58005-413-3. Jennifer Nelson—a longtime industry insider—exposes the naked truth behind the glossy pages of women's magazines, both good and bad.

Screw Everyone: Sleeping My Way to Monogamy, by Ophira Eisenberg. $16.00, 978-1-58005-439-3. Comedian Ophira Eisenberg's wisecracking account of how she spent most of her life saying "yes" to everything—and everyone—and how that attitude ultimately helped her overcome her phobia of commitment.

Single State of the Union: Single Women Speak Out on Life, Love, and the Pursuit of Happiness, edited by Diane Mapes. $14.95, 978-1-58005-202-3. Written by an impressive roster of single (and some formerly single) women, this collection portrays single women as individuals whose lives extend well beyond Match.com and Manolo Blahniks.

Bringing in Finn: An Extraordinary Surrogacy Story, by Sara Connell. $24.00, 978-1-58005-410-2. A remarkable, moving story of one woman's hard-fought, often painful, journey to motherhood—and the surrogacy experience that changed her family's life.

Essential Car Care for Women, by Jamie Little and Danielle McCormick. $17.00, 978-1-58005-436-2. Straightforward, easy to follow, and full of step-by-step diagrams and helpful pictures, this is the ultimate handbook to everything a woman should know about her set of wheels.

Find Seal Press Online
www.SealPress.com
www.Facebook.com/SealPress
Twitter: @SealPress